GAY VOICES
from EAST GERMANY

INDIANA UNIVERSITY PRESS

Bloomington and Indianapolis

GAY VOICES
from
EAST GERMANY

Interviews by JÜRGEN LEMKE

English-language version
edited and with an introduction
by JOHN BORNEMAN

Translations and introductions by Steven
Stoltenberg, J. D. Steakley, Jeffrey M. Peck,
James R. Keller, James W. Jones, James
Patrick Hill, Geoffrey J. Giles,
and John Borneman

The paper used in this publication meets the minimum requirements of American
National Standard for Information Sciences—Permanence of Paper for Printed
Library Materials, ANSI Z39.48-1984.

♾ ™

Manufactured in the United States of America

Library of Congress Cataloging-in-Publication Data

Ganz normal anders.   English.
    Gay voices from East Germany / interviews by Jürgen Lemke ;
English-language version edited and with an introduction by John
Borneman ; translations and introductions by Steven Stoltenberg . . .
[et al.].
        p.   cm.
    Translation of: Ganz normal anders.
    ISBN 0-253-33319-9 (alk. paper). — ISBN 0-253-20630-8 (alk. paper
: pbk.)
    1. Gay men—Germany (East)—Biography.   2. Gay men—Germany
(East)—Public opinion.   3. Public opinion—Germany (East)
I. Lemke, Jürgen.   II. Borneman, John.   III. Title.
HQ76.2.G35G3613   1991
305.38'9664'09431—dc20   90-43690

1 2 3 4 5 95 94 93 92 91

CONTENTS

V. **Body and Joseph**
Introduced by Jeffrey M. Peck   111

VI. **Theodor and Dieter**
Introduced by James R. Keller   135

VII. **Nicholas and J. A. W.**
Introduced by J. D. Steakley   163

GAY VOICES
from EAST GERMANY

Introduction by JOHN BORNEMAN

From its infancy in the form of East German *Protokolle* (transcribed interviews) in 1978 to its rebirth as an English translation with introductions in
1989, this book has been enlivened and sullied by individual circumstances,
by politics, and by sex. The English-language version was born of a meeting
between Jürgen Lemke and myself on September 3, 1986, in Zur Letzten
Instanz, the oldest bar in greater Berlin, on the third day of my ethnographic
fieldwork in the German Democratic Republic—what English speakers continue to call East Germany long after the natives themselves quit using the
term. I was new to the city; Jürgen was old to it. I was exhilarated by him,
his knowledge, and the audacity of the project he was undertaking: a book
of interviews with fourteen homosexual men, ten of them from the working
class, in the GDR, exemplifying and encapsulating an officially buried history. Jürgen, having worked on the project for seven uncertain years, was
still doubtful that it would be allowed to come to fruition. Yet of the work's
importance neither of us had any doubt. One month after our conversation,
on the second of October, a man named Erich died in an East Berlin hospital. His life illustrates the range of this repressed past: an unskilled industrial worker born in 1900, he had survived not only an orphanage, two
"hot" wars, and one "cold" one, but also imprisonment in the infamous
quarters for homosexuals in KZ Sachsenhausen during World War II. Erich
is the author of the first autobiography in this volume.

It is to Jürgen Lemke that the credit must go for perseverance in bringing
these men of various homosexualities to share their experience with us, to
speak its name and names in the context of their own lives, and to bring
their histories to print. Jürgen earns his living teaching market research at
a university in East Berlin. His own life is initimately connected to the
biography of his society. He was born two years before the final defeat of
the Third Reich, six years before the founding of the socialist East German
state. In 1945, in that initial, chaotic period after the war, his mother was
accidentally shot while fleeing a Russian soldier. His genetic father, released from an American POW camp in 1946, remained in the West Zone
and found work as a cook for the American army. The founding of two
antagonistic German states in 1949 made the division between father and
son permanent. Else, the childless sister of Jürgen's mother, took Jürgen
in and raised him as her own, an act for which he still feels indebted. Else
married an officer in the new GDR army in 1956, and they formally adopted
Jürgen in 1961, a few months before the Wall was built, providing him at
the age of sixteen with a new name, Lemke, and a new legal father.

In the early seventies, Jürgen's life seemed destined for the "straight and narrow" track of *Kader*. The term, taken over from the Soviet system, refers to the training of bright, loyal youngsters to be future leaders of socialist society. The GDR labels itself a "Worker and Farmer State," and in the fifties, the state initiated aggressive affirmative action programs for women and working-class children. As an adopted child in a working-class family, Jürgen received the best training his society had to offer, and he seemed sure to become a leader in marketing East German goods abroad. Already in his twenties he was negotiating trade agreements in China, Czechoslovakia, and the Soviet Union. He dutifully married in 1970, and his future looked bright.

The word *deviant*, ironically, was his downfall. In 1975, while serving on a trade mission to China, he learned that a book on political history sent by the GDR as a gift contained a sentence calling Chinese communism a "deviant form." Jürgen took the initiative of apologizing for this to the outraged Chinese. On his return home an equally outraged GDR ordered a security check on Jürgen, revealing his own, more intimate type of deviance: Jürgen was living not only with his wife but also with his male lover, a black student from Cuba. This discovery ended his career, and with it any chance to travel outside the socialist bloc. He "retired" to teaching and began the long search to understand the nature of this sexuality that seems so threatening to states both East and West.

Yet Jürgen cannot be understood merely, or even primarily, as a homosexual, though that "deviance" has played a primordial role in his life. His unflinching commitment to a humanistic, democratic socialism and his selflessness in relations with a wide range of friends are equally important to him. During the time I was living in East Berlin, his genetic father contacted him, asking to see him again after some forty years. Now old, sick, and lonely, he wished to put things back in order, to see his son once more—blood ties being strong enough to withstand the slights of time. I encouraged Jürgen to take his ex-father up on it, for at that time travel outside the GDR was mostly restricted to *Familienzusammenführung*, occasions of family reunion. But Jürgen, though moved by the letter, remained adamantly against a reunion. Although he had lost three sets of friends through emigration to the West (and would lose a fourth set in fall 1989), he considered his home to be in the East, his ties to the society there. For him, the blood ties to his father were alone no counterweight to a forty-year absence.

Jürgen speaks but once in this book, and indirectly at that, in the first page of the interview with Winne, a section deleted from the German editions. There, as elsewhere in the texts, he has edited out his own voice, his questions, his probing statements and nods of support. But Winne, a man twenty years his junior, responds directly to him; playfully, Winne lets us know someone is there with a tape recorder, clues us into the dialogue that constitutes these interviews. The interviewee reassures the interviewer: "[A]sk me anything. There is no such thing as a stupid question." He *wants* to talk with Jürgen; the interview is a form of empowerment for him also. On both sides the dialogue grows out of individual needs, neither identical nor mutually exclusive. No, Jürgen is not going to ask about "war and peace," not about "the most important questions, . . . at least not yet." And thus we are invited into stories of "personal fate."

This book is about a range of such personal fates. Its interviews, reconstructed by Jürgen, were originally published in March 1989 in East and West Germany under the title *Ganz normal anders* (Normal, but different). It was favorably reviewed in nearly all the major German-language newspapers. In addition, several of the transcripts were rewritten as a play, which opened in January 1989 in Theater im Palast, the theater in the House of Parliament in East Berlin. Now the interviews have been translated into English by a team of eight men, all American scholars with an expertise in Germany and an interest in Berlin. In addition, each translator has written a short introduction to his translations, elaborating on and contextualizing specific aspects of the life stories. These introductions enrich the interviews by drawing attention to important questions: use of the protocol as a literary documentation of everyday life in East Germany, the nature of homosexualities under socialism (Stoltenberg, Jones, Steakley, Keller, Hill, and Borneman), remembering and German history (Giles), and even the project of translation itself (Peck).

This collection of interviews represents the fourth published *Protokolle* in the GDR. Initially defined as the recorded minutes of a meeting and often identified with written, legal testimony, the protocol is now one of the main literary forms (along with fiction) for talking about everyday life in East Germany. Maxi Wander, an Austrian who in 1958 resettled from Vienna to East Berlin, introduced the form in 1977 as literary narrative to talk about women's lives under socialism. Considering this sort of documentation too politically sensitive, the most prestigious literary publishing house in East Berlin, Aufbau Verlag, rejected the manuscript, and Wander then had it published by the East Berlin Morgen Verlag. Publishing decisions in the GDR are not normally based on considerations of short-term profit but on assessment of long-term "social needs." Wander's book became an immediate best seller for Morgen Verlag in the East and Luchterhand in the West, was rewritten and performed on stage, and received widespread praise in both Germanies. The mistake of that initial rejection by Aufbau seems to have played a part in their consequent acceptance of Jürgen Lemke's protocols. Yet the acceptance and publication of these interviews was by no means automatic. Nearly three years marked the time between their initial submission and publication. With Lemke's book it was the taboo not on everyday life but on "homosexuality" that stalled the publication, with the publishers at Aufbau most often dividing along gender lines about whether to print the book: women nearly unanimously supported publication, men nearly unanimously resisted. One is struck by the extent to which, in socialist as well as capitalist societies, feminist and gay movements find themselves in alliance, partake in similar forms of expression and resistance, and are united more than divided by experiences and tactics.

What GDR author Christa Wolf writes in the introduction to Wander's protocols applies equally to Lemke's: "Not seldom we rob spirited activities—like learning, researching, working, and also writing—of their spirit, whenever we are forced to produce a result at any cost. This book was important to its author, but working on it was much more important to her. And these texts have been worked on."[1] Wolf makes three relevant claims: the primary function of *Protokolle* is to document, not to prove; their significance for the interviewer/writer as an activity of bringing nameless people to speak is not secondary but paramount to their significance as a publication; and the interviews, while *ipsissima verba*, are not verbatim accounts: they are edited into narrative form. In fact, the editing of the interviews—rearranging the prose, correcting grammar, making the flow of utterances rationally consistent with the life story as a whole—transforms them into a *Protokoll*, a dialogically constituted life narrative. While this final reconstruction does not fulfill some historians' ideal of "raw data," these stories are nonetheless documents of primary historical value.

The removal of the texts from a pristine concern with authorial intention, their early sedimentation by Wander and Lemke in the *Protokoll* form, is, moreover, a condition of any text in history. "The meaning of a text surpasses its author," writes Hans Georg Gadamer, "not occasionally, but always. Thus understanding is not a reproductive procedure, but rather always a productive one."[2] Understanding these texts, then, requires neither our objectivity and distance from nor our sympathy and communion with the authors, but rather our participation in a continuing dialogue with the author, with the interviewee, and with the set of historical circumstances in which these texts were produced and in which we read them. I can vouch that the documents are based on actual recorded interviews, since I sat through several myself. Lemke interviewed thirty-three men before deciding on the final stories. In addition, I had access to the original transcripts of several of the interviews and know the process by which they were edited. Before the final publication, Lemke submitted each *Protokoll* to his discussion partners for further negotiated corrections, so that the final version is a reasoned account agreed upon by the writer and the person being described.

Documenting the everyday lives of fourteen homosexual men in the GDR, the *Protokollierung* of ordinary life, is a very limited form of struggle, humble and without pretension—yet it was in its time at the center of what is political. With no bourgeois state to topple and little space for dialogue with a central state that doesn't hide its intent to rule, many individuals in socialist Germany committed (or resigned) themselves to playing different roles in different contexts, hence in effect debunking the ideology of coherent identities—and this long before the appearance of postmodernist strategies in the eighties in the West. These individuals do not advocate a civil society that stands in opposition to and free of the state; they demand a more radical critique of the civil domain and hence effacement of the very boundaries between public and private—an artificial division that the theorists of socialist states themselves have long denied. The political manifests itself most acutely and pervasively in the routine of everyday; it achieves only periodic ritualized expression in state activity.

Following the work of Michel Foucault, many individuals in the contemporary West have come to realize that the political activity of the late sixties, insofar as it concentrated only on governmental and formal institutional change and not on structures of everyday life, did not radically change the kinds of domination peculiar to Western democratic capitalism. As Foucault argued in his later work, efficacious political activity must begin with or at least be accompanied by the rebuilding of selves. In the socialist East this realization did not grow out of theory but was presented to citizens as a fait accompli; for already by the mid-fifties the fusion of public and private life had become part of the doxa of the socialist everyday. From this perspective, to think of separating the political consequences of private action from the private consequences of political action is a bourgeois sleight of hand, a factitious distinction: it is impossible to isolate the point where one begins and the other ends.

The process of translation is too often ignored in thinking about the meaning of translated texts; it is popularly considered a mechanical process, more dependent on technical ability than interpretive prowess: meanings come out of the text just as they went into the original document, only in a different language. To be sure, without technical skill, translation is impossible, but likewise, without the ability to situate meanings in their own time and milieu, a text loses its historical specificity and its unique range of understandings. In translation foreign concepts and practices always risk either overdomestication or overexoticization. A good translator must not dissolve but maintain a tension between the two. The goal is to bring the alien home into one's own sphere of linguistic and pragmatic equivalences while avoiding an overly eager assimilation of difference into one's own conceptual world. In reading the protocols before us, we are liable to subvert this process and thus misidentify two concepts: socialism and homosexuality. Hence it is essential that we remain in a dialectical relationship with the interviews in considering "what is socialist?" (and thus what is nonsocialist or capitalist) and "what is homosexuality?" (and thus what is nonhomosexuality or heterosexuality).

Many of the translators seem to be disappointed that the men who speak in the interviews do not readily distinguish themselves as living in a socialist world. Most of the interviewees fail to mention the naturalized aspects of their world that for an American might seem radical: rents are state-controlled and subsidized, and it is nearly impossible to evict someone from an apartment; all citizens have state-provided health insurance; labor law so favors workers that it is nearly impossible to fire someone; and homosexual practices (except for and with minors) have been decriminalized since 1968. Moreover, in an August 1987 decision, the GDR Supreme Court overturned the conviction of a man who had consensual sex with a minor, arguing that homosexuals had to be treated exactly like heterosexuals with regard to sexual relations. Only if harm or nonconsensuality were proved could an adult man be convicted of a sex crime.

What most of the translators do dwell on is the range of experiences similar to their own; East German concerns seem just as parochial as ours, their prejudices nearly predictable. Our expectation of a "socialist difference" is difficult to reconcile with the perverse banality of much homosexual experience. In part we can avoid this reading discomfort by not falling victim to the Marxist assumption that our most essential identities are economically determined. The socialisms that developed early in this century united around the primacy of the economic and naive belief that radical restructuring of these relations would result in liberating us from other forms of identity. Instead, we have in this century witnessed a proliferation of identifies of noneconomic ilk: ethnic, sexual, familial, national, and religious. This holds true for socialist and capitalist worlds. It may be the case, however, that capitalism stamps its citizens and homosexualities much more uniformly than socialism, that, in fact, capitalism in its late twentieth-century Western form can be seen much more as a "total system" than socialism.

In point of fact, we can identify a general tendency to eroticize sameness in the capitalist West and a general tendency to eroticize difference in the socialist East. The central, identifiable state in socialist Germany has, in its policy oriented toward the production of sameness and uniformity, paradoxically provoked an opposing set of desires. Many of the interview partners in these East German protocols unwittingly indicate heterogeneous desires and the eroticization of many forms of difference. Without powerful marketing systems, socialist states have not been able to resort to single, standardized versions of the erotic in selling their goods and peoples to each other. This lack of visually manufactured standardization allows for more experience-near and situation-specific fantasizing about possible erotic forms. On the other hand, although free-market, capitalist societies represent themselves as anarchic, differentiating systems, the forms of legitimate and desirable differentiation are meticulously coded and mass produced in standardized form in omnipresent advertising. The tendency in sexuality, at least in the United States, is to search for replicas of the self: sameness in age, sameness in erotic fantasy, sameness in class and occupational status.

We may then note a second, parallel difference: a tendency to display differences between known erotic codes in the capitalist West contrasted with a tendency to mask differences between unarticulated erotic codes in the socialist East. Many of the men in the interviews are still engaged in masking their sexuality, either by hiding it or playing on its ambiguity. One might summarize these two observations as follows: in the West sexual codes are highly articulated and displayed, and individuals eroticize others only within the same code; in the East sexual codes are less well articulated and involve forms of masking, and because of the ambiguity of codes and uncertainty about which code one belongs to, individuals eroticize many forms of difference. This rather free play of unarticulated signifiers in the East, contrasted with the semiotic display of known, unambiguous codes in the West, can be accounted for by three factors: the lack of a gay and lesbian movement of self-identification along sexual preference lines in the GDR, the minimal exploitation by the media of particular images of a proper sexuality, and the lack of a large apparatus of educational, psychiatric, and research institutions oriented to explaining people's sexual identities to them and getting them to articulate (and fix) their own sexual orientations. On one hand, lack of political organization (a situation now changing in the GDR, as Peter speaks about in his interview in part III) did not diminish the practice of homosexuality in these years, but led to its practice in a multitude of unarticulated forms. On the other hand, homosexual practices did not cohere into a socially recognized identity. Without the identity, homosexuality could not be understood as a group phenomenon that might lead to political organization, meaning the recognition of organizational interests in setting membership standards, recruitment strategies, appeals for social and state support, and strategies of institutionalized reproduction.

Finally, let us ask what sort of object of study are homosexualities in socialist Germany? Are they a totality about which one can speak? Does homosexuality have characteristics either singly or in a combination it can call his own? Or must we reconceptualize this thing? Among our interviewees we find these occupations: industrial worker, druggist, collective (dairy) farm worker, antique restorer, editor, export product salesman, library worker, economist, waiter, painter, art restorer. Their political orientations (as far as they are expressed or can be inferred from the interviews) range from apolitical to committed socialist to disenchanted socialist. Their social styles of presentation include macho, queen, married man, and single. Their homosexualities find expression in monogamy, polygamy, pederasty, bisexuality, transvestitism, and narcissism. Their self-images range from self-pity to self-satisfaction to defiance. There is no single underlying principle that fixes or constitutes their identities. One might conclude from these interviews that homosexuality excludes no particular political identity, no particular occupation or class identity, no social style, and no form of sexual practice. Yet diversity or *différence*, that buzz-word of the postmodernists, is in itself no virtue. Homosexualities, like heterosexualities, can coexist with nearly anything—good and bad—under any circumstance.

Homosexuality, I suggest, is neither a set of inclusive practices nor a stable identity but a shifting signification negotiated over time, which in interactions with genetic potentialities and environmental and cultural processes constitutes a person whose attributes, among others, include eroticizing the same sex. The ability to describe homosexualities, however, and the recognition of them as one among many human potentialities, is a quite different task than that of justifying gayness as an identity, as something with a social function deserving not simply respect but social support and institutional encouragement. Unlike most modern identities, gays can make no convincing claim to an Ur-history (however mythologized such histories may generally be), no appeal to essential characteristics of person or practice (however tendentious these may be); we worship no common religion and, of course, we cannot physically reproduce ourselves. We are, simply put, merely historical and cultural constructions, and that alone, I would like to suggest, does not suffice to justify demands for social nurturance and institutional support.

The social potential of a gay identity lies precisely in its ability to invert some aspect of normality and thus illuminate the "proper" for what it is not. In a dialectical process, gays can achieve social acceptance and support while simultaneously maintaining a critical relation to this acceptance. By refusing total assimilation gays help clarify not only their own raison d'être, but, equally important, that of nongays. We are quite "normal, but different"—we represent a kind of unexceptional otherness. To the extent gay becomes "normal," meaning that one particular version of homosexuality becomes regnant and nonreflective, we lose our social function. For only practices and identities that establish some kind of contradictory relation to the normal function as historical motors, only in contradiction do practices become self-referential. Without the ability to see oneself, one lacks critical distance and is therefore blind to possible permutations and alternate ways of being. With this in mind, I invite the reader to enjoy these *Protokolle*.

1987 and 1989

Since I wrote this introduction, the particular world described by the men in these pages has vanished. Not only has the German Democratic Republic as a state collapsed, but the society within it, which had its own norms and mores, has also been transformed beyond recognition. Needless to say, both East German socialism—variously and vaguely defined in the past forty-five years—and homosexualities under socialism are no longer recognizable as such. Hence this book is about a disappearing or disappeared object; its descriptions are of a world now being quickly overtaken by West German corporate capitalism. I have chosen to leave the introductions to the book and its various chapters unchanged so as to keep the text within its historical context, for whatever that East German world was—a subject that will long be disputed by both the participants in it and the scientists who try to describe it—one can only begin to understand its shape and contours by beginning with the words and experiences of those native to it.

Capitalism—an economy based on relatively unregulated market exchange oriented toward profit—is now entering East Germany with a vengeance, hastily erasing the last vestiges of any distinctiveness created during the existence of the GDR, tenaciously bringing East German men out of their walled-in, provincial universe into the light of the world market. If Jürgen Lemke were to interview the men in these pages today, their stories would undoubtedly differ from those they told before. Their relative innocence, pervasive dependency, and intermittent fear would now be replaced by concerns about job security, competition, collapsing infrastructure, and AIDS, and perhaps by stories about new adventures traveling in Western Europe, a privilege most had been denied until the opening of the Wall on November 9, 1989. As East German men meet West Germans, they are quickly introduced to a semiotic system considered superior to their own—all things West are considered superior to all things East—that codes "homo" and "hetero" as opposite, mutually exclusive orientations, only abridged by a few "bisexuals." The range of sexualities in the East portrayed in these interviews, much like the range of political opinions one could find up to the opening of the border, is already taking on West German contours. Before contemplating what will be, however, let us begin by examining what was.

May 1990
Cambridge, Massachusetts

I. Erich and Karl

Introduced and translated by
Geoffrey J. Giles

To be gay in the Third Reich was to live in constant terror of arrest. The knock on the door came early for Erich, but Karl escaped police scrutiny until 1941. The two interviews make an interesting contrast: Erich spent an appalling ten years in prisons and concentration camps, while Karl remained free for most of the period, being placed under military arrest only for the latter part of the war.

Yet Karl does not speak much of his life between Hitler's murder in 1934 of one of the Führer's few intimate friends, the homosexual Ernst Röhm, and the outbreak of the war. One has to read between the lines to sense his fear. Karl's vivid memory of Hitler, screaming the words "but pederasts we will punish!" in his rabble-rousing speech to parliament following the Röhm putsch, is in fact entirely illusory. Hitler said no such thing. He did not even use the word *pederast* or *homosexual* in the speech, talking instead in euphemisms of "the circle of those of this particular disposition." Such forthright comments as "It is any race's own fault, if it does not find the strength to destroy these pests" were directed to the victims *not* as a putative, homosexual clique, but as alleged putschists guilty of high treason.

Nevertheless Hitler had referred to the question ten days earlier in a proclamation to the Storm Troopers (*Sturmabteilung*, SA) published in the party newspaper on July 3, 1934. Among other guidelines for the future of the SA, Hitler ordered:

> I would especially like every mother to be able to offer her son to the SA, the Party, or the Hitler Youth without the fear that he might become morally or sexually depraved. I therefore request all SA officers to pay scrupulous attention to the fact that misdemeanors according to §175 [of the German Criminal Code, i.e., homosexual acts] are to result in the immediate dismissal of those guilty from the SA and Party. I want to see men as SA officers and not disgusting apes.

This, together with the evidence of arrests of homosexuals reported in the local newspaper, led to a mistaken belief among many about the primary reason for the purge. In the case of Karl, gay himself, the illusion was so strong that in his mind he put words into Hitler's mouth that were plausible

(Hitler often worked himself up into such a frenzy when talking about Jews) but fictitious.

And Karl admits that he had voted for the man! He has the courage to admit it but suffers understandably from massive guilt feelings about that cross on the ballot sheet. Karl attempts to generalize his emotional burden by explaining that gay people did not put up a fight against the Nazis, did not organize themselves as a group, because a deep feeling of guilt about their homosexuality, ingrained through centuries of persecution, somehow made the aggression and brutality of their persecutors appear to be an acceptable reaction. Only extensive research on the Jewish holocaust showed that not all Jews went "like lambs to the slaughter." We do not yet know much about the experience of homosexuals in the Third Reich. Yet the hierarchy of the camps suggests that gays were even less integrated into society than Jews, whose assimilation was often accepted. Any organized political campaign before 1933 would have been lost among the hundreds of ineffectual interest groups at the end of the Weimar Republic. Any organized resistance thereafter, in a police state with burgeoning power, would certainly have been futile without the support of a numerically powerful group such as one of the churches. But for those who suffered and even died, this seems a poor excuse for having done nothing.

Of course, many people did not think that the Nazis would be as draconian as they said they would be. Or, like Erich, they believed themselves too insignificant for the Nazis to bother about. And after all, the unemployment question, the economy—these seemed to require the firm hand that the Nazis promised. That was the important side of the Nazi program that would touch everyone's life. Karl seems almost to have joined a Nazi organization. What held him back? Hitler's ranting in his book *Mein Kampf*. But it was not the remarks about the Jews that offended him so much as what Hitler had to say about some of his favorite artists.

Once again, Karl's memory has played tricks on him. Hitler was himself a competent if unexciting artist who had applied unsuccessfully to enter the art academy in Vienna. Hitler does discuss art in his book. But he does not mention the artists Zille, Barlach, or Kollwitz, let alone describe them as lavatory graffiti artists. His venom is reserved for the Cubists and Dadaists, whose paintings, says Hitler, are "the sick excrescences of mad or depraved people." These were not movements to which Karl's favorites belonged, although, since Karl eagerly followed the contemporary art scene, he may well have admired the work of these groups.

An interesting point that comes out in both interviews is the robust hungering after culture in the lower classes. Both Erich and Karl devoured all the books they could in workers' lending libraries, the former then starting up his own. The theater, the cinema, the art galleries, all played a much bigger role in working-class life than they do today.

Although both interviews provide valuable insights into everyday life in early twentieth-century Germany and into the life of gay men (such as

Erich's amusing reminiscences of the drag balls in Berlin), these vignettes are overshadowed by the theme of persecution under the Nazis. And here the story of Erich is an utterly extraordinary document. Because they were capriciously picked on, made the victims of cruel medical experiments, or deliberately worked to death, the majority of the "175ers" did not survive the end of the Third Reich. I use the contemporary slang rather than speaking of gay prisoners, because a number of those convicted under §175 of homosexual offenses were not gay. The paragraph was also used as a tool of political persecution when no other criminal charges could be dreamt up. Whether the charge was true or not, the pink triangle on your sleeve sent you to the bottom of the camp hierarchy.

To have lived through this hell for an entire decade is a remarkable achievement of sheer tenacity. What kept Erich going? We do not really find out. No succor from philosophical beliefs, no comfort from religion, it seems. Certainly no personal ties, for he deliberately denied himself emotional bonds with his fellow human beings either inside or outside the camps during those years, and he comments on the often fatal consequences for those who did. Above all, though, he seems to have maintained an unshakable, impenetrable, obstinate refusal to surrender to the will of his masters.

We gain more insight into how he did it than why he did it. Erich's often harsh upbringing forced him to learn the art of survival early on. As one learns from other memoirs of those who lived through the camps to tell the tale, it was often possible to do so only by utter selfishness, thinking each day of your own survival alone. There were those who showed Christian, Jewish, human virtues—but often not only did they die, but so did those for whom they had sacrificed themselves. Usually it was not the heroic ones who lived, but the wily ones, those often without much self-respect who were willing to sell out completely to their masters. After 1945 such people often suffered terrible feelings of guilt for having survived when so many millions of dead were left behind them in the camps. But there is a kind of courage in what they did, in not dying when the Nazis wanted them to die, in fighting as artfully as they could for their lives.

The interviews tell us little about the substance of the Nazi campaign against homosexuality, only about its extent. The amount of time and money spent by the police and law courts on convicting persons of homosexuality—for these were often anything but summary proceedings—reflects a bizarre obsession. The goal was to round up every last homosexual in the land. All too many of those unfortunates who were arrested had maintained relationships only in private and had committed no criminal act according to the law in force before 1935. They were rooted out by denunciation, by torture, and by chance, and the law was bent in order to punish them. *Nulla poena sine lege* was not exactly the guiding precept of Nazi legal practice. And then, even at the height of the war, as if they had nothing better to do, the Nazis pursued policies of deliberate entrapment.

Alas, Karl's experience of that might also have occurred with a policeman from any number of countries in postwar Europe.

The continuity of oppression is a sad fact. After their suffering in the Third Reich, both Erich and Karl thought they had reached nirvana after 1945. The expunging of Karl's criminal record for homosexuality was a just act by the East German state, for which West Germans in similar situations waited in vain. But an overall assessment of the lot of gay men in the GDR can only emerge after reading the other memoirs in this book. Certainly the societal pressures did not vanish. Many 175ers chose suicide when confronted with arrest. We read here of an unhappy soldier driven to suicide by the cruel insinuations of his comrades during the war. But even after the war homosexuality was not so openly accepted in the GDR that Karl's cousin did not also feel that suicide was the only way out for him. It sounds like a sick joke, but medical scholars in the Third Reich used to say in all earnestness that the high suicide rate among homosexuals simply further confirmed that gay people were mentally ill.

That such attitudes have still not vanished entirely from society as a whole is what continues to burden gay people in many countries. Karl cannot even bring himself to use the words *homosexual* and *gay* in his interview, because of their negative implications. If the state authorities can lead the way in dismantling the old prejudices, as appears to be happening in the GDR today, then there is at least hope for the future, for the slow construction of a more tolerant society.

1. "You won't hear heroic tales about our kind"

Erich, 1900–1986, worker

When I left school in 1914, we used to sing: "The course of our life / goes uphill and downhill, / we are merely guests on earth." And that's the way it went, with this earth acting as a pretty brutal host for me. I often sank so low down that moving upwards was something unimaginable.

I was born in the Schönhauser Allee No. 70a. The house is still there. When I was a kid, there was open ground on the other side of the street. From Eberswalder to Gleim streets there stretched a parade ground where the Kaiser's Guards Regiments clicked their heels. The Colosseum Movie Theater was still serving as a station for the horse-drawn trains. Behind the Schönhauser S-Bahn station in the direction of Pankow was also just open ground. To Pankow and back by foot was almost a whole day's journey for us. The S-Bahn still had steam locomotives and was only electrified years later. If you didn't have a place to stay, you just got on board and rode round and round Berlin.

The "Three"—that was the great ring route on the tram. Once around lasted almost three hours. Over the Hindenburg Bridge (today called the Bornholmer), through Wedding, Moabit, Charlottenburg, and Wilmersdorf to Neu-Kölln. The Three still goes via the Bornholmer even today. Prenzlauer Hill was always a workers' district.[1] The Communists and Social Democrats drew most of their voters from there. If the KPD (*Kommunistische Partei Deutschland*, Communist party of Germany) were up to something, the streets become a sea of red flags. Today, when the Communists are in power, they only hang the flags out on public holidays in my street at the baths, the cooperative store, and the fire station.

Round the corner in Kastanienallee I used to go to the movies for 6 pfennigs. Six-penny movies they used to call them. One of those jiggly silent movies used to run from morning to evening nonstop. When the movie came to an end, they would call out your number and you had to get out. I once found a 20-mark piece. It was such a fortune I had trouble spending it. I invited five kids to come to the movies with me, but that only got rid of 30 pfennigs.

When my parents split up, I was sent to the orphanage and got out when I was fourteen. The First World War was underway and no apprenticeships were available. So I sold newspapers on the tram. I hopped from car to car all day long and was hungry the whole time. There just wasn't much to eat then. So it was always a great temptation to cash in one of the dimes for a quick bread roll. When I came back short one evening, I got the sack on the spot. There were plenty of others waiting for my job.

In the meantime my mother had died and my father was living with another woman. It wasn't long before I landed in a juvenile delinquents' home. We were brought up there with the motto "Whoever spares the rod, hates his son. Whoever loves his son will flog him!" And then pious words from dawn till dusk, and nothing to eat. So I skipped out.

I traveled all the way from Berlin to Cologne on a platform ticket without being checked. I'd picked Cologne because I wanted to join the Foreign Legion. But they caught me in the Cologne Central Station and dragged me before the judge. Ten days' jail or 100 marks' fine.

That was the first time in my life that I was inside. On the tenth day I was just sitting, peeling potatoes, when I heard someone yelling: "Hofmann, Hofmann!" It took a while before I caught on that it was me they meant. With no identity papers I'd given my name as Gustav Hofmann. And this was the name in which my release papers were made out. I was free again and I was Gustav Hofmann. And finally I had papers in my hands again.

So then I went down the Rhine on foot. From one village to the other. You weren't without company for long in those days. The roads were full of young lads like myself looking for work. One reckoned that he'd heard prospects were pretty good farther down the Rhine; upstream, another would say. If you took to each other, you'd go along together, no matter whether up- or downstream. You'd face everything together and sleep in the hay or on piles of potato leaves. Whatever happened to be dry. The next morning nobody breathed a word about what had gone on during the night. When it's dark and cold, people snuggle up together. Besides which we were young and in our prime. While we rubbed the sleep out of our eyes, our thoughts were already turning to how we could give our stomachs what they deserved.

With one or two you might spend some time tramping through the area, but with others you'd part after one night. After some weeks I found work with a farmer. There was a Communist in the village. One day he asked me, "Hey, kid, how much do you earn with your farmer?" "Oh, I don't know," I said. "Now and then he gives me a mark."

So he took me along to the shipyards in Cologne. I worked in the harbor till I was sacked—three whole months. When there was no more work, you got your notice. That's the way things were. Then I went on the road again for several months, until I felt a hankering for Berlin again. Even before that my Communist friend had talked me out of the Foreign Legion. I traveled back just as I had come. With a platform ticket.

The inflation was in full swing in Berlin and people were going crazy.

The city was like a wildly spinning carousel: people tumbled off it and others jumped up to the vacant spots during the ride. There was no possibility whatsoever of regular work for someone like me who had not learned a trade.

In those days I often let myself get picked up. Try luring a boy into your bed today with the prospect of a job. That sort of thing only happens in the movies now. Of course one thing has not changed even today: there are many who are hot for young proletarians, and there is no shortage of men who want to love them and educate them.

I used to read whatever came into my hands. I had no money to buy my own books, and where could I have kept them anyway? I found Leonhard Frank riveting, and I just devoured Bertha von Suttner's antiwar novel *Lay Down Your Arms*. Tucholsky, Kästner, everything that was in vogue. Bertha von Suttner impressed me so much that I became involved in founding an antiwar museum in the Parochialstraße and helped set it up. The men who gave me the books to read have long since vanished from my memory.

The Romanisch Café held a great attraction for me. You could find them all there: Ringelnatz, Toller, the well-known actors, the cabaret artists from the Friedrichstraße. I went to every one of Toller's plays, usually at the People's Theater near the Piscator.

In the twenties there was scarcely an occupational group that was not represented at the famous drag balls in the big Berlin ballrooms. We "simple lads" came dressed as Asta Nielsen or Henny Porten and let ourselves be served champagne by coarse, cursing taxi drivers or menservants.[2] It was part of the craziness of the setting that these tough servants and taxi drivers exchanged their gear next morning for the judge's robe or the doctor's white coat. It even happened that an "Asta" would be sent to the clink for shoplifting a week later by her "manservant."

Like most people in my neighborhood I voted Communist. As a young man I had hung around for a while with the Wandervögel[3] and had now and then gone to meetings of the Socialist Workers' Youth group, but I didn't join formally because their way of doing things seemed too prudish to me.

At the beginning of the thirties I opened a small lending library. It was logical that most of the work fell on Fridays and Saturdays. Others buzzed off to the countryside while I had to sort books. After two years I suddenly decided to sell out. The Nazis would have closed up shop for me a few months later in any case. I had a stack of the very books that they burned on the Opera Square shortly after they seized power.[4]

Those of us who live out our gay disposition always fear violence and oppression. It seems to be one of the ironies of fate that the repressed and secretive among us are drawn toward violence and submit themselves to it. The more militant the crowd, the happier they feel. Boots and belt finally turn them into real men, like the rest of the lads. If many had already fled to the Nazi Brownshirts before 1933, a lot more were ready to do so after 1933.

Things really got hot for us after the Night of the Long Knives.[5] There were already rumors long before the putsch that some of us had disappeared. I realized that was a possibility for me too. But what could I have done? Flee abroad? I didn't have enough cash for that. I could have gone into hiding—for a month, or even two, but certainly not for years on end.

Like many others I convinced myself that I was too unimportant to be checked off on their list of those to be run in. I had been working at a coffee seller's for quite a while and had not done a thing to blot my copybook. On July 5, 1935, they picked me up. I was just about to go to work when the doorbell rang. Two men at the door informed me that I was under arrest. Out in the street a third gentleman waited at the wheel of a big eight-cylinder Horch coupe.[6] A Berliner would say, "Very posh!" I got in the car and we drove one block. I knew immediately who was meant to take a seat beside me when we stopped at number eight—in a way we all kept together. They came back without him and we roared off in the direction of Pankow. More precisely, the Pankow weekly market. I was surprised to see him busy among the cucumbers, tomatoes, cabbages, and radishes, because he was known by everyone as Daisy. I saw from afar how he took off his apron, hung it on a hook, and bade a friendly farewell to the ladies lining up to shop at his stall. I shifted over, he sat beside me, and all the way to the Gestapo headquarters in the Prinz-Albrecht-Straße we acted as though we had never ever set eyes on each other before.[7]

The situation was clear from the very first day. Of all those the Nazis had herded together in the cellar, we were the lowest of the low. We were left in no doubt about that within the first five minutes. When it came to "homo hatred," the Nazis could give free rein. Whereas they had to organize hatred against Communists and Jews among their henchmen and followers with a massive propaganda effort, whole centuries of Christianity handed them homo hatred on a platter. Before they beat us up, they would bombard us with the same words that I had already heard so many times in my life.

And always the same question. Do you know so-and-so, or so-and-so? And then they would leaf forward a couple of pages in their list of names. The ones in between they had already caught. And then again, do you know him, or him? When I ventured to ask why I was being held here, they all roared as if on cue and almost collapsed from laughing.

From the Prinz-Albrecht-Straße I was sent to the Columbia-Haus, a former military prison.[8] Up there by the Tempelhof Field. I stayed there until September. The trials against us 175ers all ran exactly the same.[9] Indecency, procuring, off to the concentration camp. Nobody was to be given the opportunity to corrupt healthy, adolescent German youth again.

From the Columbia-Straße off to Lichtenburg—an old prison near Prettin that the Nazis had turned into a concentration camp. Sachsenhausen and

Buchenwald were still being built. Esterwegen was already finished. That was my next destination. Esterwegen on the moor, the hell on the forest's edge, as we called the cooler. Day in, day out, digging drainage trenches on the moor. Down came the cart, and as soon as it was there, our orders were shovel it full to the top again. I remained here from 1936 to 1939.

Being deprived on the outside stood me in good stead in the camp. In the orphanage I had learned very early on to look after myself first. My mother had died early, and I had never really gotten close to my father. I had not had a love affair with another man for several years. I was one of those people who felt more comfortable unattached.

I had no strong emotional ties to the outside, so I could concentrate fully on survival. Those who had left their lover on the outside seldom discovered what had happened to him. Where could they have gotten such information? After all, the parents often found out about their son's double life only after he was committed to the concentration camp. How could an inmate have his mother make inquiries about a person she did not know at all and who may have been interned in another concentration camp? I met inmates who had neither a hint whether their lover was alive nor any sign of life from their parents, who had demonstratively disowned their offspring as soon as they discovered the reason for his sentence to the concentration camp.

I was summoned to the commandant about a family matter in 1943. I reported as ordered, suspecting the worst, whereupon he bellowed at me: "Your old man's dropped dead, get out!" As I left, he yelled after me: "If you want to write a letter, have them give you some paper in the office." But to whom could I have written?

It may well be that for someone who is sitting out a normal sentence, his family helps him keep going. Under our circumstances that was not the case. Anyone who had spent five years here and could see no end of it was well advised to gather his strength for the next day and not waste it on dreams that lay outside the reality of the camp.

When Sachsenhausen was finished, I was transferred there. To the 175ers' block. Sachsenhausen was a nightmare. Many of us did not come through it alive. The battalion that was most severely punished lived alongside us. Both of us were sent into the clay. For us, clay pits became grave sites. If it was raining, you couldn't even lift your shovel. But the wagons for the brick works had to be full the whole time. In the camp we called the clay pit the death pit.

Always and everywhere, in every camp, the hardest and shittiest work was reserved for us. They constantly stuck it to us. The intellectuals were the first to crack. From the café to the camp—most of them were unable to handle that. They were not used to physical labor and deprivations on the outside. They did not know wretched grub either. And now such overrefined, high-strung types here in the middle of the filthiest muck.

The Kapos always enjoyed picking on them.[10] The Kapos never tired of finding new ways of proving to these "queer clever shits" that they were dumber than the dumbest broad. If some of the guards had had a few drinks and wanted a good laugh, they would order one of these "Lord Mucks" to the orderly room or would drop in to see us. One of the most harmless jokes was the nail test. In front of the assembled company the person selected had to knock a nail in the wall. That was all.

The victim stepped forward, was given a hammer and a nail, and then had to state the occupation for which he had been trained. The organizers became attentive. How many blows of the hammer would it take? Although the maximum number, seven blows, was allotted to a hairdresser without discussion, a pharmacist, for example, gave rise to some speculation. How many blows of the hammer could he be expected to need? Three? four? five? The guard who had lost at dice in the tavern beforehand and now had to bet on the victim asserted that the femininity of the pharmacist's trade demanded six hits. The rest of his colleagues shouted him down. Five at the most, the profession was not *that* effeminate! The unlucky gambler barked at the prisoner: "Get your jacket off, show us your biceps!" Roaring with laughter, the others generously conceded six strikes.

Of course it didn't happen very often that you could get the nail properly into the wall at all. From sheer terror and trembling you simply couldn't set it up right. Someone who even under normal circumstances would not knock a nail into a wall straight was suddenly the star attraction. And, unpredictable as those brutes were, such a little game could mean the end of the prisoner.

On one occasion I was picked out. True, I didn't have a profession, but I knew how to knock a nail into the wall. I bashed it in with three hits, quicker than anyone before me. There was an icy silence, until the one who had bet on me snorted with laughter. Had I been too quick? Had I provoked them with my skill? Had I disregarded my principle of always being unobtrusive? I got away with it this time.

Of medium height with an average kind of face, I had always marched in the middle of the column till then. If you were at the head of it and you stumbled, you would never rise to your feet again. At the back they kicked you in the ass. You were by far the safest in the middle. That was how I survived.

They picked on the tall, strong, handsome guys just as much as on the real queens. Both types did not live long. But I had amazed them. So one of "those" types could knock a nail in just as it ought to be done. Just like them. No occupation, also like them, at least like most of the guards. I think that at that moment I became classified in some of those skulls as one of the reformables. A guy like that could perhaps be brought to mend his ways. In the next few weeks I noticed tiny changes in their attitude toward me. I had not risen in their respect; it was just that they despised me less.

Later on in the camp at Flossenbürg I was put to work boring holes for the explosive charges in the quarry.[11] The blaster came up to me and said, "From today on you will bore the holes for the charges. You are the only guy who doesn't have two left feet. If you make an effort, you'll get on okay with me. Your predecessor had no cause for complaint."

It was a real piece of luck that I was transferred from Sachsenhausen to Flossenbürg at the end of 1940. I spent the final years up to liberation in this camp. Flossenbürg saved my life. A small camp, with better food than Sachsenhausen. We worked in the quarry. In films about these camps they often show the work in the quarries. Pick up a rock, down to the tip, deposit the rock, back at the double. Pick up another rock, down to the tip, deposit the rock, back at the double. And so on, the whole day long. The work became easier when the camp shifted to war industry. Airplane parts—for Hitler's Luftwaffe.

Buddies, human contacts, solidarity? Why didn't I find myself a dear little friend? Shared suffering is merely half the suffering. Only someone who doesn't have a clue asks such questions. I'm sorry, but now I'm becoming agitated again. This homespun wisdom may well apply to all the prisons and penitentiaries in the world, but not to a German concentration camp, and certainly not to a 175er.

I had no close contact with anybody. That was always too dangerous for me. Only the bare essential that was unavoidable among so many people in such a confined space. I also did not know anyone from the outside. Those who knew each other from the outside stuck together constantly at the beginning. Right until one morning they were called out together from the parade and sent off together for "special treatment." Relapsed, refractory, ran the justification.

Perhaps the hut orderly had caught them comforting one another, perhaps another inmate had caught them making love at night and blown the whistle on them, or it could just have been that it did not suit the Kapos that the two stuck together. Whatever, they either never returned from their "special treatment" or they starved before our eyes because their rations were eliminated.

It was hunger that finished us off. The fact that we were met everywhere with "Ha, you queer swine" did not make us suffer long, but we suffered constantly from undernourishment. You won't hear heroic tales about our kind. At any rate I don't know of any. Everyone becomes his own good neighbor when it's a question of hanging on to that last shred of life. The Communists had their party, but what did we have? Where the Communists were able to draw their strength, we just reached into a black hole.

The hierarchy of the triangles was a reflection of the outside world. Among the low we stood beneath the very lowest. Red, green, violet, then for a while nothing, at the very bottom pink.[12] The criminals could have pulled off the most appalling crimes, but they easily ranked above the homos. Only the Russian POWs, who began to be shipped to the camp from 1942 onward, stood lower than us.

Of course we laughed as well. No human being can live through ten years like that without laughing. In Flossenbürg we laughed about our camp commandant behind his back. We called him "Dusty"! His every second sentence was: "When I come along, the dust will fly! Watch out!"

Bedmaking in a German concentration camp was a story in itself. Not a wrinkle on a single blanket. If Dusty was doing his rounds, it could happen that even the Kapos would suddenly tweak a cover straight here or there. If Dusty was in a bad mood, he would rip all the bedcovers off and scream at all of us, including the Kapos.

On parade he would play his favorite game at least once a week. Number So-and-so, step forward! Then Dusty, slapping his right leather glove on his gloved left hand, would ask his adjutant: "Faggot?" The adjutant answered like a ward doctor to the chief surgeon: "Of course, Herr Commandant, all of them here are." Whereupon Dusty would ask the adjutant, pointing to the inmate with his glove: "That one too?" The adjutant: "All of them without exception."

Dusty to the inmate: "You're a bright enough guy, at least you look like it at the moment, you ought to know that one doesn't do such things. Unpunished, I mean. You're an engineer, not some drag queen who can't count to three. Well then?" Whatever the inmate answered, "Yes, Herr Commandant" or "No, Herr Commandant," the punishment was always the same: "special treatment." The new ones suffered the most. Before they had learned to keep their mouths shut, they were done for.

Before Dusty gave his adjutant the order to fall out, he warned everybody: "I know that you'd all like to do it here. Make it with sweet, young German boys. Am I right?" And then he'd say to the inmate as though he were especially disappointed in him: "Well admit it at least, you swine!" I was tougher than most in taking abuse. I'd already had to put up with a lot as a child. I was deaf in my left ear; the ear drum had developed a callous in the meantime.

In Flossenbürg there was a kind of camp self-government. The head of it was one of the criminal inmates. If he gave you the thumbs down, you were a dead man. A 175er could not even become a block scribe in this system. The camp head was responsible for the "camp jollifications." On Sundays we were allowed to play soccer. The criminals, if they'd had their way, would have put on a competition every Sunday. At the bottom of the league the 175ers always played against the Jews. If the guards played too, the criminals dropped to second place.

Besides this there was a sixty-man band. Lots of brass. Operetta melodies were particular favorites. "Rosamunde" and "Be on your way, you're only a private" were their signature tunes. If Dusty happened by, they would strike up "Lili Marleen," his favorite song.

The camp also had an inmate's whorehouse. Whoever wished to go there in the evening had to put his name down at the morning parade. One day I said to myself, "Give it a try, it can't harm you." My booking was *the* conversation topic of the day. How would they react to it? Everyone had a different opinion. If they regarded it as a provocation, I might as well say my prayers. If they saw the whole thing as a big joke, I might keep my skin. At the evening inspection I heard my number and "granted." Without any comment. My heart continued to race.

On that evening in the fall of 1943 I got to know Else. She did not survive. Else from Potsdam, twenty-six, a waitress by trade. The only person with whom I became friends in those ten years. The Nazis particularly liked to put lesbian women in brothels. They reckoned they would shape up again there. At first glance we saw through each other. We gossiped so long and hard that I was finally thrown out by her boss. As the old fury saw my pink triangle, she could scarcely believe her eyes.

Else arranged it so that we were able to get together now and then and have time to chat. It was tough for me to cope with the fact that Else didn't make it.

In the fist years after liberation I was often asked the question: how were you able to survive this hell? My life before 1933 is part of the explanation. Way back then it didn't bother me to sleep out on a park bench and have nothing to eat for two days. As a child I had to make my own way through life. But the older I get, the more certain I become that whatever reasons I put forward, they don't all add up to an explanation. There's something inexplicable there too, something I can't express. A miracle.

In September 1944 it looked as though after nine whole years my time had come. Together with a young painter from Vienna I was detailed to a battalion for SS members who were being punished. The chances of surviving this SS "punishment battalion" were even worse than those of someone in a KZ. Even today I don't know why nothing came of it. The transport just never took place. Two weeks later they hanged the painter from the gate of the camp. Allegedly he had made advances to his latest customer, a young SS man. I hate to think in how many "good German homes" portraits that he painted for the guards' company hang above the sofa. The whole gang of them were begging to be painted by him. In uniform and in color. The dimensions of the picture were strictly regulated by the rank of the sitter. If a lieutenant demanded a size to which he was not entitled, the artist had to convince him with much cunning and diplomacy that some of the cardboard he had brought along needed to be trimmed off. Because the colors were in short supply, he could only splash out with them on the higher ranks. Why he was hanging one morning from the camp gate, perhaps only the young SS man knew. It could be that it did not suit him that others could commission a picture after him. Or perhaps he could not stand it that the painter had chosen a smaller format or had not used enough color. So he had him hanged; it was that simple.

The tension in the last months was unbearable. Nobody wanted to be seen as a slacker so close to the collapse. One question was on everyone's mind. How would Dusty react? Given the size of the camp, he could eliminate all witnesses at one stroke. The worst rumors circulated. They would poison our food, they would drive us into abandoned tunnels and wall them up. In the morning we would anticipate the first scenario, in the afternoon somebody else would come along with a completely new and even more horrifying version. Everyone was on the lookout. Our guards reacted more and more nervously.

The day of freedom always comes as a surprise. Even if you have waited an eternity for it. You feel a mixture of joy and disappointment. Your fantasy has bathed the day in so much chocolate that you feel sick when it arrives.

After ten years I stood again on the Alexanderplatz.[13] Right in the middle of it, among distraught people poking around in the rubble with one eye on the black market. I felt sorrow for my Alex, but I regarded these interlopers with satisfaction. Many people have said that the city was unrecognizable. That only applied to those who didn't really know Berlin. I recognized every house in my neighborhood, whether it was totally burned out or only partly destroyed.

From the Alex I went to the Münzstraße, from there to the Grenadier, through the Schendelgasse to the Mulackstraße. The Mulack Gap was still standing, and behind the bar the same landlady who had always served me. I was thoroughly delighted, ran up to the boss, and received quite a blow when she did not recognize me. She had scarcely changed at all . . . unlike me.

On the way to the Schönhauser I whistled to myself: "The course of our life / goes uphill and downhill, / we are merely guests on earth."

In the years afterward I seldom encountered familiar faces. When I'm talking to you, faces and names occur to me from every period of my life. More faces than names. I found out that one of them had died in Buchenwald. Another fell at the front line. I can only guess what happened to most of them.

Sachsenhausen was turned into a memorial a long time ago. The last time I was there was ten years ago with some boys from my street. I caught myself talking about another me. The post-1945 me was speaking about the pre-1945 me. In a thoroughly detached way. Almost as though I was reading from a history book in which I happened to be mentioned. I can't hold it against young people if the statistics of those killed don't mean anything to them. The everyday business at the Buchenwald facility where people were shot in the neck is something you just cannot grasp. What is the use of saying: I suffered terribly.

I'm telling you about my time in the camp and I realize that I want to convince you of my suffering. That's something I haven't done for a long time. You sit down as some old codger in a bar or a café, and who is willing to listen to you? I am not even invited as a veteran to the Free German Youth groups anymore with this story of mine.[14]

I stayed at work until my seventy-seventh year. On the production line, not as a doorman somewhere. My minimum pension was one of the reasons, but I quite enjoyed working. You remain somebody. I opened my mouth when I thought it necessary. I always knew how to defend myself. If one of my many colleagues couldn't realize that I wouldn't stand for being offended with hackneyed insults, I stood up to him. It just aggravated me. If somebody asked me in a reasonable way, then I answered him. If a new guy came along and they told him about me, then I didn't have to go to the trouble myself. Factory workers differ from white-collar workers in that they shower together after their shift. Not all of them went two stalls down!

I moved into this apartment at the beginning of the fifties. Before I did so, the building supervisor went around to every household where there were young men living to inform them: "In the first rear courtyard in the middle, up two flights of stairs to the right, one of 'those' is moving in on the first of the month, so watch out." He couldn't have given me a better advertisement. After two short weeks I heard the first timid knocks at my door.

There will always be people who turn away when you tell them the whole truth about yourself. That's just one of those things. And no amount of complaining is going to change that. Those who do open themselves to you, they're the important ones, they're the ones with whom you can live your life. Whether friendship, love, or just acquaintance grows out of it depends partly on what you want from each other. There are so many jerks who would really kick themselves if they one day came to realize just how many people they have kept at a distance by sitting tight in their closet.

I scarcely had any relationships with other homosexuals in all those years. Their squeamishness got on my nerves, their constant fear of discovery, the terror that someone might shout a rude word behind their back on the street. It's quite possible that many were afraid in the postwar years that the whole horror story could be repeated. But I had enough of a political education to know that that was out of the question under the new circumstances. There were still conflicts, but your life was no longer in danger.

In the middle of the fifties I bought a good-sized boat and for the next twenty years spend my weekends on the water. Sailing was not all that went on.

Most of the guys you can see in these photos have long since married and had children. Sometimes it happens that the doorbell rings, and I open up, and outside there's someone I have to look at three times before I recognize him. A child hanging onto his left hand, a child on his right, and he with beard and potbelly. And he'll say, "Do you know what so-and-so's doing, I ran into him, and old what's-his-name has bought a car, he's doing such-and-such." Today their younger brothers fetch the coal up for me in the winter and help me when something needs to be repaired in the apartment. They've all got jobs today.

Some years ago a woman from the building out front spoke to me and said, "My Frank tells me you're a good cook." I did not know what to say.

She went on: "If what I serve up on Saturday doesn't suit him, he stands up from the table and says, I'm going over to Erich's, he can cook better!"

Every year in February I'm as old as the century. I'd like to become ninety. Twice forty-five years. Nothing wrong with that, is there? After the first forty-five I leapt out of the jaws of death; at the end of the second forty-five I'll be content to stay put. What do I care if it's a "quiet funeral"? I won't be around anymore.

Interview completed 1984

2. "This is my young friend; we're in love"

Karl, born 1907, druggist

When I was your age, the most difficult chapter of my life was coming to an end. As it happened, the following years turned out a lot brighter for me and for most people.

For somebody like me who lived through the madness of the war from the very beginning, was severely wounded, and then spent the final year of the war under military arrest, the path to the prisoner-of-war camp seemed like the road to freedom. I felt a sense of release. After all, I had just managed as a homophile to survive the martyrdom of the Third Reich. After twelve years of trembling, and by now thirty-eight years old, I finally felt free from mortal danger once more, and as a POW, I experienced again some hours of happiness after a long abstinence. You must know that wherever men live together and are not immediately threatened with death, they do it with one another. When men no longer feel death crouching over them, they eat and they smoke, they come back to life again, and that is quickly followed by love and by sex. That's S–E–X.

The French didn't do anything to stop it. Au contraire, those Algerians who had to guard us were not disinclined themselves. And what that meant, I'm sure I don't have to tell you. Yes, those Algerians! As often as I could manage to, I would shower together with them and . . . well, you know. Ah, those North African Arab tribes!

It's true that the French are a nation of great culture, but the way they handled their Algerians does not speak well for them. As a reward for getting the French out of hot water, all they received were numbers instead of names and the privilege of nonstop guard duty. I didn't think that was very fair—and made no secret of my view to the Algerians.

Mother wrote to me: "You have survived the war, son, stay a while over there if you can. According to your letters you obtain eggs, red wine, and once in a while even real coffee. Back home we're starving." I heeded my mother's words and succeeded in stretching out my stay in northern France until the end of 1948.

In the camp I had my eye on a cute little number. We called him Ducky. But I don't even think he was homophile. Well, that didn't matter to me. Incidentally, I don't like the other words for it. We get dragged in the mud so badly with them. So I said to Ducky, "Why don't you move into my room?" Straight away he said yes. Well then.

Apart from that we had a handsome camp doctor. A nice guy. You know what I mean. Thank God there were some others who had survived with me. People who had gone through those tough times suddenly opened up to each other.

Shortly before Christmas 1948 I was released. My hometown had been badly knocked around. The big factories had made the place a favorite bombing target. What little remained of them was dismantled. My twin brother returned home five days before me. Mother was beside herself with joy. Only one of my three brothers did not return home. The war had left deep scars in the families on both sides of us in our street.

All my brothers and my sister got married and provided the grandchildren, so my mother never really had a problem with my childlessness. I don't think much of these Freudian insights. But I must say I agree with him about our relationship to our mothers. I had a wonderful, deep, and intimate relationship with my mother. Mothers feel and recognize very early on which of their children need a little extra maternal affection in order to cope with the world. Fathers are ashamed of our sort. But in the Nazi period there were mothers too who turned their backs on their children on discovering that they were homophiles. I think that a mother becomes a tragic figure when she hears a voice telling her to withdraw her affection from her child. That is the outside world talking, not the mother.

My childhood memories go right back to 1914. On April 1, my twin brother and I started school. Just four months later the First World War began. The Kaiser proclaimed cockily from his palace: the German people will celebrate together under the Christmas tree, by which time the war will long be forgotten. But five Christmases passed by with less and less under the tree from year to year, and fewer and fewer people came together. The suffering was great. The whole country was starving. Ration cards for clothes and for food, shoes with wooden soles, turnip dinners, the black market—everything as it was to be again thirty years later.

Mother worked a sixteen-hour day. The war allowance only covered essentials, so she knitted everything for the children. Caps, scarves, gloves, socks, pullovers—and all that five times over. Six really, because she had to look after herself too. And then washing, ironing, and darning on top of it all. The self-sacrifice of a mother for her children is unbelievable.

I liked going to school. I didn't hate my teachers; on the contrary I got on well with them, I liked them. I must admit that I was never thrashed with either the thin cane or the big stick. My grades were always almost too good. Perhaps that was the difference between me and the other boys. I remember that every year during the war there were more and more pupils in the classroom. The reason for that was that teachers were also called up for active service and fell at the front.

The Weimar Republic introduced mixed classes. The boys and the girls used the same school entrance from then on. And suddenly the talk was all of pupils' councils. I was elected to such a committee for the first time at the age of twelve. I do not believe that they altered things very much, because the same old teachers remained.

Our history teacher restricted himself to a single topic for a whole year: the Great Elector. Time and again the Great Elector. I remember that at the end of the year the father of a fellow pupil suddenly turned up in the classroom, red in the face, and informed our history teacher: "Let me tell you something, sir, just you shut up about the Great Elector, there are plenty of much more important men who have made history in Germany, apart from your Great Elector!" Then he ran through a list of names that we had never heard before but that left our teacher speechless. He stood before us so stunned that, thinking back today, I am sure Marx and Bebel must have been among those mentioned. The teachers back then were still enthusiastic about the Kaiser, even though he had long fled.

Five minutes away from the school lay our university. I wanted to go there at all costs. All I could manage was a lab technician's course, and that only because parents no longer had to pay fees for an apprenticeship after the revolution. Two of my brothers became apprentice builders, the third went into printing, and my sister worked in a clothing store.

Even today everything about a university holds a great attraction for me. I was already considerably over seventy when a dream of mine was fulfilled. I enrolled in the university and attended my first lectures. I'm speaking of the senior citizens' courses. Apart from my fellow students everything was just as I had imagined it would be all my life.

You'll notice that I have not said a word about my father so far. My parents' marriage fell apart right after the First World War. Wars destroy everything, but above all people. My father returned from France and suddenly demanded from my worn-out mother sexual variations that he had discovered and developed a taste for during his campaign of conquest. My mother had meanwhile turned forty and had no time for such things. Since neither would give in, the marriage broke up. Years later she touched on the reason for the divorce with the words: "When he came back from over there, he demanded you-know-what from me." And she dropped a hint, shuddering. "So you can imagine, son, what sort of a slut his new flame must be." I could not very well tell my mother that I had meanwhile also become a follower of the un-German practices of my dissolute father.

We were always short of cash at home and the divorce made things worse. Admittedly he paid for new suits for our confirmation, but it was mother who bore the burden of the children. I was never able to bring myself to a reconciliation with Father while he was alive. I could not forgive him for leaving Mother in the lurch. Today I wonder if I was not too hard on him. I'm sure I was.

As the son of a farmer and a weaver, he crossed more insurmountable barriers in his youth than I did. He worked his way up from bricklayer to foreman and tried to make a go of it alone. But he didn't get anywhere. I felt I owed it to Mother to reject the hand cautiously held out in reconciliation. My other brothers and sister were less hard on him. But then they were not so close to her.

When my twin brother and I brought home our first wages, we invited Mother to the movies. Seats in the balcony. Mother in the middle, to her right and left a tall, strapping blond twin son. She was proud of us both, and I don't think she took in the movie at all, out of sheer excitement. Then we went home in a taxi. Mothers after all are never extravagant on their own.

During my apprenticeship I had a good-natured and fatherly boss. I thought he was terrific; my boss became my idol. In the college of commerce I received the best grades. Whether it was calligraphy, handwriting, letter-writing, or civics, I was full of enthusiasm for every subject. Naturally I received an "A" for attitude and diligence too.

My boss was not totally indifferent to me either. I had a funny feeling, but I couldn't put my finger on it. He dropped hints, like: "My wife doesn't want anything to do with me, but, oh well, there are other possibilities." That just confused me, the topic was embarrassing to me. What's he talking about, he's got a wife and kids? Today I could kick myself for acting so stupidly. But whom could I have asked.

One day I told him that Frederick the Great was my favorite king. The very next day a nicely framed picture of Frederica was hanging above my workplace. That our Frederick was also a Frederica was something I did not of course discover until later.

Back then every proper German household had a copy of Pilz's medical encyclopedia, which mothers placed within easy reach of their children as soon as they turned fourteen. I'm talking about the reference book with the colored, fold-out charts. I managed to save it across the years. If you look on page 136, you'll find the child in the womb. We were permitted to study the makeup of the organs. What you were to do with them was dismissed in the exhortation to wash them regularly. You will not find a single word on any one of the five hundred pages about bisexuals or about love between men. For me years went by before it came out that even married men sometimes seek out other men.

In 1930 there were millions of unemployed. At the age of twenty-three I had to feed three out-of-work brothers and my mother. My sister was married and had her own family to look after. When I came home during the lunch break, my brothers would climb out of bed, desperate for a ciggy. They would brighten up as soon as I pressed a breakfast cigarette into their hands. Between 1930 and 1932 our wages were cut 10 percent twice.

Many other German families had the same experience as we did in 1933. The years of suffering had forged us together, but they had not taught us to recognize what was happening around us. My three brothers found work and food again. Finally they were able to marry and start their own families. By now it was high time for them.

For fifty-two marks I was able to travel to Hamburg, and from there by ship past Heligoland across to the Norwegian fjords.[1] At home I had never eaten such fine meals as I enjoyed on board. I'm telling you this in order to explain why we voted for the man. I am honest enough to admit it. Apolitical people always judge events by pragmatic, petit-bourgeois standards. The new regime brightened Mother up. She could keep house properly again. All of a sudden the rent was no longer a problem.

I must come back to my boss again. He gave me Hitler's *Mein Kampf* as a Christmas present in 1933. I read it straight through. It was what I read there that held me back from joining the whole racket. On top of that there was all the talk about degenerate art. Zille, Barlach, Kollwitz were dismissed as lavatory wall graffiti. Other renowned artists were besmirched too. When it came to art, I had developed my own strong opinions with the help of my boss. Until 1933 there was an extremely active cultural scene. I went to see the exhibitions of important painters, and I could always be found in a workers' library. I read everything that was recommended to me, all the way from Thomas Mann to Karl May.

"A man like you belongs in the SS." Those were the words with which the recruiters entered our shop. My boss stayed in the background and rolled his eyes knowingly. In a purely physical sense I was certainly a prime candidate. Tall, well-built, blond, and blue-eyed. I no longer know how on earth I managed to stay out. Perhaps they laid off me because I looked too slovenly to them.

When the whole dilemma became more comprehensible after the war, I tried to face the question of my own complicity. You're there, on a list of the guilty, even if only at the bottom of it. Why didn't we homophiles put up more of a fight? It's not the first time I have been asked the question. We did not resist an all-powerful enemy, let alone organize ourselves against him, because a deep feeling of guilt inside us endorsed our murderers' desire to kill us. The short breathing space during the Weimar Republic was not sufficient to reconcile us homophiles to our sex life. The persecutions of millennia have built up this deep feeling of guilt within us. Most of us fell powerless into the hands of the Nazis.

We stood before the newspaper display cases stunned and read the names of the SA leaders Hitler had shot because of their degeneracy. I can still hear him today as he screamed at the howling mob in his Reichstag speech: "but pederasts we will punish!" The next day I opened the local newspaper and was petrified. The names, occupations, and addresses were given of men denounced as homosexual polluters of the German people. At the head of the list was a professor of art. The owner of the top cigar shop in town, the well-known tailor So-and-so, and many others. The Nazis rechristened a central square in town as "175ers Square," because four of the accused had their businesses there.

It was a proverbial load off my mind to discover that my name was not on the list. Had I gotten off by chance, or did they not yet have me on any of their lists? Every ring or knock at the door put me in a deathly panic. I did have contacts, but I was exceptionally cautious and guarded. I did not attach myself to any of the cliques that had formed around some of the people at the university and the theater. There was a real vendetta against these people. If the Nazis found during their house searches a picture postcard with greetings from a certain Klaus, they would torture you for as long as it took to get the confession that they wanted. All these people were deported. Word got around that the Nazis were making short work of us and locking us all up in the camps.

I had an acquaintance of many years, R., whose name was not published in the newspapers. Three days after the scandal he was standing in front of my shop counter, his face all green and white like one demented. Beside him stood his sister looking just the same. Without saying a word he pushed a note across the table to me and gestured me to read it. I took the letter, went into the back room, and read: "I have been accused of §175. You have to give me some poison. That's the way my sister wants it. If you don't help me, then I shall have to turn you in too." Automatically I reached for the Veronal, went up front again, and handed it over the counter.

R. had joined the Nazi party voluntarily in 1933. That was what kept his name out of the paper, but it did not save him from deportation. We ran into each other again at the beginning of 1949. We were both pleased and gossiped about this and that. He had had no opportunity to take the poison, because the Nazis were waiting for him in his apartment. He was sent to prison and then years later to Buchenwald. There he was told to report to a high-ranking SS officer on the very first evening. R. was a handsome young guy. On the surface you would never have figured him to be a homophile. The SS man took advantage of him and made him his secretary. R. did not have to wear his pink triangle and caught on very quickly. That was how he survived.

The Third Reich was a martyrdom for us homophiles, yet we were not only destroyed in Hitler's death camps, but also in less organized ways. In my company in France there was a nice young guy: one of those pretty, dreamy blonds. Even among men there is gossip. Above all, when they have nothing to do. "Look at the way he walks and holds his weapon. Bet he's a 175er!" This supposition is then complemented with a further detail and passed on. The rumor had not yet got around to the last man in the company before everyone was saying: "We've got a 175er in our unit." A 175er, born on the 17th of the 5th, in other words, a warm one—those were the expressions in use back then. As far as I know, the term *gay* did not yet exist. I think it didn't arise until after the war in Berlin. Of course it's a term of abuse. Anyway, this real nice guy was now accused of being born on the 17th of the 5th. People did not say it to his face. They just fell quiet and stopped talking whenever he came by, looked surreptitiously for further evidence, and broke out laughing as soon as his back was turned. It is possible that he, like I, wanted to keep his secret at all costs, but I suspect that he had not yet come to terms with things. In any case, he cracked up and chose suicide.

Now nobody admitted saying anything. "That's not what we wanted." But what was the use of being sorry. He was dead. Driven to his death by his comrades, abandoned by the church, which will not accompany such a person to his last resting place. We had a sensible commander who took no notice of all that. He stuck with him and made sure that they fired a final salute at the graveside of the dead comrade. His remarks at the funeral have stayed with me: "The ways of God are mysterious."

Shortly after that our motorized flak division received our marching orders. We traveled by train to Pomerania. The whole of eastern Prussia was an enormous army camp. We thought we were going on exercises. Nobody knew what was really up. Until some soldiers marching past us shouted to us: "War with Russia!" We looked at each other horrified rather than shouting hurrah. Most of the men in our company had been in the ranks since the very beginning and had already formed their own opinions about the whole madness. One comrade summarized the feeling of many: "We'll all get our ass shot off in Russia." It was clear to me that with this the lines were now drawn for the ultimate defeat.

After I had gotten within one hundred kilometers of Moscow with my motorcycle unit, I was wounded and taken to a military hospital in Smolensk. All around, nothing but suffering, dreadful suffering. From Smolensk I was transferred to Warsaw, and for final convalescence I was sent to Breslau, where my troop had been transferred in the meantime. And there something happened to me that looked at first like the end of me but that in the end may have saved my life.

I had some free time and went into town now and then. Well, we have a sixth sense for meeting places of our kind. I was drawn there against all reason. And one evening I met up with a nice civilian. At least he made a nice impression. The ritual game began. He kept circling round me, I brushed against him lightly, and suddenly he bellowed at me: "You're under arrest!" Out came his ID card, and he turned out to be an SS sergeant. "I am arresting you under §175. You made an indecent assault upon me." I said: "All I did was to brush against you." "The fact that you are here is sufficient proof," was his reply. He held me there until a patrol came by. With my shoulder in plaster I couldn't very well run away.

While millions were bleeding to death at the front, the Nazis were still hunting us down. I was locked up with people who had exceeded their leave. When they asked about me, in my distress I answered that I had been three days overdue. In my unit everyone was informed about my arrest. I was transferred to a military prison. My escort delivered me, made the proper report, and then added for my new guards: "You ought to know that this prisoner has been run in for §175." They sized me up from head to toe and greeted me with the words: "Aha, aha, now we've got everything here! Well, come along, you swine!"

Four weeks later the case came before the court-martial. The SS sergeant was the main witness for the prosecution. He showed up in court in uniform and acted as though he had, with his heroic deed, captured one of the most important enemies of the German people. A degenerate element, corrupter of German youth, a foreign body in the German race that must be eradicated. I can tell you how the proceedings in court ran, but the atmosphere prevailing was indescribable. My captain sat in the courtroom and just kept shaking his head. Before things got under way, he had whispered to me: "This cannot be true, such an intelligent man as you."

The court did everything in its power to wrench the confession from me: "Yes, I am a 175er." But I fought for my life, swore by every bone in my body: "I am not a 175er! I have nothing to admit." Meanwhile they had made inquiries in my hometown. My name was not in the homosexuals' index. So it was my word against theirs.

The prosecutor leafed nervously through his Nazi laws. I am convinced they were too lax for him in light of the threat I posed to the healthy racial consciousness. For him I was a particularly devious example, exceptionally dangerous because I was outwardly so difficult to identify. A wolf in sheep's clothing. They all shuddered with disgust. And their disgust was real, not just show. I was stripped of my rank and condemned to one year.

At first I was alone in my cell, then they put someone in with me who revealed to me straight away that he was supposed to report on me as soon as I made any indecent advances toward him. I experienced the prison world in which we ranked second from the bottom. Below us came only the child molesters.

After three months I was transferred to the fortress G. I noticed at once that the reception officer was a man with whom you could talk. We fell into conversation and he asked me right out: "Are we going to win the war or not?" I told him straight to his face: "No! And if you possibly can, get yourself transferred back home." It could have gone badly for me, but he made me his secretary. I now helped him with receiving prisoners.

In the fortress the general mood was that this was the last act. Then I discovered that my superior had put in a word for me with the commandant so that I would not be transferred to the field punishment unit. Those were the so-called journey-to-heaven commandos—sooner or later they led you to a certain death. I owed my life to him. The order from above ran: all 175ers into the field punishment unit. Of those of us serving our time in the fortress, I was the only one who was allowed to remain.

The Red Army came closer and closer, and we broke up to march in the direction of the river Elbe. Meanwhile I had long since realized that it was not the Americans, or even the Russians, who were my deadly enemies. My enemies were the Nazis. And with the help of my vote, too, they had come to power. During the march to the Elbe we were liberated by the Allies.

A technical college for my occupation was founded after the war. I applied there and received a tremendous slap in the face. In my police record stood the notation: indecency between males, one year's imprisonment. I got in touch with the appropriate public prosecutor and requested that the offense be struck off. Once again I opened up the whole story. But shortly afterward I was informed in writing of the deletion of my criminal record. You really look on a state that does that as a benefactor. The state enabled me to have a college education in my old age. I will never forget that. For me it was the last thing I might have expected.

I really relished being reunited with my mother and family during the first years. My mother understood how to hold the children close to her affectionately without forcing us. I went to work and provided for necessities. But still I lived with the lie. I cannot tell you how many times in my life I heard the question: "What, you're not married?" And then they look at you as the penny slowly drops, their head on one side: "—and no one ever sees you going out with women." I really can't count the number of times. A distant relative of mine even killed himself in his mechanics shop. They'd caught him *in flagrante* with a coworker.

Gradually I became too confined at home. It was high time. What had I experienced until then? A few encounters, devoured on the spot like hot chestnuts. They did not satisfy me, they simply spurred me on to obtain more, to experience calm and fulfilling relationships. I wanted to get away, if possible to Berlin. And, at the age of forty-eight, I did it through an ad. I liked the sound of work in a large drugstore, and I obtained an apartment too. And the inevitable happened. No sooner was I there than I was right in the thick of things. I got to know a whole crowd of people, and West Berlin was open at that time too. Some of them often came to me. There were some real nice types among them. You know the way it is: the years after 1955 were the wildest in my life. Of course I had to be careful. Paragraph 175 was still on the books until the end of the sixties, and blackmail was not uncommon. But then what was that compared with the period from 1933 to 1945. Nothing at all! A fair amount of superficiality came my way during those years, but still they were happy ones for me.

And so now I must not neglect to tell you the most wonderful experience of my life! Some years ago a young man came up and spoke to me. We were natives of the same region and took to each other instantly. And would you believe that the boy simply fell all over me—me, of all people, who was by now getting on in years. We had a wonderful evening together, and I took him along to the railroad station afterward. Twice he looked back longingly at me, and then vanished.

The following days were dreadful. The promised phone call never came. Days later, when I had already given up on him, I found a letter in my mailbox. From a tiny spot up north. He had not been able to bring himself to tell me that he was only visiting the city for the World Games and now had to serve the remaining months of his military service in this provincial town. I radiated love for him. Every third day we wrote to each other. If he got leave, he came to me. I really had to insist that he visit his mother now and then.

His period of service came to an end and he wanted to go to school somewhere in the south of the GDR. I moved heaven and earth and succeeded in getting a place for him in Berlin. For the duration of his studies he lived with me. After that he steered off toward K. but soon came back to me again. Soon we were off on vacation to Bulgaria. Dashing here and there to buy the very latest jeans. And not just for him. When I walked through the streets with him, I felt like shouting out to everybody: this is my young friend; we're in love! I really enjoyed going to the theater with a partner at my side.

I would say to all young homophiles, have a relationship. Perhaps it's better that you don't live together. But well, move in together, it'll work out for as long as it works out. The conditions for you are much, much more favorable nowadays. Only the butterflies among us will flutter about all their life.

I was sixty-six when I got to know him. The day began just like any other. Not a sign, nothing. I had long reconciled myself to my loneliness. And now it was there—for me too—le grand amour. A feeling that makes you float on air. I always told the following story in order to explain how I felt. A woman has been longing for her own baby all her life, but for various reasons she does not have children. Then one day, when she is already sixty-six, she wakes up and knows: "I'm pregnant." She is going to have a child like other women. From now on she lives for this child and looks after herself during her pregnancy like a twenty-year-old never would.

Of course I'd had boys before. But beyond the sex there was nothing. As soon as I began to fall for someone, I blew the whistle on myself. What on earth can possibly come of it, I asked myself. You're the one who'll be taken advantage of. I mean, when you're past fifty?

I felt no anger when we parted. We did so as friends. I still feel a great deal of respect for the man who granted me the six most beautiful years of my life.

So, I'm alive, and as you see, doing pretty well. When I open the window, I have a lovely view of the city. I go to the opera regularly, and in the most beautiful season of the year my hiking friend and I roam through the magnificent countryside outside the city. I even have opportunities with women still. Downstairs there is a club. Just recently an older woman was pursuing me so importunately that I simply had to run away!

Interview completed 1984

II. Reinhold and Bert

*Introduced and Translated
by Steven Stoltenberg*

Picking up a book on gay men in East Germany, one probably expects to be introduced to an exotic world far removed from the progressive, tolerant atmosphere of a Western metropolis. And yet, what strikes the reader after meeting Reinhold and Bert is not the difference but the universality of gay experience, the common problems of identity, relationships, desire, and discrimination all gay persons face no matter which social system we happen to find ourselves in.

Bert is especially remarkable for the maturity and insight into the central questions facing gay men. Here is the path to self-awareness so many of us have traveled: the stultifying atmosphere of small-town life, the furtive relationships shamefully hidden from the intrusive eyes of neighbors, the escape to the metropolis in search of community, the disillusionment with transitory sexual encounters and the superficiality of the "scene," the transition to a stable relationship, the courageous attempt to integrate an open gay identity into the contexts of work and community. After reading Bert's account of his coming to gay consciousness, one cannot help but admire the ability of gays everywhere, in whatever sociopolitical or cultural milieu, to establish meaningful, open life-styles for themselves.

Reinhold presents a different picture, since he remains content within a small-town setting, with the duality of an existence split between a marriage and family on one hand and a secretive gay relationship on the other. Such a compromise is perhaps understandable given the difficulties of being out under such conditions; yet more importantly, what is evident here is Reinhold's sense of responsibility as husband and father. To be sure, he has not resolved the moral dilemma of leading a double life and the dishonesty it entails, but nevertheless he seems to have effected a compromise that satisfies his needs for both male companionship and the important ties of family and community. Though we may not agree completely with such a compromise, preferring instead the alternative of a large, urban setting with the freedoms and anonymity it provides, Reinhold's example does highlight an important and often denied truth: a gay man is just as capable of raising and maintaining a family as any heterosexual male. The next time we hear demagogic statements to the effect that gay males are irresponsible, promiscuous, and incapable of long-term commitments, we should recall that there are innumerable Reinholds out there, each performing the roles of gay man, husband, and father at the same time. It may be time for gays to revise our prejudices concerning such men and to accept their coexistence as an alternate homosexuality. Their decision to live within two worlds at once may be conscious and not merely an example of preliberation adaptation to social pressure and custom.

If what I have said about the universality of our experience is true—if we do indeed find it so easy to recognize ourselves in these life stories—then perhaps one may be optimistic about efforts to reach across borders and ideological curtains. This book, in fact, is one such effort in border crossing, not as an example of transgression but of unity in establishing ties and building an ever-expanding international network of gay people.

3. "I've got a headache from all your questions"

Reinhold, born 1935, worker on a collective dairy farm

I tell you, I have to watch my step. People know me. People from my wife's new place of work too. People say hello to me on the street who I can't place right away. This town isn't all that big. Sometimes only after I've gone on a ways down the street does it occur to me, oh yeah, he's the one from my wife's last party at work. One of her friends; he sat right next to me at the table. I feel a lot better when I know where I can place somebody.

When I've got something to do near the train station, I stop by there, it's the only place, the train station I mean, where you can meet somebody who might be interested. I can't let myself be seen there too often. On Sundays there's something going on there, late in the afternoon, when everybody goes back to work to the cities. A lot of people come by bus from the small villages, spend some time in our town, and have a look around. Sunday afternoons you can't budge me from my coffee table. That is, most of the time.

What I'm going to tell you about happened years ago. There's this old, gray-haired, disgusting type of guy who hangs out at the toilets, even today. His biggest pleasure is watching people. I heard from F. that the old guy talks a lot. I swore to myself I would grab him the first chance I got. He won't wreck my life with his gossip. A few days later I went up to him and grabbed him by the collar and yelled: "You bastard, you're just like us but you go off and spread stories around. You've got a big mouth, you bastard." I twisted his queer little collar on his work overalls until his face went white as a sheet. "From now on you're gonna let people be and stop giving them a hard time with your big mouth; here's a kick in your ass. Now beat it, you hear."

After that things were quiet.

Since then I take a beer over to him now and then and I'm certain he doesn't blow the whistle on me; he keeps his mouth shut. I told you, I only go by there once in a while, and it's even rarer that something happens. It's not like in the cities where you live.

If there were a few thousand more people living here I'd feel a lot safer.

This is a small town when you count how many live here. In the sixties, they built the factory, then the new housing units, but it still stayed a small town. I came here with my family only, let's see, four years ago.

Before then we always lived in small villages. They were small enough that you knew everybody, and you knew the situation a lot better. That's what I mean when I say I have to watch my step here. Somebody's looking at you and it seems they have nothing on their mind, and you don't know whether later on they might pull a fast one on you when you least expect it. I'm always living on edge.

If it came out and my wife and kids knew about me, I'd hang myself. I know what I'm saying. I couldn't handle the disgrace. It doesn't matter where you show up. After that everybody'll say: "He's one of those."

It doesn't matter that my wife and kids are basically good people. If only bad people were against us we'd have it easier. I can't expect more understanding from my family than from the teacher or mayor, or for that matter from the pastor. And I know their opinion on the matter even though I've never spoken to them about it. And for good reason.

I know my wife. As good as she is, she can be a real bear. If she was 100 percent sure about me, from that day on I wouldn't be able to look her in the eyes. Believe me, she would really spread it on thick.

It's so crazy. You don't get into dangerous situations just because it might be kind of fun, or maybe it's out of pride. If it were so I would have stopped a long time ago, like others are able to do. I am one of those—who knows how many there are—who have this deep need inside themselves. Quite often I've really suffered from a guilty conscience, and I decided I'd try to quit the whole thing. I imagined what my wife's reaction would be, and the shock my kids would have when they'd hear someday from other kids at school that their father was that way. There were times when I thought someone was following me when I went into the nearest big town. I quickly got out of the train, hid behind a newspaper kiosk, and then watched to see who was getting out of the train. It was a kind of persecution complex. I think if I hadn't quieted down, I would have been in the crazy house by now.

I haven't stopped yet, up to now, and I don't intend to do so either. I've gotten to know myself too well. If everything's gone fine so far, it'll keep on going that way. It has to.

It doesn't matter a bit to you guys in the city what your neighbors think about you, but for us it's different. In this apartment house we're sitting in now as many people live here as in our entire village. You go up and down the elevator twenty floors, and I walk up and down the village street. A bit of a difference, wouldn't you say?

There's one guy in our village who makes no bones about being open, and everybody knows about him. But he's even a bit too open. A few weeks ago I went with my wife for coffee, after we'd first taken a walk. We hadn't been sitting too long when the same guy comes in and sits down next to our table. He's capable of doing things like that. Five minutes later the waitress brings us two drinks. My wife asks: "Who sent these over?" The waitress nods in his direction and says a bit maliciously: "That one over there."

My wife looks at me with glaring eyes you wouldn't believe. I just said "hello" and nothing more. Everybody knows about him. Half an hour later I go to the bathroom and he's right there after me. I growl at him: "Get out of here, they're onto us, you idiot. You'll wreck it for us all."

I've already been through a lot with him. That was all a while ago, when I drank one with him in the Schloßkrug Bar. We weren't by ourselves; at the table was a neighbor and somebody else who I can't remember. At any rate, he started to fumble around under the table, getting more and more pushy. All of a sudden one of the guys at the club table stood up and placed himself in front of the guy and yelled at him: "Leave him alone"—meaning me. "He doesn't go for that kind of thing. If you don't take your paws off of him, you gonna get thrown out of here on your ass."

I was so embarrassed I could hardly talk. But later on in the evening I left with him anyway. That is, we left separately. I'm that careless only after I've downed a few. The only thing I could think was "hopefully nobody saw you." When after a week no one said anything about it, I started to settle down again.

When he comes into the bar you hear remarks like: "He's looking for something again. He's out fishing around, everybody on guard!"

He manages to do the most incredible things. There's this young tractor driver in the village who's real good-looking. He invited the guy home after work, got him drunk, and put the make on him. The poor guy didn't even dare to show up at work the next morning. His team leader went to his house since nobody knew what had happened. The kid was lying in bed, crying like a baby. With tears running down his face he let out the whole story. I mean the whole story. You can imagine how fast it got around. Just the thing people like to feed on. The kid couldn't let himself be seen for weeks. His buck acted like there was nothing to be ashamed of. He just said to the crew's boss: "So what. After all, he's no minor."

Of course, people quiet down after a while; he's not a topic that lasts for long. Something else happens that diverts people's attention. Besides, they need him. He's now taken over his father's Trabant auto repair shop.

Two years ago at the spring festival he made off with some woman's husband, right in front of everybody. The guy's the kind who gets along when he's in a tight situation, who lets himself be invited when he's run out of pocket money. They were necking with each other right in front of his wife and mother-in-law. Drunk, naturally. Both of the girls were so shocked that they couldn't get a word out; they just stared at them, gripping their purses, and ran off home like they'd been bitten by a tarantula.

Three days later the old lady let him have it right in the middle of the street. "You seduced my son-in-law, you cat fucker you." She must have yelled it out twenty times. Don't ask me where she got that word. He just left her standing there; he's that thick-skinned. He's able to do so only because there isn't that law against homos anymore. Otherwise, he'd be real scared. Most people still go to his car shop rather than go twenty miles to another repair shop to get their Trabant fixed.

As far as I'm concerned, that's a lot of bull about seduction. You can get seduced the first time, and if you like it, then you yourself look for a second and third time. The guy who doesn't have a real taste for it just shakes it off afterward like a wet poodle and doesn't at all want to repeat it.

That was all years ago for me. I was in my early thirties, we still lived in Leinefelde, and I worked in the fields. I remember that day like it was yesterday. It was on a Monday, cold, in November. We had harrowed a huge section of the field, with a crew of three. The crows were always twenty meters behind us, poking around in the freshly harrowed earth.

In his coat pocket, we kept a big bottle against the cold. Once in a while only the two of us could take a shot, since the third guy had to drive the tractor. He and I took care of the harrows, and by the end of the day we had finished off the bottle. We were in good spirits by then; no one was drunk. We both got on the trailer and we headed back home. We had a good half hour's worth of driving. After five minutes it started raining cats and dogs. We sat under the canvas top, squeezed tight together. He smelled like cigarettes, liquor, and . . . something I had never smelled in my life.

All of a sudden we went wild.

We came back to our senses when we heard the driver yelling: "Did you guys fall asleep?" We scrambled out of there like chickens with their heads cut off, each in a different direction, without looking up, eyes staring down at the ground. I only noticed that the driver had taken off the canvas cover and was calling behind us: "Drinking like grown-ups, taking it like kids!"

The next morning I woke up and my first thought was: "You dreamed the whole thing." It didn't take long for me to realize it hadn't been a dream. I started to shake real hard. I was in my early thirties, married for years with four kids. Up to then I hadn't had anything to do with men, nothing at all; once in a dream, but that was years before. And I had been to America once in a dream.

And now this. I didn't want to get up. My wife practically had to force me to go to work. I was a quarter of an hour late to our meeting point. Already from a distance I could see he was there. We said hello without looking at each other. The two guys climbed into the trailer. It was my turn to drive. I was happy somehow that it wasn't raining. I was relieved to see that each of them sat in his own corner.

Not a word fell between us while harrowing the field. Only our third partner kept moaning that it was so boring, if only he could drink something. The next day went the same way, only he drove and I sat in the back. Wednesday afternoon we were finished with the patch and we drove to the next one. I waited for Thursday.

Thursday morning it was colder. We crouched in our thick cotton jackets, back on the trailer, with the canvas between us. Each one held on to the trailer's sides so that he wouldn't bump into the other guy when we went around a curve. That's the way we acted the whole day through, each one being careful not to touch the other guy. Even though it was damn cold, nobody took a swig from the bottle. The third guy saw the bottle was full at the end of the day and said: "I can't figure you guys out at all."

Finally we were finished with the harrowing. I was supposed to work with the cows the next day; I didn't ask him what kind of work he was supposed to do. Each of us went home alone.

No one could say a word to me; the least little thing and I would explode. My wife only had to look at me questioningly and I would start yelling at her. And only because I was at wit's end. I didn't know what was eating at me. I was as miserable as a dog.

After work I went straight home because I was afraid to run into him. After a week I went looking for him. I found him and made a wide detour around him. It went like that for weeks, up to the Christmas holidays. Then I went up to him: "Come with me, I'm free, the wife is at work and the kids are sleeping upstairs." Five minutes later we were at my place. My wife had cooked liver and placed it in the oven. We didn't speak a word to each other. I set the table and was as excited as a seventeen-year-old. We had a nice meal, in peace and quiet. We still hadn't spoken to each other. Not a word. Then we washed up and lay down in the bed. We went at it all night. At four in the morning we got up; we held one hand on the coffee pot and held hands with the other, like at the movies.

I wasn't any smarter after this night, but much more at peace.

In those days he didn't have a television. If my wife had the night shift he came to watch TV if he had some free time. After the kids were asleep in bed we had ourselves a good time.

We were together for over a year—until a woman stuck herself between us and broke up our friendship. I put an end to it because he didn't want to leave her. I couldn't stand it. We still met now and then, until things were completely over between us. I was impossible.

Today I know it was my mistake that I made it hell for him because of the woman. I should have waited longer and not played it so crazy right off the bat. After all, I was married too.

Get married, I would say today. Start a family, we'll see how things go. If you still agree later we'll stay together. Sharing isn't really so bad. And that's all there is to it.

For a whole year we didn't speak to each other, stayed out of each other's way, and watched each other from a distance. Like children. The people around us just shook their heads and wondered what was going on.

In late fall came the harvest festival again. He sat with her at a table in the other corner of the hall.

An hour before things were to end he came over to us, shook everybody's hand, and invited me to the bar. I was so excited I couldn't go with him right away. "Go on over," I answered, "I'll dance one with my wife and then I'll be over." I needed five minutes to get a hold on myself.

Then I went over to the bar.

"You were right," he said. "I'm sorry. It's all my fault. As of today it's over between her and me. I've had enough."

I was completely confused. I could only stammer: "We haven't said hello for a whole year; you can say that now, after I've decided to move away with my family."

"Then I'll go too," was his answer. "Why should I stay here?" He downed a shot, turned around, and left the hall. Twenty minutes later his wife was at our table asking me where he was. I left her standing there and ran out of the hall.

I never saw him again. Six weeks later I moved the family to Mühlow.

We often moved. My wife didn't understand sometimes why I wanted to get away again. "You're so restless. You can't stand to stay too long in one place." I can still hear her saying it. I never really wanted my own house. Up to now we've lived in six different districts. Here in Thüringen we feel comfortable. I think we'll stay here. You can get work anywhere as an animal caretaker. If you can do something, it's a lot easier.

I can bring my documents and certificates of award that I've gotten over the years for my cattle. Our whole knicknack chest in the living room is packed full of them. I've gotten a lot of offers at exhibitions.

More money was definitely also a reason I wanted to move again. But it's more fun to work in the state-owned cooperatives where things run smoothly. Not only because it brings in more money. Sure, money is always an argument, especially when you've got six mouths to feed. Of course the kids are on their own now.

Except for that first move, a man never played a role in my decisions. Maybe in the back of my mind I had this vague desire to meet someone like him again. Could be.

Sometimes there was a dry season, for months on end, and all of a sudden something came along. It's not like in the city. If something doesn't happen for two weeks, you think it's the end of the world and you go crazy.

I didn't run after men all the time. Besides, when you search around like a crazy man you might as well stay at home. When the kids still had to be taken care of I had other things on my mind. You only think about food, drink, and something to wear. One kid was always sick, another one had sassed back at a teacher, and the oldest one had gotten caught for the tenth time smoking behind the schoolhouse.

You should remember I always had my own farm on the side. Pigs, chickens, geese, and rabbits. There was always plenty of work. When one of us was flat on his back, I mean sick, sometimes the work came crashing down on our heads. The bigger your family is the more important it is to get along with your wife. It's possible that so many get divorced nowadays because they only want to have one, two kids at the most. That may be why. Yeah, it feels good when I look back on things. We always managed.

I'm proud of my children. All of them made something of themselves. Was I a strict father? There were times when they deserved a slap in the face. But you should ask my kids about that.

We used to say: "When the kids are older, then . . . then everything'll be easier. Then we'll take it easy. I won't keep so many cattle. Why should I? The kids will be standing on their own two feet. The wife won't raise flowers and carrots anymore. We'll have a good time with our money. We'll travel around and stay in Interhotels. We won't think twice before spending a mark."

We do go on trips, but I've still never seen the inside of an Interhotel because our sons-in-law and daughters-in-law have their own apartments. After two days at the most I want to go back home. Me, the big ox, built himself another barn, and when we're away my buddy has to do the feeding. We travel around less and less because the children have figured out that they can haul away more in their Trabants than my wife and I can take to them on a train. And my wife doesn't want to do without carrots from our own garden anymore.

Oh yeah, our money. We think just as long before we spend it. After we financed four weddings, now it's time for the socialist name-day parties.

There are remarks you hear as a young boy; they stick with you your whole life and you can't get rid of them. In my family, Father had taken on the milking, Mother took care of us—of me and my eight brothers and sisters. Sometimes Father came in with such a long face, to get the milk cans that Mother had washed out. Mother took one look at him and said, "A cow doesn't give much milk to an unhappy person. Here, let me do the milking today."

Either my father growled at her, sat down near the window, and got even more grouchy, or his face started to beam. Then he came up to me, squeezed me, went to Mother, gave her a pat from behind, and went out whistling with his milk cans out to the barn.

You know, I needed a push now and then too. Then I was able to go along on my own.

I married at twenty-two. The oldest in the family was already married, and I never would have considered not marrying. All my buddies got married, why shouldn't I? I don't mean that I didn't love my wife, but we didn't make such a big deal out of it. It wasn't the custom for us or for anybody I know in the country. Nobody says "I love you" ten times a day to his wife. Women don't expect it; they don't say it either.

I have to come back to this "push" thing again.

My mother didn't want to say anything more to my father then other than: "What would happen to us, to the kids, to the farm, if I went around with a long face, if I could care less about my chores?" Just like Father, I understood what she meant—to get something done you have to work together.

My marriage was first with me all those years. I never had another woman. She would have gone to pieces if I had fooled around with another woman. For years I worked with a woman in the barn who had just one thing on her mind. Your tape recorder would get a hard-on if I told you everything she had done with men. She threw herself onto the hay in front of me, pulled her pants down, showed her cunt, and cooed. I left her lying there and shouted, "You can beg till you're blue in the face; if you want to keep working with me you'd better behave."

She went and spread it all over the village: "I never met anyone like him. The man is hard as iron, nobody can get near him, not that one."

She was right, too. In this respect my wife never had reason to complain. At our festivals I at most had one too many to drink, but I never went grabbing after other women like most guys after they've had a few too many. If someone started something with my wife I would get jealous, downright mad. I couldn't put up with it.

I betray my wife with another man. Sounds strange. Let's assume it came out. Nobody would say, "He cheated on his wife with another man." You can't compare the two. The disgrace is much bigger. With a woman, that's something normal, happens often enough. With another man, people use completely different words, meaner, or they can't think of anything to say at all.

I often felt guilty when I had slept with a man, but I never looked at it as something that threatened my marriage. I don't mean it's not serious with a man, but to live with a man for several years, no way. There's nothing to keep men together for so long. At least I've never met anybody that I'd give up my family for.

I know it's ridiculous, but I could imagine my wife having a girlfriend. I have thought about it. She would think I was crazy if I made her such an offer. That's out of the question.

You know my buddy. As soon as he's had a little too much to drink, he lets himself go. In front of our women, at the table, he starts a conversation: "True love is only between men, right?" He bangs his knee against my thigh under the table and looks at me with puppy dog eyes. The women yawn and nod at him. I say, "Of course," and I'm happy if he seems satisfied with our answers. But he can also be quite contrary.

I had some risky situations because of him. The biggest affair was some good two years ago. There was talk about us in the village. I went straight to my wife. "That fat Mrs. Ruth has spread this and that around; people are gossiping." She blew her top and cursed: "If she says that one more time . . . the fat pig."

She went right over to my buddy's wife in her house slippers, and both of them came to a quick decision: "We'll grab the culprit. Right away, as a matter of fact!"

The cow was nowhere to be found afterward. A day later her written apology was hanging on the cooperative bulletin board. Real legible, written on a typewriter: "I hereby apologize to the members of the cooperative." There followed the name of our cooperative, beneath that both of our names, and "I take back the accusation made against them. What I said is untrue."

We kept safely in the background, my buddy and I. It was clear to us they must have watched us while we were gathering mushrooms. You know, that was our cover. We'd gone looking for mushrooms, hand-in-hand, and we threw each other kisses whenever one of us found one.

I think we got out of that situation without any problems because people's power of imagination wasn't able to follow what it was all about. They hadn't behaved so foolishly themselves, even when they were seventeen, and now this accusation against two grown men with wives and kids. That fat Mrs. Ruth could only be nuts. That was the obvious answer.

I would prefer my friend to be more reserved. If I've promised to meet on Tuesday at nine, and something comes up—sometimes I just can't get away—the next time we meet I have to listen to who knows what. If I go shopping in Suhl, he'd like a report about every move I made. He's a bit like me with my first man. Maybe it's a question of age. He's fourteen years younger than me and inexperienced.

I've let him know many a time that it can't go on this way. We both can only lose if it were all to come out in public. He always says yes, yes, he wants to change, but when we go dancing with our wives and he drinks a little, everything is different. While drunk he's even suggested we move to Berlin together: "Let's get away from this place where we have to hide." My answer is always the same: "I'm staying put."

I want to keep working in the barn. I don't want to go to Berlin and work in an office. They wanted to recruit me a few times to work in the office here. I like the barn air better than the stuffiness of an office. As far as Berlin is concerned, I think it stinks more on the intersections of Dimitroff Street and Schönhauser Allee, much more than in my stables. It may sound funny to a city dweller, but for me there's something cozy about a clean, orderly barn. I can stand the warmth of a barn much better than the central heating in your apartment. I don't mean to say anything more than this: I feel just fine in my little village.

My parents were farmers, I grew up on a farm, so I too became a farmer. I do what I can do best, and I live where I can get on best.

I have little hope that people will fully accept us in the next few years. It'll remain a wish. One thing you can say for sure: whatever the village gossip spreads around to her friends when they're cleaning up the milk-house carries more weight than what they hear on television. That's the way it is.

Do you know what I think about sometimes? I'd like to go to the police and investigate where he made off to. Maybe he doesn't live that far away from here, right in the vicinity. It could very well be.

I never smelled that kind of breath again.

So, now I have to be going. The train won't wait for me. I've got a headache from all your questions. And you get a false picture of me when we only talk about men.

Interview completed 1983

4. "The way you look, you don't have a chance of getting in"

Bert, born 1961, worker

In April I will be twenty-five. Age really doesn't matter much to me. I'm not interested in who I'll be in twenty years. It's much more important that there'll be real people and trees. I'm from Thüringen.[1] I feel fine the way I'm living now. A lot has happened in the last five years. If I were heterosexual, things would have gone differently. I would have married, established a family, the usual sort of thing. I'm not really into what counts as normal family life in this country, neither into children nor the joy of being a father. I wouldn't like to lead such a life, and I demand that my concept of life also be tolerated. I'm fully aware of the fact that the state supports young marriages.[2] If everyone would live like me, there'd be a population problem. Lucky for the state that most people aren't gay.

I expect more out of life than coming home after my shift, watching television, going to bed, and back to work again. I'm bored by the regularity my work imposes on me. There's regularity in my relationship with Rainer as well, but not that grinding day-in-and-day-out kind. Sometimes I go alone to the bar, or I make a date with a buddy. Now and then I have to be by myself—it does me good. I withdraw into my apartment and recover from my day. Afterward I need him and others I'm close to even more.

It took me several years to be clear about who I am and what I want. Who I am and what I am is closely connected with my sexuality. That's true for everybody, but for me this connection is more confused and complicated because I'm gay. I orient my life accordingly and I'll make it all right.

I discovered who I am when I was nineteen years old. There was a hussy in our town who all the boys were able to try it out with. I was really proud when I was able to join those who had made it with her. What I felt with her didn't do anything for me. Only one week later I really fell apart, my "zero hour,"[3] so to speak. Among my work colleagues was a guy, around thirty, attractive, untalkative, and reserved. There was a tension between us I couldn't make out. I couldn't help thinking about him. He still lived with his parents, didn't have a girlfriend, and that was all I knew about him. His regular seat on the bus was three rows from mine, and when I moved a bit in my seat, I could see the back of his close-cropped head and his broad neck. He never turned around, and he always sat still until the bus stopped at the factory gate. Sometimes I ran into him on weekends in the bar: he'd usually had a few too many and talked to me, but nothing more. Our tavern closed an hour later on weekends, and whoever didn't want to go home went another fifty meters to the *Konsum* (grocery store),[4] where they stayed and chatted with each other.

One evening I decided to go along. I had a bottle of wine clasped under my arm and I sat down beside him. We drank and talked about the usual things. The things you talk about at that hour. When the bottle was empty I said goodbye and wanted to go home. He got up as well and said: "I'll come along; after all, we're going in the same direction." Not a word passed between us. We went past his house, down to the lake. On the bank we undressed and jumped into the water. We swam to the other side, climbed up the embankment, and just as quietly and deliberately as he got off the bus, he pulled up to me and said: "You must be cold." At five in the morning we went back to get our things.

I had a deep crush on him and was completely confused. Monday afternoon I waited for him at the bus stop one minute before the bus was to arrive and he still wasn't there. I became more and more nervous. The bus rolled around the corner, we got in, and he showed up. We set off, and I waited expectantly for him to turn around and nod. Nothing—not even once. On the way into the factory I caught up with him; he looked in the other direction. It was the same way day after day. He didn't look at me, didn't speak to me. He acted as if nothing had happened. I was burning up inside, I was suffering. He sat like a statue in the bus. Five weeks later we ran across each other in the tavern. After an hour he looked at me for the first time, I became white as a sheet, I was almost sick with desire, I could hardly breathe. I had to get outside. Twenty minutes later I went back inside, sat with my back toward his table and thought only about him. Later that night I went to the *Konsum*—he wasn't there. Feeling sad, I stuck a bottle under my arm and went over to the lake. There he stood. We made love, the way we had dreamed of for five weeks, before falling asleep. Naturally, without any guilt feelings. For the first time, I felt him inside of me.

The next weeks became more and more unbearable for me. He still wouldn't look at me in the bus, and at night on the lake he didn't want to let me go back home. I told him that I loved him. He looked at me squeamishly yet in a surly fashion, cuddled up to me, saying with a sulky voice: "Oh, we're not gay, that's impossible!"

I wanted to get away: "Come on, let's split, to another city, let's get away from here, we can find work anywhere." He was stubborn: "I'm staying here." I pictured our future together: we'll live in a highrise, on the top floor under the clouds, just by ourselves, no neighbors to bother us. He remained stubborn and kept babbling the same sentence: "I'm staying here." I felt we'd suffocate in that environment and I kept begging him: "Come with me." But in vain.

I'd made my decision, and I wanted to get away. Get away. It worked. Without saying goodbye to him I moved that fall to Berlin.

Later when I visited my parents I'd meet him sometimes on the street, I'd say hello, and I always thought the same thing: just keep riding that bus, keep pretending you're straight, and wither away.

After those first encounters I was still angry with him; later on I became indifferent, and now I think of him as a pitiful creature. Even the old women have stopped asking him when he's going to get married.

You can't explain it all away by fate. But if you can count to three, you should be able to figure out what's going to happen to a gay in a village or small town. There are two possibilities: stay or move to the city, stew in your own juices or live. Those who stay and live only on the weekend will for sure see their life go by without taking part in it.

After a month one of my friends from work offered to introduce us provincials to the Berlin nightlife. We met on Alexanderplatz. Our guide looked us up and down, shook his head, and said in an annoyed voice: "The way you look, you don't have a chance of getting in. Hopefully, I can get you in. We'll go to Dimitroffstraße. Take your few pennies and pay for the bus. Man, conductors check you here at Alexanderplatz; it's not like in the province."

We got out at Dimitroffstraße. Standing near the newspaper stand, we formed a half-circle around him and he began to explain: "Now, see that bar over there? It's open till five, but only divorced singles hang out there. Twenty meters further on's a place that's open till six; that's where people our age go. Across the street is where the homos hang out."

We were astonished. We nodded, murmured respectfully, "Uh huh," and were sure he had arranged it all, that everything was so fantastic. At least that's how he sounded.

The next morning my head was throbbing, and like a broken record one sentence kept repeating over and over in my head: "Across the street is where the homos hang out." It was only months later that I got up the nerve to go there.

On the weekends after that I wandered alone through Berlin. I always ended up on Alexanderplatz, where someone always came up to me right away. I always went off with him immediately, with big expectations. Once, twice, three times, and the craziest thing about it was that I had a crush on each one I met. There was never a second meeting. After half a year I had enough. I felt good at work, I liked the city, but I couldn't deal with superficial gays.

I got up the nerve to go into the "appropriate" bars. At first I was dazzled by what I saw. People came in, went from table to table, greeted someone with "hello," someone else with a kiss. It was incredible, everything seemed so natural. Like one big family that sticks together, no mean words, and people called each other names I had never heard before. It did seem odd to me when someone called the person across the table "Suzi," and then "Suzi" responded as if this name was the most natural one in the world. I realized that most of the people were my age. Oh, I thought, here's where you'll make friends. In the evening you go for a beer, chat with people about your problems, they understand you because they're all in the same boat as you. This is your place. Inside I was angry that it had taken so long to get up the courage to join. I had been such an ass to spend half a year with some half-closeted guys who wanted to have sex with me and then just split. Here people were sure of themselves and didn't hide out in dark corners. Better to be a little crazy than have those fly-by-night encounters in dark parks. Those were my thoughts.

On the second evening there I sat down at a table where there was still a free seat. I listened for a while and introduced myself: that I was from Thüringen, came to Berlin through the Berliner Initiative,[5] and liked it here very much; it seemed that we could all do a lot more together, we could love each other more and pull closer together. The people at my table smiled at each other. I was glowing with enthusiasm like the times when I built houses out of leaves with other kids. The guy sitting on my right poked his neighbor's side and whispered so that everyone could understand: "He means group sex."

Everybody laughed. The one who quieted down first moaned: "Wonderfully naive, and this dialect, it's just too much."

Afterward he took me to his place. The next morning he said goodbye as quickly as possible: "See you, it was great, take care, maybe we'll see each other tonight!"

I went back that night, still flushed with my experience from the night before. I still believed what people told me. He stood at the bar, looking bored. I went up to him, glowing; he nodded quickly at me and let me know that at that moment he didn't want to be disturbed. Even here I lost my illusions from evening to evening; I quickly picked up the rules of the game.

People constantly change their partners; they're constantly greedy, after something new, more exciting; and they're unreliable. The whole bar scene is at best a place to have a good time. It's totally superficial. Whoever hangs out there for a long time automatically gets hurt. Once you get caught up in it, you get addicted to the rush of being in the scene. Maybe most of these guys were let down when they were really young, so they can't find a way out of their frustration, or they've never expected anything else out of life. Whoever's able to show up every night in the latest fashion holding a glass of champagne and is good at engaging in empty chatter fits right in. It was soon clear to me that I wanted that as little as I wanted life with a woman or going back to my village—although the guy from the company bus appeared more and more often in my dreams.

I'm positive I would never have made the leap out of the bar scene so easily if I hadn't met Rainer. I had been in Berlin for a whole year. I had seen him several times on the weekends in one of the bars. He stood in a corner as if he had nothing to do with what was going on around him. I was attracted to him, but I had become more cautious. His attitude seemed to me to be just another game—the lonely, hard cowboy. With him it would end up in the same old way. The way it had been up to now. Luckily it all turned out quite differently.

Rainer is nine years older than me, was married for six years, and has a son. I'm attracted by his seriousness, and I find him very masculine. I sometimes watch him at home while he's cooking or reading—he's down to earth and that's why everything about him is so right. When I talk to him he listens. I can't deal with guys who go on and on and always have to prove they're right. With him I feel complete. His thighs are hunky and he's got lots of beautiful body hair. Of course, that's important. I'd better quit.

We want our relationship to last, so we live accordingly. Our daily rhythm is set by my workshifts. We spend most of the time at his place, since his apartment is better. If I work graveyard shift, I sleep at my place. For me love is strongly connected to the expectations I have of life and of my partner. I had a deep crush on the guy from the bus—yet I couldn't love him because he was finished with life at thirty. Whoever expects nothing more out of life can't love, he pulls you down with him. A lot has happened with Rainer. We live together, each one gets something from the other, and there are new expectations, shared dreams. This is completely normal, common, but totally important. Each is responsible for the other and for himself. I can't demand too much from him, certainly not everything. I'm also self-reliant. Do you understand? Today I know more exactly what I want and what's good for me. It's also important when in love to feel proud of the other person.

I often see men who appeal to me, but love means something more. I don't believe in love at first sight. Desire, yes, but love? Sure, all connections between people can unravel. The danger's always there, but it doesn't have to be inevitable, like a law. I'm not old, and I don't want to see things that way. I have to make my life, not just talk about it.

I try not to aggravate him if he's in a bad mood. For example, when he talks about his favorite dream over a glass of beer—about the bar we're going to open together—I play along, for his sake. You shouldn't be lazy or indifferent, and, and, and . . . We, of course, agree on war and peace.

I rarely go back home. If I'm there I devote myself exclusively to my parents and brother. I told my parents about myself. My mother said right to my face: "You never stop talking about your male friends and acquaintances. I don't understand it. Don't you have a girlfriend?"

I went and got my father, asked them both to sit down at the table, and

I let loose. I didn't use the word "homosexual," but I kept talking about Rainer, about my "inclinations," and to such an extent that Mother also had to understand what I was getting at. Father stood up, fetched a bottle of his favorite schnapps, took glasses out of the cupboard, and filled them up. I looked out the window, Mother looked at her hands, finally Father said: "Well, it's good he told us. Cheers."

Five glasses later it came out that he had already known and had seen through me for some time. I had underestimated him.

I could speak about it with my parents because I was together with Rainer. Before him I wouldn't at all have known how to pull it off. How could I have explained to them what I had experienced in Berlin in that one year? Now I could tell them that we were living together, about our projects and our friends and acquaintances, and about what worries us. When they met Rainer they were skeptical. To Mother he was a playboy, not a sound investment for the future. How can one drink so much champagne in one evening and smoke the most expensive cigarettes? Father spent a long time sizing him up. Since then they've both accepted him completely. They know where I stand when it comes to Rainer, and that I'm going to stay with him. What's important is that they've understood that he's "serious" about their boy. When I'm alone with Mother sometimes she starts all over again: "Boy, if you do go ahead and marry, then . . . " I say: "Then what? Then I'd be totally unhappy and would go around with a frown on my face. Aren't my brother's kids enough grandchildren for you?"

My brother and sister-in-law know about me. She can't deny what she is—a teacher—and teachers are, well—.[6] Of course she doesn't have *anything* against it, but she'll keep an eye on her son just in case, and as soon as she notices anything, she'll take the proper steps. She told my mother this right away. The idea's never struck her that her daughter could also turn out that way. Besides, she can't imagine that doctors today are helpless against it; most probably it just has to be discovered early on. Scientific progress and so on.

My relationship with Rainer is apparent to those around us. After the late shift he picks me up from work with his car. Such things get around faster than the latest pay plans. I'm sure the whole plant knows about us. Even though there are several hundred employees and a lot goes on, a man who's picked up by his male lover after the shift is unusual, a sensation. *Was* a sensation; not anymore in my company.

My colleagues [at work] are predominantly young people. Up to now, my openness hasn't caused me problems. On the contrary, it creates trust. I didn't lie about it, and they quickly came to terms with it. At least those who are important to me. It's possible that they say things behind my back, but that doesn't bother me. In my presence, they don't say a single unpleasant word. If someone tells a gay joke during break, I listen. If I find it funny, I laugh. But our women, now they are even better objects for hetero jokes. Most jokes are aimed at women. With gay jokes even the women finally get a chance to laugh freely. Recently I threatened at breakfast: the time's coming when women and gays together will crack jokes about the straight bucks. Most of the women didn't understand me, but the men did.

Some of my friends at work wanted to know more exactly, total discretion, one on one, of course. I let them ask me questions. They beat around the bush and found it hard to ask the questions that were really on their minds. Do you pool your money? Do you also feel jealousy? Up to the most important question: which one of you is the man and which the woman?

I told them we have a single budget, spend vacations together, that Rainer does more housework than I do because he's a better cook and works a regular daytime job, that no one's the man and no one's the woman, that actually there are four of us, to use a figure of speech, two men and two women. Why four? The question came immediately, spontaneously. As I gave more details they started to grin. Through these conversations I realized that most of them couldn't imagine what two men do together. The possibility that men might dance together tenderly because they enjoy it doesn't even enter their minds. That's the way it is with a lot of uptight gays as well.

I'm convinced that some of my colleagues think it must be really good to be gay. Gayness means that I always have money, I don't need to borrow, I wear cool clothes, I have no obligations, things go well for me. Let's not kid ourselves, the majority of people think in practical terms.

Four weeks ago our work section went on a steamboat trip. On the way back one friend started talking to me, an older guy who I'd hardly spoken with till then. A real businessman type, over forty, married. Already graying. Already drunk.

He: Would it bother you if we had a conversation?

I: No, why?

He: I think it's great you've managed so well. Are you still together with your lover?

I: Yes.

He: I don't think much of gays.

I: A lot of people think that way.

Now it was clear to me what he wanted to say. He was impressed that I didn't conceal myself from my work friends and that I had gained some authority. He was impressed even though he personally rejected gays. I turned the tables on him.

I: Let's talk about you. How's your life? Do you feel good? Are you happy?

He: Well, I have my wife, you know.

I: You sure do drink a lot.

He: That's the way it is in a marriage. It's not so bad.

I: Besides that, you're fat. As a gay you wouldn't stand a chance of picking anybody up.

He: Stop talking to me about gays! What'll happen when you're older, or you have an accident? I have my wife.

I: I have my lover.

He: A lover's not a wife.

I wanted to answer, but he had stopped listening. Satisfied with himself, he returned to the bar.

I'm respected because I don't miss any shifts, I'm achievement oriented, and I'm materially well situated. If you have nothing to offer as a gay, and someone sees that things aren't going well for you, you'll be the last ass. Some of these tormented types are in the plant. The pressure to be better than others can be a stimulus, depending on whether you're successful at it. Sometimes it's enough to do something for someone just to lift their spirits. As a simple worker I haven't had any problems because of my sexual orientation. Of course, if I tried to qualify as a teacher I might run into discrimination. People like me seduce their young students—that's what people think. When it comes time to promote somebody to an important position, the fact of being gay is taken into consideration by management, behind closed doors. That's the way it seems, though I can't prove it. Maybe it doesn't make a difference anymore in restaurant work or in the ballet company, but in "higher" professions we're not looked upon too kindly.

A year and a half ago a friend at work came out to me. He went out of his way to make sure nobody else was in the dressing room before he let loose: "You won't believe it, but I've done it with men. Surprised, aren't you? Not just once. Whether you believe it or not, you know one of them; guess who? You see him all the time, in our work brigade!"

I couldn't believe my ears. I was flipping out. My blood pressure went way up. He became more and more frantic, cracking his knuckles nervously. No, no, no! Scared by his own shouting, he came closer and closer. His face was covered with red patches. He couldn't hold it any longer: "Lothar, it's Lothar."

I was completely surprised. Lothar, of all people. While he was checking the second row of lockers for possible eavesdroppers, I managed to get some words out: "Congratulations, how did you manage to get him? He's such a *Stino* [stink normal]."

His face was red as a beet, but he said proudly: "No, he talked me into it. He thinks you are 120 percent gay."

I was flabbergasted. Why hadn't I noticed anything? With either of them? I thought about them and saw right away how obvious it all was. At breakfast in the cafeteria Lothar held his coffee cup in a way that was suspiciously elegant; the other one stood kind of queenish in line during the lunch break. It occurred to me that they were always last to leave the shower room. It was obvious, and I wondered why I wasn't able to figure it out on my own. It struck me the way Lothar was always flirting with the women, sometimes pinching them, other times slapping their behinds. And he was married.

Now I know, the same thing that happens to a lot of people happened to me. I had fallen for the usual prejudices. If someone's gay, it should be visible to anyone. I heard the fact and automatically felt that need to have my prejudices confirmed. I looked for the proof and found it. It's like when you find out about someone you've known for some years that he has Jewish parents. All at once you see him differently, you're embarrassed, you look at him more carefully, and then it seems his nose is slightly crooked. It's like a compulsion. The stereotype I carry with me had fooled me into believing I could make out any gay man no matter how concealed. If not at first sight, then minimally by the third. It turned out I was wrong. My next stereotype became apparent as I examined Lothar and his colleague in light of typical gay characteristics—and, of course, then my stereotype was confirmed. The truth of the matter is that neither of them appears gay, and therefore I couldn't have discovered anything about them earlier. I did the same thing a lot of people do in other situations: make experience fit your preconceived notions about life. Because they're so easy to use, so practical.

Out of the 800,000 gays statistics say exist in our country, only a small number of them can be recognized from the way they appear. You might say it's one-sixth of the iceberg that's above water, the other five-sixths can only be guessed at. And most don't have the need to behave effeminately and don't want to be like women.

The more I think about sexuality, the more stereotypes burst like soap bubbles. Straight, gay, *Stino*, *Stockschwul* [120 percent gay]: those are all labels, little boxes to fit people into. Everything clear and nicely ordered, but a hindrance in real life. For Lothar, I must be out-and-out gay, because he still wants to insist to the others that he's not so gay. He can sleep peacefully since there's somebody who's gayer than he is. He's only . . . a little bit gay, and that's okay nowadays. Who wants to be *Stino?* That's boring. But to be *Stockschwul?* No, that's not right either.

The other colleague who came out to me, he's tried a hundred times to go to one of the bars in order to find a steady lover. Always the same scene: during the shift he asks me over and over what he should wear and how he'll know whether the guys there are really gay or not, and on and on. Then it always follows the same pattern. At home he carefully gets dressed up, smells like a French horse, and heads out. In his favorite bar on the corner he quickly drinks a beer to get up his courage, then another beer and another, things get more and more cozy there with his buddies. By midnight he's drunk, and thank god he's not far away from home. I wouldn't like to know how many guys use the beer table strategy to deal with their sexuality.

I already talked about how my relationship with Rainer is apparent to people around us. For the people living in front and in back of our apartment building we're lovers. When Rainer moved into the place six years ago, he didn't put on any airs about who he is. He went from apartment to apartment, rang the bell, and introduced himself: I'm the new tenant, from now on I'll be living here, in the left wing of the building, on the third floor, I'm not married any longer. He had a bottle under one arm, a few sentences were exchanged, and a toast to good neighborliness. That way the ice was broken, at least with most of them. He didn't bother to keep in touch with the ones who didn't return his visit. There's always the kind of person who's proud of the fact he doesn't socialize with other tenants.

Rainer didn't push the fact that he's different, but he also didn't pretend anything, since in the end they'd have stumbled onto the truth anyway. He trusted each person's intelligence, that they'd figure things out. And that's the way it was. Nowadays everybody in the apartment building knows what's going on. At the first party I thought I was seeing things. My lover was dancing with a man from the building behind us. His wife was chatting with another neighbor and didn't even bother to watch.

In the summer we hold our parties down in the courtyard to the back apartment house. These courtyards in Berlin are cold and gray; they don't get much sunlight. We all pitched in and planted flowers and creepers—they're not expensive and it's beautiful when they sprout and blossom. Already in March everybody in the building was talking about the parties that would be held soon. Two men from our building built the benches and tables, an electrician from the building in front of ours installed a string of lights. Most of the tenants here have practical professions.

Weather permitting, we hold our tenants' breakfast on Sundays. Around half past eight Rainer and I set the table. Then we open up the windows and somebody shouts: we're bringing the cake! And from another window somebody calls: today's our turn to bring coffee! Everything comes together without much organization. From the window no one says what they've got wrapped under their arm. They set it down by the table leg, and when the coffee's all drunk they pull it out—a bottle. It's always fun, I don't ever want to miss it. Not everybody takes part. One person out of stinginess, another is missing for several Sundays because he's not talking to someone else in the group.

Unfortunately our building is practically temporary quarters. The young married couples mostly have just one room and a kitchen. Once they have children it takes at most two to three years before they move to a new apartment building—and then they leave. Now and then they drop by for the Sunday tenants' breakfast. They always moan: "If only we had stayed here, it's so cozy. If only the apartments were bigger."

We have closer contact with three of the families. They come to us when they think we can help them with something. Most of the young wives can't cook well; they often ring and stand at the door: "Say, Rainer, what's your secret with that sauerbraten? Come on up and taste my sauce, otherwise my old man'll be grumbling again." Or they ask for a clove of garlic or a shot of vinegar. Last Christmas our neighbor from across the hall stood in front of the door, completely at her wits' end: "Hey, you guys, we've got a turkey, do you know what to do with it?" When there's trouble he or she comes to us and cries their heart out. We're no different ourselves.

A constant subject these last months has been AIDS. People feel the same way we do—they're worried. The first information made you think that we're up against a devilish disease. A scourge of God, punishment for the immoral life-style of those people. The many sensational reports created a barrier that's meant to divide the good from the bad. It worked, too. Those on the respectable side are once again pointing their finger at us, and on the other side the old guilt feelings are enjoying a revival. We can only hope that the virus won't have the last laugh, ' cause the majority rests comfortably in their feeling of security, which is a false one, and the minority finds itself in a state of anxiety.

I didn't hold it against some people at work or in our building who made a detour around me at the beginning of the hysteria. The real dangers are only recognized much later or not at all. Many people feel less threatened by missiles than by the doorbell of two gays' apartment. You could get infected by it, you know! Luckily the hysteria has subsided since then, since the information has gotten more objective.

When I first heard about AIDS I was incredibly happy that I'm together with Rainer. The disease forces people to take a stand, and whoever feels in danger strikes back, no matter whether the enemy is real or imaginary. The main thing is for there to be one. Intolerance always seeks out an enemy. I think it's crucial for people to have some direct experience with us, if we don't hide ourselves. I myself had to come to terms with the fact that my feelings are completely normal and just different than the majority's. And if a heterosexual's going to understand that, I have to go to him and try to have a conversation. He has fewer reasons to come to me than I have to go to him. There's no other way, otherwise nothing will change.

What can still happen to me nowadays? If someone turns away from me with disgust, go right on ahead. No boss can fire me from work, and I'll leave my aprtment only if I can't pay the rent. It's only whining when us gays always complain that no one understands us. Of course, I'm talking about relations in the city and not the provinces, and some amount of misunderstanding will always remain.

There are amusing situations too. In the plant we had a youth forum on the theme "Socialist Morality and Life-style." After the prepared questions were quickly used up, the Presidium, with great difficulty, tried to keep the discussion going. "No taboos, no limits on discussion, we're honest and open here. Surely, young friends, there are problems everywhere."[7] But no discussion arose. I had gone over my question in my head all day long, practiced it at home, and now my heart was in my throat; I was sweating, and I had lost my confidence. I still managed to raise my hand. I stood up and started: "I have a question that fits the theme, in my opinion."

The Presidium members from our plant winced, the guests looked at me with encouragement, expectantly. My throat was completely dry and I sounded like a crow cawing: "What does our youth club do for its gay members?"

An embarrassed silence filled the hall. In the corner some snickered. The highest ranking guest nodded at me cautiously; everyone else on the Presidium stared up at the chandelier. I took advantage of the situation and let loose: "You said at first"—I was speaking directly to the guest who had nodded at me—"you said that here in our country everything is for the good of the individual person, the whole person. I like that, and I think you meant all persons, gays included. I'd like to hope so. Talk is one thing but. . . . " I started to botch it although my voice had recovered.

The hall was very quiet; no one was laughing anymore. The guests looked from one Presidium member to another, but they were still fascinated by the chandelier. The pause stretched on; some in the hall snickered again. I know it's dumb, but at that moment I felt sorry for him and I really felt how he must be sweating. At any moment laughter could erupt in the hall—I knew my work colleagues.

Luckily he started to speak: "Now, you don't mean to say that, my young friend. Objectively speaking, that comes up extremely rarely, and not at all in such a forum; this isn't the place, but the question has been noted." In the last row a voice called out, "Taboo," and a wave of laughter broke out. The forum was over.

Afterward a friend patted me on the back respectfully: "You really gave it to him." I didn't give anything to him, I didn't provoke him either. I just asked a question and nothing more. If such a question is considered provocative, then that's definitely not because of the question itself. I wish that those who always talk about honesty and openness would themselves be so and not insulate themselves from the real world.

People are at the center of all activity—that's something I feel is true. Somewhere I read that the first and most important human need is work, but for me that would mean my three different shifts a week. From wisdoms like this I begin to make sense of my world. Where else could I begin? This is, after all, one of the most often used ideological axioms in socialist agitation and propaganda.

If this assumption is true, doesn't that also have to be automatically true for my own life also? I believe that every person must strive to find a "center." For us gays, it's especially true that we will have to find it by ourselves. In my own life I have had only my friends, parents, and a buddy to help me with my problems.

At the beginning of our discussion you asked me, "What would you like to be at forty?" I can't answer that directly because it doesn't really interest me. But I can tell you what I do not want to be: not as frustrated as many married couples I know; not as disappointed in life as so many gays at that age.

I hope in the next few years that people will begin discussing their problems more openly with each other, at home with their parents, at school, at work, everywhere. For now, while their pot's still full, they should use their minds for other things. Oh, that sounds fabulously clever.

Interview completed 1988
Translated by Steven Stoltenberg

III. Lothar, Peter, and Volker

*Introduced and translated by
James W. Jones*

"Coming-out" literature is a necessary aspect of gay liberation. The term *gay liberation* may perhaps seem out-moded for us in the United States at the end of the twentieth century, but it is still an appropriate and necessary term for the process every gay person must undertake if she or he is to create a fulfilling life within a homophobic society.

The degrees of homophobia and its cultural roots certainly vary between the United States and the GDR and within regions and cities inside the two countries (for example, the possibilities for gay life in East Berlin are quite different than they are in Halle, as Peter and Volker discuss). The GDR does not have a cultural tradition of puritanism, of laws condemning someone to life imprisonment for "sodomy" (although until 1968, paragraph 175 did allow for shorter-term jail sentences as well as fines), or of "interest groups" seeking to change laws to make society more hospitable to minorities. The GDR does, however, have a German tradition of gays and lesbians seeking legal equality and social integration. This tradition began around the turn of the century with the creation of a homosexual emancipation movement using the new view of homosexuality as a fact of nature, an innate characteristic for a certain percentage of the population. Dr. Magnus Hirschfeld, whom Lothar mentions for his book *Transvestites* (1910; second edition, 1925), led the part of this movement which was centered in the Scientific-Humanitarian Committee (1897–1933) and which Hirschfeld himself co-founded. This group vigorously fought for abolition of paragraph 175 and for social acceptance of gays and lesbians as equal members of society. It based its arguments on Hirschfeld's theory of homosexuals as a "third sex" in which male homosexuals were defined as male in physical gender but female in soul or character, with the reverse being true for lesbians. Although the Third Reich put an end to this first movement toward "gay liberation"in Germany, its history serves as a tradition for both West and East Germans today, thanks to the efforts of many scholars to reclaim that past for the present struggle.[1]

These *Auskünfte schwuler Männer* ("particulars of gay men,"as the German subtitle of this book states), then, are part of a coming-out literature that has been developing recently within the GDR.[2] This literature has certain common characteristics no matter what the nationality of its authors. In it, we explain ourselves to ourselves and to others. In it, we are forever telling those stories that gay men share with each other in bars and bedrooms, and living rooms, too, throughout the world. They serve as a first step toward creating the community that is evoked by the use of the word *gay* in the book's German subtitle.

And yet the coming-out literature that we read here, as much as it seeks to break down barriers by making "them" familiar with "our" differences, also serves to define "us" as precisely that Other who is not speaking "our" experience. Herein lies an essential difference between the experiences Lothar, Peter, and Volker describe and "our" American (or even West German) experiences, be they heterosexual or homosexual. While coming-out literature seeks to lead the majority to tolerance of "our" open existence within "their" midst, some important aspects of these men's attitudes and experiences illustrate the distinction that sexual orientation creates for these three men in this country at this time. Such distinctions also demonstrate how their discourse of gay life differs from that found in the United States.

All three men conceive of gender roles as rather fixed identities, despite their own transgression of the very borders they perceive. Lothar, in particular, assigns certain qualities (the desire to be "conquered," to have children) to all women. Perhaps this can be ascribed to the way he conceives of his own identity, namely that of a transvestite, gay man. His own identity permits, even demands, for him, these fixed bounds, which he may step over by putting on women's clothes. Peter and Volker believe that every gay man ought to be involved in a committed relationship. They seem to think that, if they can manage it, anyone can. They also view all gay men as focused almost exclusively on sex as the sole motivator of social interaction between gay men.

All three see themselves as relatively separate from the gay community in their cities and in the GDR. Lothar, with perhaps a bit of flamboyant vanity, speaks of the disbelief younger gays evince when he tells of the erotic attraction he exerts on some men who desire transvestites. He also describes other gays' discrimination against him because he does not fit their definition of what a gay man should be. Volker and Peter mention how gays will not even greet each other when passing on the street.

Yet their stories focus on their integration—or at least their attempts at integration—into the larger heterosexual world. They all achieve this through their involvement in the majority society. Lothar has his museum through which he guides tourists and school groups. Peter achieved a measure of integration into heterosexual society through D., a close female friend, and into a gay community through his involvement with a gay discussion group. Volker describes his openness to his colleagues at work about being gay.

Yet what makes the experiences of these three so different from those of their American counterparts as they are chronicled in the popular culture, are to my mind precisely those elements that make their experiences typical for men of their generations (over thirty-five) in the GDR. Indeed, they share with them some "conservative," even "old-fashioned" (by American standards) attitudes about gender roles and love relationships. What I find also markedly "East German" about their experiences is exactly that estrangement from the gay community (which, it must be remembered, has only existed a few years as an open, organized group) and their turning to the larger, nongay community for modes of integration. Gay ghettos do not exist, not only because of the youth of East German gay culture but also because of German social traditions, living arrangements, and socialist cultural norms. Yet even in integration they maintain their identities as gays. They want to make society change to suit them, not make themselves conform to its decrees.

Many people in the GDR, especially in East Berlin, know Lothar and Peter because they have been willing to profess their sexuality publicly in order to fight for gay rights. Lothar has achieved a certain renown because of his unrepentant flamboyance, making him a kind of East German Quentin Crisp.[3] Since this interview was conducted, Peter has taken even greater steps in living as an openly gay man. He was elected as one of the leaders of a Berlin parish of the Evangelical (Lutheran) church. In this position, he has bravely stood up for gay rights in the face of official opposition.

Since 1985, gays and lesbians in the GDR have organized "discussion groups" under the protective umbrella of the Evangelical church. Initially numbering twelve (with a thirteenth existing outside the church and with state approval), their number has continually grown. These "discussion groups" serve a wide variety of purposes for gays and lesbians, chief among them consciousness-raising, emotional support, and political action. Recent events have demonstrated how such groups, organized beyond the control of the state, have helped bring about changes in the nature of political power in the GDR.

What makes these men's experiences similar to those of American or even West German gays? Peter's experience with the seminary will come as no surprise to any gay person who has had any dealings with the Lutheran churches in America. Volker's description of the reaction of his colleagues will also ring a bell. The well-meaning utterances ("Some of my best friends are . . . ") as well as the moment when a male coworker started to tell a fag story also represent incidents common to many cultures. The violence against gays, which lies waiting to erupt at moments of "provocation" or relaxation of social barriers (via alcohol), forms a further common theme. But the violence takes a particularly German tone, for its vocabulary is that of German fascism.

In reading and translating these interviews, I am reminded of the changes in gay identities and gay lives that have occurred over the past twenty years. The role of drag and the signal of effeminacy as necessary aspects of male homosexuality have decreased under the influence of the cult of masculinity, increased visibility (if not tolerance) of the multiplicity of gays, and changes in the social roles of women. In some ways, Lothar is perhaps a relic of a bygone era, that preliberation, even prewar, era of homosexuality. But he is a charming relic, and one that reminds us of what we have lost. Peter's and Volker's emphasis on committed, usually monogamous relationships for gays reminds us of how AIDS has changed definitions of gayness. Perhaps few would subscribe to their exhortation to "partnership" as an agenda for all gays, but there is no doubt that one effect of the health crisis has been to move gay men toward such relationships.

While they remind us of the changes, their words demonstrate, for us, for them, and for their readers in the GDR, that individual gays acting together can create a gay community. Peter, especially, voices the need for group action and describes how he and Volker have confronted official homophobia again and again. Their reports document that some gays have taken a stand and that they have started to band together in order to effect social change. Their words demonstrate that gay spirit continually arises and shapes its own forms of expression. That lesson rekindles hope on both sides of the Atlantic at a time when the chance for new beginnings seems brighter than ever.

5. "I am my own woman"

Lothar, born 1927, curator

With the least amount of pathos possible. All right, I'll try.

This house is my fate. In it, I have realized a part of my dreams. As a child, it captivated me.

It was constructed around 1750. In 1920, it went into the possession of the city of Berlin and, in the ten years until 1930, it was a municipal home for children. For the older people in Mahlsdorf it is still the old estate. After 1930 it was, by turns, a country school, youth welfare office, employment bureau, revenue office, office for issuing ration cards, criminal investigation office for the police, registry office, office for street cleaning and for trash disposal. In 1957 the house was supposed to be torn down. I heard about it, quickly decided to go to the authorities, and succeeded in getting the house rent free. It took me thirteen years to put a house back in order out of those ruins. I succeeded in what I undertook to do. I made a museum out of it. In early August it will be twenty-seven years since the collection was opened to the public as a private collection.

We are now in the Gothic Room.

When *Gründerzeit* fell out of fashion in the twenties and thirties, many people chopped up their old furniture and used it as fuel in their stoves; more prudent ones stored it in the attic or in the cellar.[1] People bought new furniture—that is, modern. In this period all the turrets and the ornamentation on the *Gründerzeit* furniture simply didn't fit in.

If we were redecorating at home and it was decided that the conch-shell ornamentation of the mirror had to be removed after all—in my mother's eyes it had just become a useless dust catcher—my lament began: "Oh, mommy, that looked so pretty, that lovely conch shell. Please, mommy?"

She would answer: "Take it up to your trash collection then!" Beaming with joy, I squeezed the ornament under my arm and took off to my kingdom, to the treasures with which I had carefully decorated my attic chamber. Mother tolerated my fancy for collecting.

Naturally, I couldn't tell one style from another as a child. I was crazy for everything that was old, yet for *Gründerzeit* I had a sixth sense from an early age. *Biedermeier* tallboys I also found pretty, but they had to have columns.[2] Elaborate feet, a little delicate carving in the shape of a wooden ball here, and I was transported. Many things on *Gründerzeit* pieces can be dismantled. When you couldn't decide whether to discard the whole piece

of furniture—sometimes you didn't even have the little bit of money required to pay someone to haul it away—you'd dismantle the piece you
thought was junk and cart it off to the dump. With heart racing, I sorted,
as a ten-year-old, through the trash left there and examined turrets, knobs,
and smaller ornaments to see if I had any use for them. Whatever I thought
was pretty came into my treasure trove.

At the age of four or five, I played with puppet furniture; at six I dragged
chairs and a little sewing table through my great uncle's house and I continually rearranged and decorated. I couldn't get enough.

My great uncle was a kindly fellow. As an automobile engineer, he belonged to the upper middle class. He was a bachelor and lived with two
unmarried sisters in a household that had been founded in the last decade
of the previous century.

School friends brought along old pieces for me when they visited. If I
was invited to their houses, I was allowed to dig around in their attics. I
also went up to people. Don't you have an old gramophone, even if it's
just the horn? If I was tossed out, that didn't discourage me. Just in case,
I had my savings with me to pay for it.

Just take a look at this gramophone. The working parts are encased in
a cute chest of wood. The music comes out of an exquisite flowered horn.
Certainly all of that has little to do with art, but it is nice to look at. From
my earliest days, a horn, for me, belongs to a gramophone. The equipment
after 1920 does not interest me in the least. Music has to come out of a
horn. Maybe I'm crazy. That's just the way I am.

I'd rather be in an old barn with all my pretty things than in an apartment
with modern furnishings and with district heating and a bathroom. I am
allergic to mass-produced stuff. In a clock, a house, for all I care even in
a chair, I always look for its face. Objects fashioned without love make me
sick. Even the silhouette of a television set makes me shudder.

Fifty-one years have passed since I was examined by a school doctor in
this house. I was six years old. The next meeting was much more unpleasant. Children who were not vigorous enough and only very irregularly
participated in the pleasures of the Hitler Youth were summoned here. We
black sheep were permitted to line up in front of the house, and first of
all were herded into a group by a stiff and stern squad leader from Lich-
tenberg before we were then removed individually. This guy had the first
formation of boys take a step forward, the second one backward. Then he
chewed each one out.

Me he mustered with an especially stern look. Then he barked out:
"You're standing there like a simple country girl! Do you even know what
squad you're in?"

My god, I thought. Squad, squad, what in the world is that? In my mind's
eye I saw a little flag fluttering in the wind.[3] At that moment he was called
by another Hitler Youth leader. I exhaled. I glanced at Kurt, my loyal friend
from school who was standing just to the left of me. In my excitement, I

hadn't caught what he'd been whispering to me. Finally, I understood him: "Lothar, it's sitting right there on your epaulettes."

That cretin turned to me again and spoke imperiously: "Well, let's have it!" I cast a sidelong glance at my right epaulette and saw an 18, a slash, and a 124. Promptly I replied: "Squad 18 through 124." The boys burst out laughing. He planted himself, legs apart, before me, stuck his hands on his hips and bellowed: "Boy are you generous! So I can just pick out the one that suits me?" I was so flabbergasted, and we'd always been told to answer with "Yes, sir," so I blurted back at him my "Yes, sir."

Everybody collapsed with laughter.

"Quiet!" he screamed into the rows. Since they didn't want to quiet down, he crowed like a rooster: "No talking! That's an order."

After that we had to go into this room. I stood in a corner near the grandfather's clock. The room was jammed. I only vaguely listened to the twaddle and looked at the doors. Delightful. Cornices on the doors, these magnificent windows. Was it ever nice here. Suddenly Kurt poked me in the side and whispered: "Watch out, that creep's just been talking about you again." I broke away from the glories of that room and wanted out, to go home.

There were enough children and adults at this time who found me, with my little head full of golden blond locks, deeply contemptible and spoke up loud and clear. Just because I adorned myself with barrettes, I was beaten up. "Golden blond nanny-goat," they called; "you look just like a girl." I was astonished. Why were they so ill-mannered? I'd done nothing to them. Later I could feel this wall between me and many others. At that time I had no explanation. Helplessly, I stood before my father one time when he beat me with the riding whip and roared like someone possessed: "You're not a girl, you're not a girl! You have to be a boy and become a soldier—remember that, once and for all!" After that he rushed to the attic and threw my belongings out the attic window.

Certainly nobody looking at me would ever have thought of Krupp steel.[4] Of that I'm quite certain today.

I was happy among my treasures. I continually rearranged things, polished my furniture, dusted, laid down a crocheted doily here, removed one there, and repaired little bits of damage.

Boys interested me a lot. Not the big, brutish wood-cutter types. Boors were never my type. The blond, slim, quiet boys awakened wishes inside of me. If I played with them, I was bubbling over with merry notions and had the most prickly ideas. But girls I only took notice of if they wore a pretty skirt or if an especially sweet bodice caught my eye. What I liked about them I would gladly have worn myself.

Once my great uncle took me to Berlin to buy me a new coat. We went into one of the biggest department stores. My uncle knew where you could buy good things inexpensively. The salesgirl tried a Loden coat on me. I turned in front of the mirror and was dissatisfied. "You don't like it?" my uncle asked. "No, uncle, I don't like it at all. It just hangs there like a sack. It should be fitted at the waist and have a belt that you can pull nice and tight."

"We have boys' coats with belts, too," said the salesgirl to that. I slipped into that coat and pulled the belt as tight as humanly possible. In front of the mirror I shook my head. "No, it just doesn't fit right either. You see, here there are wrinkles all over the place. No, it's just got to be fitted at the waist." "Well, little boy," said the salesgirl, "only girls' coats are fitted."

We went over to the girls' department. The very first one fit like a glove. A dream. Fitted at the waist, darts, a cute bell shape.

Me: "Oh, is it ever pretty, that's the one I'd like to have."

To that, my uncle: "A girl's coat? Just don't let your old man see that."

Luckily he didn't understand at all that I was shivering through the neighborhood all winter in a girl's coat.

In the attic, I secretly tried on my mother's mothballed school dresses. I thought I was cute and fit right in.

In contrast, my first suit was a disaster. I received it for my confirmation. Long pants. I struggled against putting the thing on. My kind-hearted great uncle coaxed me, my mother tried to persuade me: "Child, you simply cannot go in short pants." I remained firm: "I am not putting that suit on! A white shirt and a bow-tie look stupid."

I fiddled around in front of the mirror for such a long time that our maid's patience ran out. "I've had enough of you now!" Very red in the face, she whacked me on the behind with her carpet-beater and said curtly and strictly: "That suit is going to be worn! I am not about to allow you to stand before the altar wearing short pants." I whined some more and said defiantly: "I'd much rather put on a dress." She answered: "That'd suit you better too."

In the church, I kept looking at my pants legs and always thought the same thing: How idiotic, how idiotic. But how pretty the black dresses of the girls in my class were. Little white pointed collars on black velvet. And fitted at the waist too. At that moment, I decided: Sometime, somewhere you are going to buy yourself a dress too.

At fifteen I discovered the most magnificent treasures in a room on my great aunt Luise's estate in what was then East Prussia. Old costumes, ball gowns, extremely tailored women's riding outfits. To my great joy, the things fit me as if they had been made just for me. Every year I went to my aunt's for vacation. She called me "Marielly" or "my mistress" and didn't care at all that I so thoroughly enjoyed trying on these valuables. During the entire vacation I dragged about in her old clothes. Of course only inside the house.

At the end of the forties, I bought my own outfits and to my own taste. Skirts, blouses, coats, and accessories. I had a hair dresser do my hair.

During a moment alone, Mom said to me: "Lothar, you ought to start thinking of looking for a woman and getting married. Of course I am happy to have you at home, but you must think of your future."

I answered her: "You know, Mommy, I am my own woman and your oldest, unmarried daughter. Your Lotharina."

At that she laughed and said: "That I don't understand."

"You know," I said, "you must know. I am happy this way. I have started on my path and I have absolutely no desire to depart from it. Tremendous misery would befall me if you were to take your love away from me."

I read aloud to my mom passages out of Magnus Hirschfeld's *Transvestites* and told her much about my psyche and that of my friends. My great aunt Luise had been a friend of the sexologist Magnus Hirschfeld and had received the book as a present, with a dedication from him. She left it to me in her will, and to this day it holds a place of honor in my bookcase.

My sister found out when she was helping my mom with the laundry during one of her visits. It was at the time when washing machines appeared. While sorting the laundry, she happened to notice black garter belts, little silk panties and very sheer nylons. Amazed, she asked: "Just who do these belong to?" Mom replied: "Those are Lothar's." My sister got very red and yelled hysterically: "And you permit that? You must forbid him to do that! A man is not permitted to wear that!" To that, Mom said: "He is old enough, he must realize what he's putting on."

On shopping trips to Berlin I went in the women's dressing room. Occasionally people looked askance, out of the corners of their eyes. When I expressed my desire in the shops, the salesgirls did not always quite see eye to eye with me, but they waited on me. On the other hand, if I showed up wearing men's clothes, sometimes the salesgirls secretly poked each other and laughed somewhat stupidly. I was never exactly sure what made them laugh. Was it my voice, my pocketbook, or the basket with handles that I carried on my arm? What man carried a basket like that on the street? If I wore a dress, I seldom attracted attention because everything was right, everything fit.

Today I still avoid shirts, a suit and tie like a devil avoids holy water. To wear a beard—ghastly.

Like so many women, I would like to be conquered. What a beautiful feeling, when you are noticed on the street, in a restaurant. Aha, someone's following you with his eyes, desires you, that confirmation that a human being does not bloom in vain. I've had many admirers in my life, even masculine women have loved me. Since I'm no child of sadness, it goes without saying that this also went beyond admiration. I have never liked excessively masculine men. Their brutal aura repelled me.

There's one experience I should like to report. Even homosexual men look up at the ceiling with indignation and disbelief as soon as I speak about my erotic effect on men. They laugh to themselves whenever they hear how panic-stricken men search for wide-open spaces after they have followed me down street after street and I respond to their proposition by telling them that with me there is just a little hitch. That there are also, however, men who get even wilder in response to my words dumbfounds some gays who then just look up at the ceiling.

Apparently, only a few people can deal with a reality that they have not experienced themselves.

Within my four walls I usually go about in sackcloth and ashes. I get into a housedress that fits me well and I get the urge to clean and to polish. Anything that doesn't fit me fairly well I can't stand and I never put on again. In a man's jacket I couldn't lift a finger in the household. My great uncle always said: "You'd have made a gem of a maid around 1900."

I find today's women's fashions unbearable. Yesterday I wanted to buy myself a housedress in a clothing store. Nothing on the racks but shapeless, one-piece things that just hang on you. I had the same experience three, four years ago when I wanted to buy a woman's coat. The saleswoman simply could not offer me anything fitted at the waist. In neat rows on the racks hung the potato sack model, the sugar sack model, and the flour sack model. The saleswoman advised me to buy some good material and gave me the address of her tailor. I went to see him. As he was measuring me, the old gentleman was mumbling to himself: "Well, you haven't got much bosom left either."

The fittings were a lot of fun. I really got on his nerves with my demands. There another dart, the left shoulder a little higher, the whole thing a tad more bell-shaped.

"Aha," he said, "you want the old-fashioned style, bell-shaped, why didn't you say that right away?" "Well," I said, "I insist on tailored clothes, fitted at the waist." I still wear that coat he made today.

Well, what can I add to that? I wear size 44 off the rack, I have narrow shoulders and, luckily, a tight behind, which can fill out a few things. I prefer lime green, sky blue, and black. I never wear makeup. The way you are is just the way you are. As far as jewelry goes, I am rather restrained. In no way conspicuous. I take pleasure in old costume jewelry. Perfume is unimportant to me.

I have dresses and skirts that are over thirty years old and still fit me. Oh yes, there are memories bound up with many of them.

When I am invited by friends to a small ball at someone's home—today, of course, it's called a party—I go to my hairdresser, then I stand in front of my closet, pick something out and take my time making myself pretty. When I am invited on short notice, everything has to happen in a flash. I choose a wig that matches my dress, quickly get dressed, and hop on the streetcar.

I think it was always life-threatening: except in Berlin in the twenties and today. Throughout the history of mankind, countless effeminate men have been destroyed, spectacularly or in complete silence. If they weren't killed by someone else, they saw to it themselves. Often their family faced a riddle. He simply didn't have any reason at all to do that. Why did he do this to us? I am happy to be alive at a time when living openly doesn't mean death any more. If I had been born a few years earlier, I would have gone to the gas chambers. It's as simple as that.

The year 1945 brought even to us that freedom we longed for. At last we could admit who we were to ourselves. Many of us even had the courage to do so. That most people harbored the most sinister prejudices against us was just a trifle compared to that fatal persecution and was even down-right normal. What for centuries had been considered criminal, sinful, and degenerate can surely only gradually be changed in people's thinking. Besides that, the "Golden Twenties" had left behind fewer marks on the consciousness of the populace than people like to assume. I quickly understood that this new time was also supposed to be our time. That sounds sentimental, but I really mean it. Living together, planning together, traveling with your partner: just living. With a little civic courage, now that too was possible for us. The day-to-day living is not so gray at all. It degenerates into that if you do not take charge of it yourself.

In my memory, the difficult postwar period is not so difficult at all. Work was never a strain in my life, I was young and clever enough to grasp that on May 8 I had been liberated two and three times over.

I was supposed to be shot in the early days of May. SS watchdogs combed through the air-raid shelters looking for teenagers and old men in order to put them up against the wall because they had supposedly shirked their defense duties. I was saved by an army officer who appeared on the scene and chased the young watchdogs away. An hour later I was buried alive in the next air raid.

Deep in the bottom of my heart the war engraved a fear of the outdoors. I stand in fear of the uncertainty that suddenly grabs hold of you when no escape is possible. I have never gotten rid of this fear. I need a person who, in critical situations, will say to me: "Now look, dearie, it's going to work out. Just calm down, wait and see, don't be afraid, I'm here with you. Let me take care of it." That's how I take heart.

But back to the past. In 1938, my great uncle arranged for me to attend a school in the center of Berlin, Berlin SE 36, the old Berlin Luisenstadt. I had to take the Jannowitz Bridge streetcar through Brücken Street, Neander Street, Annen Street to Dresdner Street 90, an exquisite *Gründerzeit* house. That was my new school. We entered the room of the principal and inwardly I leapt for joy. On the ceiling hung an electric gas chandelier with a white shade and green beads. Behind the gigantic desk, a clock with weights ticked away. A round table covered with a dark green plush tablecloth was placed in the corner for visitors. On the table stood a magnificent tray for visitor's cards.

When the term *Hitler Youth* was mentioned, I concentrated again on the conversation between the principal and my great uncle. When my great uncle said, "Well, that's just the way things are," the principal made a dismissive gesture with both hands and murmured: "I understand, I understand."

In 1944, the school was bombed out.

The Luisenstadt was *the* discovery for me. Between the Jannowitz bridge, Frucht Street, Koppen Square, and where the East train station stands today, there was literally one secondhand store after another. As a little boy I'd already gone from secondhand dealer to secondhand dealer in Köpenick, but so many exquisite shops within spitting distance—that was really something!

Bit by bit I got to know the secondhand dealers. Soon I knew exactly where the best things were. Here the old victrolas, there historical records, next door Edison rolls for player pianos, and one street beyond dressers, sideboards, and buffets. After school, I regularly traipsed round the shops, and it didn't take long till I was allowed to make myself useful here and there. It was in the secondhand goods basement of Maxe Bier, Köpenicker Street 148, that I stayed put. I took care of whatever came to hand. Polished table tops, put in gramophone needles, made minor repairs on clocks. In 1942, at the age of fifteen, I could already carry pianos. Moving a piano as part of a household move brought in an extra ten marks, after all. A lot of money for that time.

Together with Maxe Bier, I pulled the flat-bed truck over the asphalt of Luisen Street. The open truck was two and a half meters long, one meter thirty wide, had leaf springs and wheels with wooden spokes. With the leather reins over our shoulders, we pulled our treasures into Maxe Bier's secondhand goods cellar. For a fifteen-year-old, that was really hard work. But what's hard work if it's fun? The other boys went swimming and played soccer—things that did not interest me.

Mom had long ago given up thinking my passion was a whim, a fancy that I would grow out of as I got older.

At Maxe Bier's I got things cheaper. A small chest of drawers that I'd fallen in love with cost me eight marks retail. I made my wish known and after a glance at his list of used goods, Maxe Bier said: "Well, you did help carry it, six marks is what I paid for it. That's what you'll have it for too."

That evening at six I went home, my book bag on my back, the chest of drawers on my stomach. First thing, on to the streetcar, the 87. Every ten meters I had to set it down and catch my breath. In Köpenick I had to change trams, to the 83. The conductors already knew me. When they saw me standing with a heavy piece of furniture, they climbed out and helped me store my load on the forward platform. They always made some kind of remark: "Man, little boy, you're already on the move again today," or, "That's bordering on child labor, I'm going to report it."

The streetcar rocked slowly through the forest to Mahlsdorf-South, and I never needed to ask a conductor to help me. They lent a hand as a matter of course.

Well, that's how I put together the ground floor of the Mahlsdorf Museum.

In 1942, Maxe Bier had to hire a young man to carry the furniture. He just couldn't do the work anymore. The Nazis charged the secondhand dealers with managing the so-called Jewish estates. To put it plainly: it was their job to take over what was left after the apartments had been ransacked and to clear out the horribly ravaged rooms.

Mrs. Bier called the new guy our little Levinson. He received his place at the dinner table in the kitchen, and from then on I pulled the wagon with him through Luisenstadt. In the meantime Maxe Bier had turned sixty-two and couldn't carry heavy things anymore. Levinson and I were bosom buddies after a few days.

One day, it was the beginning of 1943, I came into the store after school. Something had happened. Mrs. Bier was crying and moaning: "Where in the world are they going to take the boy?" Maxe Bier was standing helplessly behind his wife and trying to console her: "They'll take him to Poland and put him on a farm, as forced labor."

I believed him. That Maxe Bier, at this time, still also believed it, I dare to doubt today.

Up until the first years of the war, the world of secondhand goods dealers went on within Luisenstadt as if the Nazis didn't exist. That changed when the dreadful deportations of Jews began on a large scale. Anyone who had to enter one ransacked Jewish apartment after another could not ignore the Nazis anymore. And, of course, many secondhand dealers were themselves Jews.

As an adolescent, I experienced that world of secondhand goods dealers as an oasis in which I could speak openly and freely. The atmosphere at Maxe Bier's and the experience of the sorrow of our Jewish fellow citizens made me into an enemy of the Nazis for the rest of my life.

After 1945, I exhibited a large bookcase that I had acquired from the assets left behind by a deported Jewish family. The family never returned to their house on Engel-Ufer; all traces of them disappeared, as with most of their comrades in suffering, inside the extermination camps. I mounted a little plaque on the bookcase and on it I noted the fate of this Jewish family. Up until this past year, the bookcase was in this house. When I heard that the synagogue in Oranien Street was going to be rebuilt, I donated that bookcase and a few other things to the Jewish community.

I've never tied my fate to heaven but, rather, always to what is here on earth: to my century, to my psyche, and to this house.

When the house was at its hour of greatest need, it summoned me and I was there, and it was not torn down. For five years I roamed through Berlin houses about to be torn down in order to procure missing doorknobs, doors, stucco rosettes, skirting boards, historically accurate door moldings, windows, and window handles. No water, no light, mountains of rubble everywhere. A lot of work. I couldn't afford craftsmen. I paid the farmers a small sum to cart the rubble away. The roof I covered myself.

"That crazy guy with his old junk is wandering around like a ghost in his ruins." Or: "The nut with a thing for *Gründerzeit*." That's how the neighborhood reacted to me. In the first months, I sat inside this big house alone with my fear during those dark nights. Scarcely had I glazed the windows when they were broken in again that same night.

A lucky coincidence came at the right time for me. Right next door, the company where they fattened up pigs was looking for a night watchman. This part-time job for a couple of weeks turned into a whole six years. Farming of course was not foreign to me. The very first night I had to feed the pigs. I didn't sit around all night, I pitched in where I saw work to be done. You convince simple people best through your work. It didn't take long before no colleague cared anymore if he came to work early in the morning and met me in an apron, wearing a scarf on my head.

After the war I was employed for some years as a curator in the Märkisches Museum. I mainly restored clocks and mechanical musical instruments: music boxes, orchestrions, musical clocks. When I was a child, a clockmaker in Köpenick explained to me what was driven by what inside a clock. I built on that. An art college I only saw from the outside, but all along I could tell walnut from oak. Work was always a lot of fun for me, and I learned a lot from watching my other colleagues. Then I carried out special assignments for the museum for years.

It was a long, arduous path, but if you want to achieve something, you have to stick to it. The joy I provide people through this collection returns to my own heart. Whenever young people spontaneously express their enthusiasm and astonishment after a tour, I am happy. Twenty-year-olds tell me how great they think it is that a person built up this collection in time of war and in the postwar years. What more could I want?

In our country there are all kinds of museums that preserve our German history with much love and care. I created one about the life of the simple middle-class in Germany around 1900. How things looked then in the front parlors of those people they can see here. As we Berliners say, "At my house."

Well, what else is there to say about myself? Resolute people impress me. Men and women. People who hold the reins in their hands and stand with their power at my side in life's difficult situations. Like most women I of course have not found the ideal man. At least not yet. But it's never too late!

I wished for a man with whom I could have shared bed and board for the rest of my life, who wouldn't have teased me, to whom I could have been a faithful wife. With effeminate men, the urge to feel tender toward someone, to cuddle someone up to oneself, is strong. It's the old song: wishes and reality.

My lover of many years, a blond who also liked to dress in drag, died last year. He was not faithful. We shared bed and board on weekends. He had his household, I had mine. Now and then he'd spend his vacation here. We had lovely, happy hours with each other. Much of the unpleasantness that heterosexual women experience was spared me. I think there are lots of unhappy women—women who in their marriages are pushed into a corner, humiliated and beaten by their husbands.

Like every female being I like children. As a child I just went crazy whenever I was allowed to push the baby carriage or take care of a child. That I wasn't able to have any I have to accept. Many women of course do not have any either, for various reasons.

When I take children through an exhibit, I let them touch everything. I remember all too well what a craving beautiful things evoked in me at this age. I do not boss them around, and in a flash they are hanging on my apron strings. When I look more closely at a little face, sometimes sad feelings come over me. What will the future bring them, these little creatures? The weapons are getting more and more monstrous. I fervently wish that it does not come to a third world war. Let's hope that smart and reasonable people preserve us from it. I myself side with Luther. If I knew that the world was going to perish tomorrow, I would still plant an apple tree today. That's the way I have always felt. Otherwise I would never have been able to lift a finger for sheer misgivings. They'd never have been able to make a war with me. Throw a hand grenade into a house? The chandelier could shatter or a lovely piece of *Gründerzeit* furniture could break. The only thing I am suited for is preserving things and making them whole.

Well, how do I affect those around me? I know that I am a provocation. People either reject me completely or they accept me, and usually vehemently at that. The times have gotten decidedly more favorable. Who would even have dreamt about a sex change decades ago? At my age it is pointless to discuss being for or against a change. My well-being does not depend on the kind of genitalia I have. A change would be absurd for me. I feel so strongly a woman that my genitalia do not inconvenience me. But it is a good thing for those who see their salvation in it.

Men react more aggressively to my appearance than women do. Actually they ought to breathe a sigh of relief when they see me. After all, each queen is one rival less for them on the heterosexual love market. Far from it, however. The most unpleasant attacks have come from the male front. One example. Years ago near the train station men were walking past on the sidewalk across the street. Four or five of them, not so young anymore. It was cool out, and I had a woman's coat on. I don't recollect whether I was wearing a scarf or a hat. In front of a clothing store on the right-hand side I stopped. In the window, there were women's sweaters that I really liked. Suddenly a cannonade of insults descended on me: "Faggot, guys like you ought to be burned. Under Hitler those queers were done away with."

Something even worse happened to me at the Ostkreuz train station. I was attacked by a drunk and reviled in the worst way. With Nazi vocabulary too, by the way. But, actually, that is the exception.

Once I encountered some men in a park. One of them stopped, looked me carefully up and down, and said right in my face: "Oh, honey, haven't you ever made yourself pretty? No, just what do we think of that now?" The others joined in his laughter and peacefully went on their way.

Actually, women ought to be the more aggressive ones in their reaction; at least they would have a more plausible reason. After the war, men were in short supply and, after all, every queen is one less man for them. The reactions of women have actually gotten more and more malicious. When I would enter my neighborhood store in years gone by, I'd often hear a female clerk call to the back: "Come here, quick, Lucy's here, in her red coat." Promptly they all arrived and gaped at me. I calmly took my time packing up my purchases and took my leave in a friendly manner. I acted as if all of that did not concern me.

Among homosexuals, we transvestites are treated in a variety of ways. In a bar it sometimes happens that I am hissed at: "Stupid old thing, get lost, sit down someplace else." To that I just nod in a friendly way and sit at a different table.

Our little bunnies often exaggerate. They lay it on a little thick, they "really beat on the pudding," as Berliners say. No wonder then that those homosexuals who conform more than we do fear for their good reputation. I think if worse came to worst we'd stick together.

Otherwise it's like it is everywhere else. You approach each other if you'd like something from the other one. Today less so than earlier, and it seems to me that the reasons have become somewhat more materialistic. Even our people [in the GDR] are more caught up with themselves nowadays.

I was always a devoted soul. Anyone who was the least little bit nice to me—whether he felt the same way or not—had me for the rest of his life. Whenever friendships came to an end—whether through death, through moving to another city, or for other reasons—I was always very sad.

If I were to enter into a committed relationship again—after all, nothing is impossible—it would have to be a harmonious one. Without question. I can make accommodations, can very well put up with less. Certain spinsterish traits are normal at my age. As far as the household is concerned, I will maintain my bullheadedness. If I want to put the buffet over there and the wardrobe in the corner, I will get my way. It may be that the years of great need [the postwar years] made me that way. For me, luxury goods were never worth striving for; smoking and drinking were never a temptation.

I have friends who surround me, and my public leaves me little time. Mahlsdorf is the town I was born in; my home is here. I have never considered moving away from here. Here I know every tree, every stone, and here I have my mother and my sister close by. I am firmly rooted here. It only depresses me that the place is losing more and more of its lovely old face. Young people are not concerned about that, but then again they don't know how beautiful it once was here.

Wishes? Warsaw I would like to take a look at. Warsaw is a city to which I am attached by relatives. New York attracts me too. But since I am deathly afraid of flying, it will remain a wish. I would want to take an old, local train, the kind on a narrow-gauge track, and travel through the whole world on an open platform. In my involvement as a bit player in the movies, please no male roles. Now that it has become trendy to put Prussian history on film, I certainly would not like to have to play a sergeant.

Interview completed 1986

"Married without children"

Peter, born 1944, typesetter

In the spring of '68 I got to know Volker. I was a student at the Paulinum seminary. We sniffed each other out, went for a cup of coffee, and imagined how nice a shared vacation might be. Bulgaria, sun, water, beach. Our relationship became closer and closer. But not a word, not a touch that would have been unambiguous.

Today it's hard to believe how naive I was. I had the impudence to take the soprano role in "offering the virginal wreath" at the Paulinum in the variety show we put on at the beginning of the semester.[1] Naturally in drag. The crowd roared. Had I known about myself, I would have stopped myself. Since I didn't, I was able to step out and speak up without embarrassment.

In conversations lasting deep into the night, I felt my way with my fellow students toward questions that concerned me more strongly at that time than I suspected. What would happen if you were assigned a parish in the country after your studies? To live alone, not to live alone, and whether to live at all? I chose to get engaged! Not at just any time, but right away.

She was thirty, I was twenty-four. I presented my future bride to the school adminstration, in accordance with the rules, and a consensus conversation took place. With Volker I had dreamed of Bulgaria, but it was with her that I took a trip, to Thüringen.[2] That vacation was torture for us both.

No one had warned me: "What you're doing won't work."

Besides that, my relationship with Volker was getting stronger and stronger. I dragged him along to all the events. Every Thursday an open forum was held in the institute. On all kinds of topics. If the topic was known, written questions could be submitted beforehand. One of the most exciting evenings was the one on sexuality. The presenter was a doctor. After the lecture, he rummaged through his slips of paper, stopped short, took one, cleared his throat, and read aloud: "Can homosexuals enter the ministry?" He had barely finished stating the question when our director leapt to his feet and declared peremptorily: "No, homosexuals cannot enter the ministry!"

The physician did not let this ruffle him. Just why not, he didn't understand that. To which our boss once again drew himself up to his full height and remarked: "I will correct myself. Homosexuals can enter the ministry, but only in an old-age home." He had the laughers on his side.

This "humorous remark" I considered even then to be colossal discrimination. Against homosexuals and those who care for old people and against old people themselves.

In November, then, I went to him, to the director of the institute. "Well, this is my situation: I love Volker, I want to live with him. I want things to be clear. I know what I'm saying, this is no whim. I am not getting married."

He: "So I was right! I've suspected as much ever since the 'virginal wreath'!"

Three days later, I was sitting in front of my bishop and repeating my litany. "Hmm," he reckoned, "perhaps in ten years, maybe then there will be congregations that can handle a pastor living in a homosexual partnership. Then you might stand a better chance. At the present time no path leads in that direction."

I dropped out and by return mail I received the demand to repay my scholarship within two and a half years—including the money for books that had been given us at Christmas. If only out of morality I ought to feel obligated to repay, said one of the many letters I received.

Looking back, it became clear to me that I had always had homosexual feelings. At fifteen I sometimes thought: this guy or that one I would gladly marry—if I were a woman. At seventeen, when I heard from a pastor in the vicinity that there are people who are not made for marriage, I immediately thought: that's how it'll be with you. The most beautiful life I could imagine was one inside a spiritual community, similar to the brotherhood of Tai zé. During the day everyone pursues his work; you gather for meals and the hourly prayers. In the evening, the problems of the day are discussed by the whole community.

The period after breaking off my studies was the most difficult one for me in my life. With one stroke what I had seen as the meaning of my life no longer mattered. With my exmatriculation, my residence permit for Berlin was canceled. Without a residence permit, no work; I had to leave. Volker in Berlin, me in Halle again. What would become of our relationship? What true Berliner ever really wants to leave Berlin? His parents lived here; he had become successful in his company.

Through music—I played the recorder and sang in the Paulinum choir— I had gotten to know D. She was about forty years older than me and had a successful career as a concert singer behind her. She understood better than we did what a bind we were in, and she helped us by taking us into her apartment. She liked me because I didn't have any parents anymore and I was interested in her singing. On an interpersonal level we were very close.

All of my efforts to obtain a residence permit and a job proved fruitless.

We deliberated until we finally came up with an idea: get married. Marry D. and that would finally put an end to this mess.

But we had made a fundamental miscalculation. Despite a marriage license and an apartment I did not receive a residence permit. They offered her the opportunity to move with her husband to Halle. All of a sudden she was no longer acceptable as a soloist for the Paulinum choir.

At this time, obstacles were placed in our path from all sides. By the church, by the authorities, and even by D.'s family. D. stood by us, in spite of massive attempts to influence her and in spite of a "family court." We experienced a great deal of warmth and security with her.

I cannot even describe how panicked I would get whenever questions about my marriage were asked. "Huh? You're married to a woman who's forty years older than you?" To explain that to someone . . . , that weighed on me up to the time of her death.

For me it was a trauma: Volker gets a look at Halle. When the day arrived, I suffered horribly. Really. As if I were responsible for what he was getting to see. That's how I felt. Halle looked bad at that time. Waiting for him there were a longer way to work, lower pay, and a city that would only make him uneasy. Of course I could see how this was affecting him. The crowded living conditions mattered little to me, I was at home here, but he. . . .

When Volker later received the new apartment in Halle-Neustadt[3] from his company, I didn't object, although the idea of spending the rest of my life in Ha-Neu seemed a dreadful one to me. Our Halle friends now stopped by our place less often. We made no contacts in our apartment building. The young married couples were not exactly keen on our relationship. On the contrary. Once we heard children on the balcony next door talking about us: really evil people live there.

Whenever it could be arranged, we spent every other weekend at D.'s place in Berlin. That always followed the same pattern. Friday evening arrival in Berlin, supper, cozy evening watching TV. Saturday morning shopping, visiting Volker's parents, in the evening sometimes going to the opera with D. or to a concert. Sundays sleep late, lunch, sit together a while longer, pack up our things and off to Halle.

For outsiders it was barely noticeable that not everything between Volker and me was going well. I had insisted on exclusivity in our relationship. I wanted Volker for myself alone, and at the slightest provocation I would immediately put to him the question of trust: "Are we together or not?" I was oversensitive and therefore quickly disappointed and reacted with pathological accusations and allegations. Maybe I'd been slighted too often as a child and felt that I wasn't being paid enough attention. I can't explain my behavior all that well. In any case, the result was this: I had cut Volker off from several of his acquaintances.

Earlier, I was active with the church youth group, worked with the youth, sang in the choir, played the trumpet. Even as a student, I was constantly in motion. Now I had my job in the print shop and Volker. I did not have contact with the congregation since my former institute director inquired there as to whether, in connection with my youth work, moral offenses had been committed.

I was intensely involved in my relationship with Volker; I devoted myself exclusively to him and to some extent blackmailed him into behaving exactly the same way toward me. That can be all right for a few years, but I think by enriching yourself in this way you also restrict yourself. For the time being we hardly noticed that. Rather, we thought it was the routine, the monotony that left us dissatisfied.

Into this situation came a cry for help from D. She was ill, very ill and in need of care.

I did not hesitate one second. I take responsibility for the people around me. Even if I separate from someone, I never get rid of the responsibility for him. That person continues to be there. Admittedly, that doesn't sound very logical—my pious past is certainly showing—but I cannot simply steal away from a human relationship. I did that once when I maneuvered myself out of my engagement. This feeling of responsibility is not tied to love. I know many questions remain open; you also cannot keep up, the gap between wanting and being able to will always be there. . . .

In 1976 we were in Berlin again. In the meantime, residence permits were no longer required. D. had brought us closer together again. We had a new task and a new environment, which motivated us greatly. When D. died in 1972 we were both more mature and had become even closer.

I cannot say that there was a crisis point in the eighties that we only overcame with supreme effort. No, there was never that.

I tend to misuse my partner. It's satisfying for me to talk about my troubles freely. When I let off steam, I'm over it. Well, I've plowed over Volker often and I've selfishly dumped my problems in his lap. When I did that he would pace thoughtfully around the apartment and in the meantime I was already someplace else entirely. I guess I am more sensitive than empathetic. I also cannot say that I gave much consideration to Volker's feelings. When you're so close to each other, there's always the danger of thinking more about others than about your own partner.

That you just have to accept: equality does not exist in a relationship, not even what one might term "on the whole equal." Besides, who ever changes deep down? In spite of whatever development, everyone remains the person he once was. On my first trip to the West to visit relatives, I learned that I was supposedly insufferable in my neighborhood as a child. Over nothing I could start a fight. When I wanted to get someone, I knew no bounds. I didn't think I was such a bad kid at all. I do want to say that I can't escape my shadow. I'm still obstinate and quarrelsome today. Whatever I want has to be done; if I realize that I have to retreat, I won't budge at all at first and then only very, very slowly will I move. I am not proud of that. . . .

Two of this sort wouldn't put up with each other for a week. Volker notices mood swings that to me are imperceptible. I can't do anything about that. Between us there have been points of incompatibility, and there always will be. In our first years I often got all worked up. Volker rejected me because I was too demanding of him. I changed my behavior. Now he wishes for more devotion again.

I have strong opinions about our household. I wash curtains and windows, iron shirts, pants, jackets, and tablecloths. In addition, I scrub the hall outside the apartment. Technology has done away with a part of my housework. The gas heater and washing machine were on my side. Volker does the kitchen. It makes sense that he should cook, and besides I like his cooking. For me, cooking is neither feminine nor masculine, which also goes for ironing. I come from a family of tailors. Ironing shirts goes a lot faster for me than for Volker. It takes him twice as long, and besides he doesn't do it good enough for me. It would be silly to set a schedule according to which each would have to do half the ironing. What kind of parity is that?

The sex in our relationship is of course not what it was at twenty. Sex is a beautiful thing that one looks forward to but that meanwhile one can postpone a bit too.

In this relationship there have been ups and downs, phases in which the attraction weakened quite a bit, when each one wanted to be left in peace, and then again phases in which the desire was strong. The reasons for this I can no longer recall today, but the differing demands on each of us at work are connected to it—without a doubt.

I imagine that anyone who spends his life alone is much more strongly fixated on what he never can have. In a partnership, one could theoretically have sex every day. Yet for many of those who live alone, their entire lives revolve around sex. Drives become stronger, we know, when they are not fulfilled; they end up terrorizing us.

I do have something against the overemphasis on sexual fidelity. If two people are living with each other and are of the opinion that they need to express their sexuality separately, and they don't cause the other one any pain by doing so, I accept that. Who can know what will happen to you in your lifetime? I know myself that there are a lot of things I can't handle, and therefore I cannot give a 100 percent guarantee. I can only say that I do not want to be unfaithful, but that there also isn't anybody at the present time with whom I would really like to.

One sore point between us is music. I liked and still do like Baroque music, on old instruments if possible, and Volker hasn't changed; he still likes [Caterina] Valente. To exaggerate a bit: I abhor pop music. I listen to a female singer and all I hear is screeching. Nothing more. As far as interpreting music goes, I am probably arrogant and presumptuous. Volker thinks it is carrying things too far to have five different recordings of one piece of music; I am crazy about it.

When Volker claims that D. and I helped bring him into classical music, he is right. I reproach him for not defending himself against it. Why didn't he say: "Your opera doesn't interest me, I'm going to a play." No, he'd glance reproachfully at his watch and complain: "Once again it's so late; I have to get up early tomorrow." No one forced him to go to the opera. In the meantime, all that has gotten smoothed out. He comes along to a concert if he feels like it and he also goes to the theater alone sometimes.

I do believe that we have given each other strength, even if things between us did not always occur without complications. In any case, our relationship has made me more self-assured. Gays can only resist the pressure from their environment by living their love and discovering themselves. We have both experienced that. A gay man can recite a thousand times to himself, "I am worth just as much as any person," but it still remains a phrase as long as he does not experience essential things the way the majority of people do. I include among these the love of one's partner, feeling responsible for him—in short, a life in common. If I follow that paradigm, my life is like that of most heterosexual couples, with similar inequalities— except for the fact that children, and therefore one important task in life, are missing.

Those who do not want to or cannot live in partnerships do not necessarily have to be unhappy, but I suppose that being alone forces them to have to shore up their feeling of self-worth over and over again. And that takes a lot of strength, a lot of strength. It is probably the main problem for all those people who live alone.

At work I have not said anything about my relationship with Volker. But I also have not made any attempts to hush it up. When we invited some of my colleagues to our house we learned they'd figured it out a long time ago. Even our shared household could not suprise them any more.

Today I am of the opinion that anyone who is half-way self-accepting should come out. People have to be able to get to know us.

Years ago a lecture on homosexuality was given in our community, with a discussion afterward. It was the way it always is when things are talked about that one isn't acquainted with, that one's only heard about: "Well," they say, "of course, such people do exist. . . . " The discussion proceeded in that fashion. So we both stood up and came out in front of everybody there. Personal confrontation is very important. Someone from their midst, someone they can touch. I am convinced that we must offer people the possibility for this. Opening up the conversation is important, too, because there is little sense in frightening people off. After all, we're the ones who want something from them and not the other way around.

If I were to kiss Volker on the street, we would only provoke resistance. The time for strolling arm in arm through the streets has not arrived yet. At the present, what is important, in my opinion, is that people learn to tolerate us, that they learn to live with us, without completely condoning everything we do.

"Coming out" is an expression of feeling free. And I felt free when I was able to answer the question about family status on my first travel application: a long-term relationship, for eighteen years, with a man, I wrote. Ten years ago I would not have said that so lightly to the authorities. The female bureaucrat was, however, slightly irritated, and the first thing she did was go in the back to her boss as a precaution before she entered "long-term relationship" on the application.[4]

Nevertheless, there are still plenty of feelings of constraint—for example, in my behavior toward children, especially those in this apartment building. At first, I just blocked them out because I was afraid of showing a liking that could be interpreted negatively, especially a liking for the boys. Understandably that makes me unsure of myself. When children ask questions in their naive way, I tense up. The most normal questions take on a double meaning for me. So they ask me: don't you have a mommy? where is your wife? Yes, I say, I do have a mommy, but not a wife. Before the "well, why not" comes, I close the window or divert the children to other topics. In the back of my mind, I am thinking about the parents and about possible suspicions. I totally avoid the question about Volker, or I say: "Well, one can certainly have a friend. You certainly have one too, don't you?" It would never occur to me to ask a child into the apartment or to give him a piece of chocolate. Obviously, in the company of children I am inhibited.

And so, finally then, we gays feel "unfree," even when among ourselves, and act accordingly. Just how do we interact with each other? We couldn't be more inhibited. When Volker and I meet a gay couple on the street, there's a certain ignoring of each other that takes place à la "We are goddesses." It's silly, but we simply cannot bring ourselves to smile at each other. We probably all put on the same stupid faces. Gays are very critical of each other, to the point of being intolerant. Each is convinced that the other is a total queen, and so each is endlessly happy not being one himself. That's something that has to be done away with.

At parties strange things happen too with people you don't know. Expressing interest in each other is avoided as much as possible. Of course you have no need to and, since the other person is also inhibited, the situation ends up in an exchange of blows instead of a conversation. If I exhibit some interest anyway, a come-on is immediately assumed and then there are just two possibilities: I am accepted as a sexual partner or not. If not, then things slowly begin to crack.

I maintain that gays are communicatively dysfunctional with each other and they are extremely dependent on their environment. In bars, at parties, at their meeting places, it doesn't matter where, they communicate sexually with each other, in various ways, but much remains unspoken. Whoever pops up spreads his tail feathers for all to see and wants to be the best and prettiest without question. There is détente when the fronts are clear. Then it's even possible to talk with each other. Heterosexuals may have their negative experiences in this area too, but they are trained from childhood to view sexuality as only one aspect of human interaction.

Years ago, Volker and I must have seemed insufferable to those who live alone. We were so intent on putting our happiness on parade that there was nothing for observers to think except what poor jerks they were. Yes, yes, it was a demonstration: We have been together for such a long time already. Look over here, it can't be all that hard!

Actually, I always wanted to reach the point where I could say I am content. What I have is enough for me. We have it good, like most people here. We spend about 1500 marks per month. A car and a piece of land in the country we don't own anymore. We have made a few trips to foreign countries. Oh sure, even to Bulgaria. Since the theater opened, the amount we spend on cultural activities every month has increased considerably. And we have a nice apartment. Not exactly decorated according to the latest fashion; we much prefer old things. The china with the onion pattern that we got from D. fits in so well with our taste, and, where possible, we have completed the set.[5] We are still running around looking for egg cups. The ones with feet.

Actually, we are like married without children. If there aren't any children around, then it's simply other tasks that give life meaning. Some time ago, it was caring for D., today it's my work in the community, above all in the Discussion Group on Homosexuality, which has existed now for six years.

I know about the danger that satisfaction can easily turn into indifference. You need an occasion—a report on TV, a book, a film—to shake you up and force you to grasp the fact that people still live in relationships that should make us uneasy. Things for us are like they are for many who are not professionally involved in politics or culture: the focus on the little things in everyday life often obscures our view of the really serious questions of humanity and of the pain of individuals.

Volker, born 1948, foreign trade salesman

It was at the Paulinum that I saw Peter for the first time. I was instantly interested. Right away, I questioned the friend I was visiting there. He did not know specifics. I was the lover of an older man at that time. He was surprised that I was constantly talking about Peter. I didn't even notice how much I hurt him with my gushing.

For my parents it must have been quite a shock when it became clear that both their sons had a "different" sexual orientation. Father tried for years to steer us toward his interests. In vain. His passion for handicrafts and his enthusiasm for soccer were totally uninteresting to us. No one could tear us away from Mother's saucepan. What Mother offered was much, much more exciting. I remember that my brother wanted an apron for his birthday, an apron because he liked to clean house so much. He promptly got it. He constantly wanted to straighten up the apartment, help Mom, and always have everything ready and waiting when Mom arrived.

Our parents let us do what we wanted. Neither of us were afraid of them. When my brother began his dance training, they supported him. I didn't have to hide anything from them and was certain my parents would always understand and accept me.

My coming out took place without any big problems actually. With a friend of my brother's I just went out. Cruising. Evening after evening. I was often in love. With a look and his acceptance, I'd go along home with him. When it came time to really get down to business, things would get weird for me and I'd take off—only to run again the next night, as if compelled to swim upstream: today it'll happen, I'm sure of it.

At the trade school I attended, I too wanted to stake a claim to social status and that meant having slept with a girl. In order to be able to add my voice to the general boasting, I too played up to a girl. That our date in the shed did not turn into anything more was not only because the shed was damp and clammy. She must have suffered terribly from my lack of feeling.

And then came Peter.

I always say, with me it was love at second glance. I defended myself against Peter's exclusivity. I wanted to keep meeting other people. When my brother's friend was supposed to come back from the army in November, the one with whom I'd taken my first steps in the Friedrichstraße,[6] I said to Peter that we would not be seeing each other for a while. He was indignant. Not see each other for a whole day? Meet a friend? How could I even think of wanting to experience something without Peter?

I had regularly written to this friend, including about my relationship with Peter. I felt obligated to him in another way. I did want to be together with Peter, but I did not want to give up my friend either.

My physical attraction to Peter was strong, but I reacted with greater control. Until it turned into love and I knew *this is it*, a little more time passed by. Some more things needed to grow.

I did not take Peter's engagement that summer too seriously. In September, then, we finally made a commitment to each other. We were happy from the very beginning.

At that time we felt the need to document our relationship externally. We had rings made, wore the same clothes—little games that were important to us. This innocent and unaffected quality wasn't around for long; it's gone astray. I remember one situation. We were saying goodbye to a pair of lovers at a streetcar stop. I hugged one of them, and behind me I heard one of the people waiting there venomously hiss at us: "Come here, you little fag, I'll kill you!"—that sticks with you.

In the beginning, everything was easy for me. I still remember saying to Peter once: it isn't fair that we cannot pick each other up at work with a kiss and with flowers. The next day he was standing with a bouquet in front of my office. No kiss, just our hearts beating fast. We didn't look each other in the eye either; rather, we watched other people to see how they would react to it. I think we both quickly realized that there are more important things than the freedom to kiss on the street.

At the beginning of '69 Peter was expelled and suddenly there was a black hole in front of us. Moving out of Berlin had been a topic for debate for a long time already. The prospects for a Berlin parish were zero. Now, however, things had gotten serious overnight instead of several years from now. Of course, I too was not free from this Berlin chauvinism: you simply cannot live anyplace else.

Halle was initially a catastrophe for me. I came from a well-equipped Berlin export office into a country shop. On the way to the Communist party cadre department, I got panicky because all the ducts and pipes were steaming and hissing. I did not feel well; a risk-taker I've never been.

We lived in Peter's old room in one apartment, together with his uncle and his old grandma. The apartment was big, but without a bath. It had a tiny toilet. You had to get washed in the kitchen. For Peter this was a familiar environment, his home. With his grandma and uncle he had grown up in this apartment. All of it got on my nerves. The apartment, my job, the whole city. Grandma and uncle treated me kindly and took me in, but I was still too young to open myself up to them.

I constantly pestered him; I wanted my own place. Peter did not lift a finger. When there was a chance at work to join the AWG [Arbeitswohn-gemeinschaften] to get a communal apartment through my workplace, I put in an application for a one-bedroom apartment for myself and Peter. It was accepted, to our great astonishment. Even the apartment allocation proceeded without a hitch. Shortly afterward, I was invited by the leader of the AWG to a conversation with him. As regrettable as it may be, he said, a colleague had erred. He had gone over my application again and would give me a studio apartment. My college chum could apply to share it with me, but he did not have a right to the apartment. As small as the apartment was, I grabbed it. At last a home of our own, and everything that went with it.

We lived for four years in this apartment. Our friends only came by once in a while. We were simply too far off the beaten path. We were called "Capo" by them. Castor and Pollux, the inseparables. Outwardly our relationship gave that impression too, yet I felt that something wasn't right. I think we were in that damned seventh year. A point at which many couples arrive. Somehow we had gotten stuck.

That's when D. got sick. I liked her too, but I was surprised how easy it was for Peter to simply turn his back and abandon what we had built up. In the meantime I had gotten used to Halle. I saw us as a threesome again, back in D.'s apartment, a new job, new colleagues once again. That she needed help was clear to me, but it was difficult to leave the first apartment we had shared.

After six years, then, we were back living in Berlin. My misgivings quickly vanished. Here was a task, D. needed us, and together we took care of her. D. and Berlin—that brought us together in a new way.

This feeling of responsibility, this faithfulness is what I treasured in Peter. Not only in our relationship. I never worried about his being unfaithful. I also would never question or hound him. My trust is unbounded. Many consider that abnormal. To put it mildly, they think I'm stupid. But I see Peter differently from every other man I know. A different man his age would be too old for me. For me, Peter has remained young and desirable. Timeless, somehow. I met him at a young age, developed together with him, and I know that cannot be repeated with anyone else.

I don't stay with him because I made up my mind to do so at some point in time but rather because I love him. This varies in intensity, to be sure, as far as sex goes too, but that love is there, my interest in Peter has always stayed alive. I always wanted a man like Peter, never the hard guy who feared nothing, who just oozes manliness. But not the opposite either. Peter is masculine and gentle. That attracts me. By the way, I consider both the macho man and the queen to be extremes that live within one pseudo-identity. Acculturated clichés, both.

Today I am in less and less of a position to say this is masculine, that is feminine. What is feminine, and what is masculine anyway? I do not shut myself off from the so-called feminine qualities in me. I do, however, resist such trite assumptions as the one that says we gays are all waiting for the day when we're finally allowed to take to the streets in drag. That's another cliché.

When we were in a jam together, the problems were never insoluble. A catastrophe never occurred. You don't think that just happened by chance?

There were no battles over leadership between us because I usually left that department to Peter. I cannot stand fighting and often, at certain points in our relationship, I did not get my way. That wasn't always necessarily wrong. In the face of difficulties from outside I immediately closed ranks, whereas Peter, on the other hand. . . .

Well, I must say, love breaks my usual habits. With Peter I kept myself in check too often. Today I see it that way. Somehow that is tied to the part of me that needs harmony and which simply ignores disagreements. I gave in to demands that, inwardly, I really did not want to. I never felt at ease about that.

For a long time I thought anything could be changed, altered. You just have to want to do it. That idea was drummed out of my head. I'm at a point where I can't get past my own self, and I know Peter's limits. I know what I can expect of him and what is possible between us.

I suffer from my inconsistency for a while but quickly switch over to the usual routine because, even on a day like that, there are situations when I know that Peter understands me very well. Hard to say what I was not able to make come true. What is tolerable for me today, that I do know.

I left off telling about my job. These things I settle for myself without sharing them. He comes home from his job with his pockets full and unloads—everything has to be subordinate to that. And he cannot apologize. Pointless to insist on it. I have learned not to pin any hopes to a fine verbal phrase. In this, his language is not my language, and it took me a while to get that into my head. You really have to give up that idea of wanting to have someone made in your own image.

A close woman colleague always says: in every relationship somebody gets oppressed, in every one. In yours, it's you. Yes, I sense inequalities, but I do not feel I'm exploited. It's like I am driven to have to do certain things. He doesn't demand them, but he doesn't prevent me from doing them either. Perhaps I ought to take a really firm stand just once—supper? there isn't any tonight; I've been reading till just this second—but I won't do it.

I have asked myself whether I too would be able to accept everything as routine: that he would cook every day, go shopping, come up with something to make the week a little brighter. I couldn't do it. But that's probably a general problem in marriages.

I could never pursue my hobbies while he does the housework. He is able to do that. With total peace of mind, he plays the flute while I'm stuck in the kitchen. Even now he doesn't know where things are in the kitchen and where they belong. And that is bad. To say nothing of shopping.

Other people's demands take precedence with him. If someone's visiting, he'll get more attention than I do. The fate of every missionary's spouse.

I do not see myself as an oppressed woman but rather as an oppressed man—in these matters. I have never felt myself to be a woman, but neither have I felt like a man in my relationship with him. We were always both. I think homosexuals have the chance to live a kind of "modern marriage," one lived as little as possible within prescribed roles.

I desire more closeness than Peter does. My longing for tenderness is more urgent. With him I literally have to tickle those kinds of reactions out of him. I admit there were also phases when the situation was reversed, especially early on.

As far as his music goes, he has a bad partner in me. I really regret that. When listening to music, I can't stand it as long as he can and I am also easily distracted. At twenty, music for me was primarily dance music. That changed with Peter and D., who introduced me to classical music—above all, church music. I was fascinated, and yet . . . music all day long, classical . . . I wanted to read once in a while too. If we went out, then it was to the opera or a concert. Peter did not even notice that sometimes I wanted to run away. Exactly—that's just the kind of situation in which I should have stood up for myself more. But from the vantage point of two decades, that's easy to say. It wasn't that I had no relation to music, I just didn't desire it as exclusively as Peter did. Caterina Valente was just as important to me. Peter looked down his nose at that.

Unfortunately, I only grasped fairly late that conflicts of interest in a partnership are quite normal and that it all depends on how you deal with them. There has to be a certain minimum of common interests. Beyond that, you need to take note of and learn to live with the differences. Naturally that's a learning process. One example: as far as literature is concerned, I would have preferred through all these years to have had more of an exchange of ideas with Peter. Where I did find that was with colleagues. Outside contacts are especially necessary so you don't demand too much of your partner. And I've always been able to establish them too. Luckily. At work, within the family, in the community, and now, above all, within the Discussion Group on Homosexuality.

It's often claimed that relationships between men are more short-lived because it is so much more stimulating to switch partners. I've never experienced that change, but I think those who are always switching partners do not know the charms that accompany familiarity. Short-term horniness doesn't even make it to the very edge of those intimate realms that make sex satisfying. In an intimate relationship I can let myself go, forget myself and needn't always suck in my stomach.

Sexual faithfulness is extremely important for me. Absolutely. I was astonished at a pair of lovers. When one of them went to a spa for four weeks, both took it for granted that their bodies should also get their due during this period. Four weeks of no sex? You might get sick.

Admittedly, a slip can happen, but then it also needs to be treated as that and not as a joke that just makes the relationship contemporary and modern. If I seriously come to terms with this with my partner, maybe I can restore his trust in me. And if he accepts me, such an escapade can even be an impetus for a new beginning. The freedom to do what you like sexually just becomes a cheap necessity in an already deteriorated partnership. You stay together out of convenience or for material reasons. I always say, the dilemma is just put in a contemporary package named "sexual freedom" and extolled as *the* achievement. The old-fashioned kind for me, please.

I am relatively open about my relationship, even at work. I consider myself emancipated, and yet I do not transcend my gay biography. The majority of people do not like us gays, do not accept us. That has remained stuck in the back of my mind, because that's the way things are. That thought is always present, I am always on the lookout, and am always checking myself. I don't believe a heterosexual man is constantly aware of his sexuality. Even in tough situations, his sexuality is a matter of course for him. I am striving for that matter-of-factness. In vain. Because I live in a relationship that is not tolerated by the majority. This majority cannot be unimportant to me. That's obvious, for ultimately I'm not living only among good friends.

I know my position in society is also determined by other things. My qualities as a human being, my attitude toward work, my social involvement. But experience also tells me my sexuality complicates this position and makes it vulnerable. Sexuality is assigned a place of value that it really shouldn't be allotted at all today. This vulnerability demands that I continually muster strength—strength that then is missing someplace else. It's like: *in spite of* his orientation he carries out his duties respectably; *in spite of* that, he's okay. I sense that, and I see it as a restriction.

You cannot get along with everybody. Theoretically that's clear to me. Even so, if someone rejects me, automatically the questions pops into my mind: is it possibly because of that? Earlier, such thoughts didn't occur to me. In my naiveté, it did not interest me then either. The more I know about things and the more I have become sensitized, the more oppressive this anonymous burden has become.

At my job I have learned to fit in. I tried to do especially good work, was always friendly, always courteous—the nice man who indeed remained nice in the case of his being found out. Except for that one flaw.

Within my circle of colleagues at work, weekend experiences were regularly exchanged on Monday. I always said *we*. We both . . . , we did this . . . , that happened to us . . . , until I had had it with fibbing. Without thinking about it, I just decided to enlighten them. Several colleagues assured me what a positive attitude they did indeed have toward "those people." The ones they knew were all nice, even extremely nice. Really.

I was astonished because I knew quite a few I did not find so nice. I told them that there are just as many repulsive jerks among us as there are everywhere. Yet they cast that aside; they simply didn't want to buy that. It is difficult to make it clear to people that we are neither monsters nor saints and that not all of us dream of a career as a dancer. We're just normal people.

There were practically no more questions later on. From men none at all. At some point a female colleague said to me: "You are very much mistaken; they do indeed like you as a colleague, but they basically haven't changed their attitude toward this issue. You are for us *the gay* within the whole company. They think it's a good thing that you're so open and that you've been living together for such a long time with the same man, but that you two have intimacies with each other, that you love each other, that doesn't sink in with them."

That's exactly the point where the border lies. The way we drag around our gay backpack, they carry millennia-old prejudices in their vest pockets.

A male colleague recently reported on a trip to a foreign country. There he saw two men kissing in broad daylight. He babbled on: just imagine . . . ! He forgot that I am that way. Another male colleague thought he had to save the situation and interrupted him: enough of that, let's change the subject. They don't understand that it is precisely this kind of consideration which I find embarrassing. Another male colleague is constantly deflecting the point whenever I talk about Peter. He turns him into my buddy. They don't know how they are supposed to treat me. Because too much is demanded of them, and this is also the deeper reason for their reserved attitude.

Even their compliments reveal their negative picture of homosexuals. At the firm's party, a male colleague recently whispered from behind a raised hand into my ear: "You, you aren't even a real gay at all." My feeling constrained and self-conscious arises from that kind of thing, not from direct, blatant discrimination.

And among gays too not everything is going well. The nihilistic attitude that many have disturbs me, especially when they say nothing at all works. Neither heterosexual marriages nor among gays, where everyone cheats on everyone else, and this whole to-do about partnerships—what's the point?

At their lamentations I get more and more quiet and barely dare to reply: "Your entire dilemma is your own fault." Most of all I'd like to yell at them: "Try out a partnership, experience what is possible between two people, even allow each other to have some freedom. It's difficult, but it's possible."

What we do is, for many, bourgeois, conformist. We've heard that a lot. Others say: "How in the world can two people be satisfied with just their own relationship at a time when gays are fighting for equal rights? That's just egotistical."

If I'm a conformist, then gladly so. Just what is supposed to be so attractive about a nonconformist life-style, the kind many apparently lead? No one has yet been able to give me a plausible explanation. Theoretically, they experiment with variety; in practice they do whatever comes easiest. I find there's one thing above all they're unable to do and that's to abide having contented people around them.

In our discussion group on homosexuality I have certainly learned that things in reality are often much more differentiated than I see them. My view that you only need to be willing is perhaps somewhat naive. Much of what I hear and to which I have no answers weighs me down. In all likelihood, the nihilistic attitude of many gays can only secondarily be traced back to a personal failure; it stems primarily from the way society treats its homosexuals. Just patting somebody sympathetically on the shoulder and telling them to keep their chin up doesn't accomplish very much.

On the whole that's a general experience. The older I get, the more varied the connections appear to me—in the world at large and in my own little corner of it. I'm looking forward to the next twenty years with mixed emotions. Absolutely. I am certain that my future is bound up with Peter, and that everything is going to keep on flowing. Things aren't going to get easier. That's not at all what I want either. I am conscious of borders that truly are borders. There will continue to be conflicts of interest. That's normal. In the meantime those have become clichés for me. In the past we didn't have any fewer problems, but I did not recognize them then or didn't want to see them. Today I have a clearer picture of how things are in my life. I have become more critical, I know better what is good for me, and I go after it. A lack of love or a not so nice day makes me moody. Love stimulates me tremendously.

Interviews completed 1988

IV. Winne

Introduced and translated by James Patrick Hill and John Borneman

This restructured interview is a sort of self-portrait of the artist as a young man. Winne has received his *Abitur* (college admittance exam) with distinction, so he is assured of a place at a university. He strives to do well in school and, later, to succeed in the larger world as a writer. Yet his past gets in the way, and he narrowly escapes a series of nervous breakdowns and suicide attempts.

The stepfather who tortures him gives him a victim's identity. He is from a broken family in which (step)father and son compete for the affections of the wife and mother. The behavior of his mother, a well-trained, professional woman, in holding on to her objectionable husband may in part be explained by her fear of not finding another man in a country with more women than men of her age group. But ultimately we must look to historical patterns of female dependency and male dominance anchored in the institution of marriage to explain fully her behavior. For Winne's generation, however, much has changed. This fear among women about finding and holding a partner no longer holds true: the divorce rate has skyrocketed and is now twice that of the Federal Republic, and 48 percent of all first children in East Berlin are born to single mothers.

In spite of his intellectual and academic achievements, our subject identifies himself as a loser: emotionally unstable and immature, he has never experienced love with a man. (Women seem unimportant in his life; only his mother surfaces for long in the text.) His self-indictment for lack of emotional development reveals itself at another, unconscious level in his description of the ideal lover: a kind of caretaker and psychiatric nurse who reappears as a waiter in his novel. Their fantasy relationship, much like the lived one of Winne's mother and stepfather, is monologic: never are we told what Winne might do for his lover; never is the relationship democratically conceived, mutually constructed.

Winne is obviously not "glad to be gay"—as some of us Western gays claim to be. On the contrary, he prides himself on looking "normal" and wishes to appear manly for the other soldiers with whom he was to serve in the military. (Military service in the GDR is compulsory.) Before he comes to terms with his sexuality, he studiously avoids other homosexuals and falls in love with a girl, though one guesses it was a rather superficial attachment. Even after he comes out to his classmates, all his friends are straight—the GDR slang term for them is *Stino*, stink normal—and he never once mentions other gay friends. He disapproves of himself thoroughly, buying into the negative social valuation of homosexuality, and at times even sympathizes with his stepfather's brutal reaction to him.

In a *Gymnasium* (college prep high school), one is a member of a class—a kind of homeroom—and generally has peripheral associations with members of other classes. What is most unusual, from an American point of view, is the easy acceptance ("solidarity and understanding") he wins from his immediate classmates after his coming out; they protect him from the hostile students. But this does not really make him happy, nor increase his self-esteem: he feels he must submit to their needs to please them and becomes the class clown, a curiosity that does not deserve their kindness and can never repay it.

Though he is treated more tolerantly than he might be were he an American gay boy, he exhibits no positive gay consciousness. Developing a positive homosexual identity with high self-esteem may in fact be one of the most important accomplishments of the American and West European gay movements, and it is fascinating to ask to what extent this development has been possible without a comparable social movement and a gay discourse in Eastern Europe. Certainly the other men in this volume have fared better than Winne. In Winne's case, he has begun the personal construction of a homosexuality with self-deprecating humor, irony, and a brutal honesty rarely found in the West. For nonreflective individuals, there is no doubt less need to articulate personal desires; they can ignore or deflect negative social valuations by keeping them banned, for the most part, in the unconscious through repressive mechanisms. Repression, however, does not work for Winne. Perhaps his movement from critical reflection to verbal articulation is a necessary first step to a healthy ego, one not only capable of understanding the nature of social prejudice without internalizing it, but also capable of articulating a positive alternative in its midst.

7. "What should I do with such a hot-blooded guy?"

Winne, born 1964, library worker

I can calm you down. Ask me anything. There is no such thing as a stupid question. But you do have some questions you want to ask me. Though it won't be possible to ask what lies behind certain problems—I recently read that somewhere. Perhaps you can tell me: why should I now be able to answer questions that I myself have asked in vain for a long time? Are we already being taped? You're crazy.

Shall we begin? I expect you'll not be asking me the most important questions, about war and peace, at least not yet. I suspect you're more interested in questions about my personal fate?

You wonder where I got that from? Sorry, but I will not be able to answer all of your questions. So please.

Excuse me, but I have to comment about something. I am granting this interview on the condition that it won't be printed. Above all—no names. Don't you think that a possible reader at this point would recognize that he's looking at a real joker? These are, you know, relaxation exercises.

As a child I observed life from my own corner of the world. I was three years old when my mother remarried. From the beginning, I was in my stepfather's way. Perhaps he saw in me a miniature likeness of his predecessor and hated me for that reason. That could be. My elder sister was by far treated less badly than I.

I was a well-mannered, reserved child, sweet and calm, always careful not to do anything wrong. As I grew older I shopped and helped with chores every day. I shined my stepfather's shoes and washed his car. He always treated me as a mama's boy—to him I was not a real boy. He called me "fat ass" because I was a heavy child and not very presentable. I would call him "uncle" until he would pass me something I wanted at the dinner table. Then I would finally call him "sir." (You have no other resort as a child.) He reacted by making me leave the dinner table. At night, when he would storm in a drunken rage through the apartment, I would lie under the covers, fearing for my life. He would threaten me with death often enough. I could not jump out of the window because we lived on the fourth floor and crawling under the bed did no good either—that would only provoke him more. Through these experiences I learned how to appease someone.

I will describe some episodes to you.

One morning I went to the bathroom. Everywhere there were snippets of paper; he had made a mess during the night. As I looked more closely I could see that he had in his drunkenness cut the images of me out of all of our family photos and flushed them down the toilet: I was symbolically drowned.

Another day he hung my jacket on the top of a tall chest of drawers and I was symbolically hanged. Once he took twenty cans of fish out of the cupboard and, like a madman, opened them and roared at me: "Now you're going to eat these or I'll kill you on the spot, you bastard!"

The neighbors, who knew of these goings-on and were sick of them, knew where they could find me—in the garbage storage room of the building. When he'd finished with his ranting and had fallen asleep, I would go back into our apartment. He was simply a miserable drunken pig without character who bullied anyone weaker than himself.

Sometimes on the weekends he would spontaneously inform us: "We're driving out into the country today!" I would never want to go along. First, I would never know how long his good mood would last, and second, while he was gone, I could finally watch television alone in peace. He would then say: "The couch potato, he is already so pale and now he just wants to stay home and stuff himself." He was right about that.

Mother was good and strict with me but never affectionate. She loved him, so she wasn't disturbed by his disgusting behavior toward me. Perhaps I really was in his way. Today Mother maintains that she waited too long to throw him out, but I remember well that in those days she said reproachfully that she would only throw him out for my sake.

Drunk as he'd get, he would also not leave her alone. He would regularly kneel before her the next morning, excusing himself in his hung-over voice, and he either made promises to reform or threatened to hang himself. Afterward he would, with great diligence and enthusiasm, put together all the things that he'd torn apart the night before. I believe that their perpetual reconciliations only came about because he made me responsible for his excesses and Mother didn't put up much of a fight against that argument. It was a lot easier for her.

Eight years was too long. In eight years one can create a psychopath. This situation could certainly not be good for me. When your mother brings you your food secretly, or must knock at your door and say "You can come out, he's gone," you cannot help but suffer consequences from such constant stress. My hypersensitivity is caused by nerves, not by an overactive thyroid gland. Every time he was driving his car I wished he'd have an accident.

Shortly after mother had separated from him, I made my first suicide attempt. At school we had dragged a girl into the lavatory against her will and felt her breasts. We were supposed to be reprimanded. Trouble at home and now at school too. During the middle of class I stood up, went out into the corridor, stamped on my glasses, and was about to slit my wrists with a broken piece of glass. A quick end to it all, I hoped, would mean that everyone would leave me alone. As my teacher tore the broken glass from my hand, I let my feelings go and cried freely.

What was really bothering me? I didn't express that. No one could imagine that such chaos could reign in the home of the best student in the class. At school I was the amusing one, the good-humored one, the clown. Everyone thought I was funny. Nobody knew what went on within. Until now I had secretly flirted with this contradiction, and suddenly I had displayed to everyone this other side of me. I was supposed to be reprimanded, and my silly overreaction escalated into desperation. Like someone who is starving, I longed greedily for every word of praise from my teacher. Two days later I went to the disco with a bound wrist.

My family life was not like that of other students. They gathered peacefully around the dinner table and afterward sat down cosily in front of the television. There was fighting in other families, of course, but such abuse, aimed at one person, I could hardly imagine elsewhere.

After the tenth grade I pursued an *Abitur* and also learned the trade of a skilled worker. I hadn't any problem at all in theoretical subjects, and I quickly got used to physical work. Things went well for me—that is, until I fell in love for the first time. That was during my first year of apprenticeship.

I read the Thomas Mann novella *Death in Venice*. I identified with it, and I made a fellow apprentice from my group who especially pleased me into my Tadzio. What I at first thought of as a passing fancy became deadly serious. I had really fallen in love—I burned with love. What then?

In my diary I wrote: he is my angel. Beneath this I listed his attributes on half a page in small print. Inwardly I groaned: once again something that could only happen to me. And I knew immediately that this was no longer some adolescent game beneath the cellar steps. It was something different, completely different. Among my classmates some had buddies— one preferred this one, another that one—but who sat around in the evenings like me and listed his buddy's qualities one by one? No one but me. The others wouldn't even go that far with their girlfriends.

Suddenly I remembered remarks made in passing that characterized me as gay. I had no enthusiasm for soccer. I was always orderly, clean, well-disciplined, ambitious. I made myself vulnerable to such comments. I never fought. I certainly felt easily embarrassed and somehow uncomfortable. Still I ignored the gays. The important thing was that I didn't feel I was one. On a school lot everyone is spoken to rudely and everyone has stupid comments made to them. One followed the motto: fight it out, laugh it off, forget it, and live in peace. In addition I was already in love with a girl. Now I also remembered a statement my stepfather had made while observing me secretly: "I don't believe it, he combs his hair like a woman!" Now it hit me. I was totally stunned and my speech—everything was just an affectation and couldn't stand up against this.

Through a ridiculous accident everything came out. A school friend visited me, and while I made coffee in the kitchen he paged through my diary, which lay on the table. I came back and almost dropped the coffee pot when I saw him reading peacefully. I grabbed the book out of his hands and stuttered: "I mean to write about everyone in our class. Yes, I will definitely write." And I then went on: "Writing is the greatest human activity," and talked about Thomas Mann and so on. He replied that he had no objection to writing. On the contrary, everyone goes through a phase, a writing phase, but he found it incredible that I should call R. "my angel." That he couldn't follow.

I gave up and confessed. He reacted sensibly. In our relationship nothing changed for him, nothing at all. Why should it? I had to stop myself from clasping him around the neck out of pure gratitude. I seemed almost normal again.

In my joy I told another classmate at school the next day. He had a completely different reaction. Without giving it a second thought, he told everyone: "Good old Winne is a homosexual." He spread it around, as if it were the funniest thing in the world. From then on he lost no opportunity to kid around with me. On the subway he took my hand in front of everyone, caressed me, rolled his eyes, and chattered on about his love for me. The other passengers' eyes practically popped out of their sockets, and we laughed ourselves sick.

Externally everything was okay. My friends knew what was what, and I wasn't excluded from anything. There was something special about me, and I found myself interesting. No one felt threatened or avoided me, except for my "angel." That I had chosen him in particular, well, he didn't think too highly of that. He felt threatened, and everything changed between us.

I was a welcome addition to the others. If I wanted to skip a class party for some reason, someone from the back row would call out: "Come along! We'll bring along a boy for you, sweety." Or someone yelled: "Come along! I'm at a great party where there's a *Schwuli* (cute gay), just the right one for you!" I was in my pajamas, but of course I ran over. He put down the phone, I'm sure, and announced loudly: "Hey, listen: in ten minutes another *Schwuler* is coming." You know the sort of party where a young malcontent with a beard sits around babbling about modern music, exercising his ego. Naturally I couldn't mumble even a few words because I was so embarrassed and shy. The others spied on us closely because they wanted to observe how two gays behave with one another. Ten minutes later they all went back shyly to their friends and said off-handedly: "Not my cup of tea."

I'm convinced that our primary problem is not how we relate to normal people but to each other.

I can't complain about my teachers. Only my math teacher was actually surprised: why should his model student, of all people, have wasted himself on boys? He then spoke of Frederick the Great and a certain Katte (or something like that). They say that Frederick had something to do with him. And with that the matter was settled for him. In a relaxed and friendly way my German teacher recommended to me Stefan Zweig's novella *Confusion of Feelings*.

Everything that makes its way around the class soon spreads to the whole school. And there things didn't go so smoothly. Early in the morning I would step out of the subway and be stared at. "Oh, the gay from the second year. That's him, there he goes." With a stern look and weak knees I would march by, always thinking: "Just don't look limp-wristed and effeminate." I always suspected enemies among those I didn't know and I'd act overbearing. I thought: "I still have my intelligence—that will always be mine. They can think what they want. I'll go on to the university. Who knows whether they will also? They're lucky even to know me."

During breaks in the school yard others would pick fights with me. "Ha, ha, our sweetheart!" Friends from my class would immediately resist the others, and open attacks were avoided completely.

I felt solidarity and understanding, but at the same time I suffered under a pressure I can hardly define. I constantly wished to restore my reputation and thank my classmates for their friendliness and unusual deeds. That worked among my classmates, but how should I make it known to everyone else in the school who knew about me that I was all right in spite of it? I felt helpless against them. I could have said: "It doesn't matter what they think of me. What's more important is that the people in my class like me." But that didn't work. The others' looks and insinuations were always provoking me and keeping me on my toes when I ran into them. What I presented to them was arrogant pretension. I acted casual, cool, harsh, and butch. But my fears were not groundless. I came to find this out two years later quite accidentally when I chatted with someone from the same school. He was amazed when he heard I was studying at the university. "How could that be? We thought you were a bad student."

I think this is a general situation in which we [homosexuals] find ourselves. It is the model after which society patterns itself in relation to its homosexuals. It is subtly varied under different circumstances but is found everywhere, from the school to the old-age home. In the works of one of our great authors I read: "Prejudice is farther from the truth than ignorance." In all humility let me add that prejudice is harder to get at than ignorance.

Although I flirted with being different, I felt it to be a great deficit. Soon it wasn't enough to get good grades to maintain my position in the class.

In any case, that's what I imagined. I wanted more—the more unusual it was the more effective. What could be more appropriate than writing? I knew enough examples of people from literary history who made it right away with their first book. Making it would mean recognition, independence, status, which would further mean that things about me other than my sexuality would become important to the world. No sooner was this thought than done—I will become a writer. Writing about myself would be my salvation. And my first book must be a big hit.

In a short time the first few pages of my grandly conceived novel were done. I intimated to a classmate that I was writing a book, and already I was cloaked in mystery. At my graduation party I appeared in a Stresemann.[1] In my studio I tailored myself after the youthful image of my great model, Thomas Mann.

I still had three months until I was to be called into the army. "Not a moment of idleness" was my motto. I wrote as if my life depended on it. If I wrote three pages for every day left before my call to the army, I would have a small volume. I waxed with the pleasure of anticipation. I had to write these three pages every day. More than three pages and the quality would suffer. When two pages were done, I only thought about finishing the third. It didn't matter at what time of day I produced them. If I was tired, I'd stay awake with caffeine tablets.

My novel was my great secret. Its appearance would have the effect of crashing cymbals: "Look here! Here I am! I am indeed a homosexual, but here is my great work." Overnight I would be saved and independent. Hard work pays off, and for my renunciation I'd be rewarded. It is only fitting that everyone should know me since I've renounced love, which you (my mother and my angel) refuse to give me. I also don't need to be beautiful. I knew how I idolized writers, no matter how they looked. Chemists and mathematicians were nothing in comparison.

One cannot tempt souls with formulas. I wouldn't want to be loved for money anyway. I also wouldn't want to become a braggart because of the success of my book. My vanity would be flattered much more by people whispering behind my back: "He's still the same old guy, in spite of his great success."

My fear grew with every day as my call to the army neared. Surely only by struggling would I be up to the physical challenge, and because of my glasses I couldn't hope to be a good shot. When considering how my homosexuality might become known in my battalion, my imagination ran away with me. I quickly decided to add a program of physical training to my writing program. I wanted to become as strong and powerful as the others, in the time before I entered the army. From a ninety-eight-pound weakling to a mighty German oak in three months, so to speak. I exercised until I dropped. Meanwhile, I inquired about the average time for the 3000-meter run. Rain or shine, there was no question of my lying in bed; I had to complete my daily quota of exercise. In four weeks I ran the distance in just under twelve minutes. I had started at thirteen and a half minutes. One hundred twenty bench presses was what I usually did to strengthen my arms. My fat cells had no chance anymore, and the mirror proved me right. I had a diet of margarine, crackers, and oats. And no cigarettes.

Before long my psyche was alternating between exhilaration and depression—between the condition of a racehorse for whom the gate was flung wide open and that of a lunatic who dares not go out onto the street. The last weeks before my breakdown were terrible. A childish misunderstanding was enough to sever contact with my sister. My mother lay in the hospital and I told her perfunctorily: no more time for visits! I wrote and trained as someone obsessed.

The calamity was caused by a close call. My "angel" visited me with a friend: while my "angel" obstinately stared at the carpet in my room, his friend declared, to my amazement, that he was ready to. . . . Oh well, I already knew.

It was an act of charity. We went to his place and listened uncomfortably to music while smoking and drinking. It was half past midnight and I was in a quandary: should I continue drinking and smoking, even though it was late? I came up against the ironclad rules to which I had adhered for so long. How would I accomplish the next day's tasks? If I got closer to him, he would pour another drink. Suddenly he fell asleep. I shook him awake and he was startled, looked around disconcertedly, and threw me out. On the way home I went into a panic. It was cold and foggy outside.

I must explain something else. My ability to think rationally is quite well developed, and I have an exceptional memory. I reviewed my life and came to the conclusion: what my life has been, it will continue to be in the future. At such moments I don't yield. The bottom line was unadulterated hopelessness. Without mercy. I arrived home wide awake and very calmly and deliberately prepared my end.

Three days later I came out of the coma for no particular reason.

In the clinic they prescribed therapy and gave me well-meaning advice. I was convinced that they wanted to help me, but I soon began to doubt the effectiveness of their help. I talked and talked, saying, in essence, that the causes of my behavior lie in this and that—one, two, three. . . . Well, it's no wonder that I'm like who I am! Then every four hours we'll take ten drops of this and—no cheating—then we'll try that. This we'll leave alone. And above all, fresh air. The diagnosis was so obvious, cause and effect so logically proceeded from one to the other, that I had to agree with the doctor. Days passed by. I took walks in fresh air and my brain functioned again. This and that from my past occurred to me. All day I rummaged around in my collection of memories. If I had the memory of an experience by the collar, I thought to myself, there must be a reason why this childhood memory is resurfacing, and this experience must have left an effect. But what?

Even more came back to me. I thought about the psychiatrist's words, and the line he traced so rationally through my past became a crack. Then I reached for the magnifying glass; I was down on the couch like Marcel Proust and dug deep in myself, and the seemingly clear line appeared less and less compelling to me. Finally it broke. His talk seemed to me divorced from reality. I was much more simply constituted. There was not so much there to unravel. I had no lover, that is, someone to love who would love me back. Fresh air plus a lover would work, but that the doctor could not prescribe.

My drunken, evil stepfather is not responsible for the fact that the conditions of my youth so prevented me from living in a way that I could have been true to myself. What did my stepfather have to do with the failure of my courtship with my "angel"? Nothing at all. In such moments of reflection, I find some sympathy for him. I think of him as guilty only insofar as he had sensed the gayness in me from the beginning and hated me for it. It's only an accident that I ended up with a stepfather who embodied a lot of societal prejudices. And because of that, he punished me harder for things that other fathers also punish, just not so hard.

The doctor urged me: first just mature properly. I was deeply insulted. What did he mean by that? Three months earlier I had earned my *Abitur* with distinction. I was diligent, could think, and I was an ace at math. My teachers had affirmed my qualities often enough. Those with D's on their report cards couldn't be ahead of me with my A's. I was indignant.

I hadn't yet appreciated what a great gap there can be between intellectual and emotional maturity. I had also ignored the fact that others were having fun with the last of several girlfriends, while I sat at home striving to be someone. No one is praised at school for having had several girlfriends. The high grades mean you are praised, whether or not you are a loser as a person. I am just twenty and to those around me, I'm a failure. There are moments when I agree with them, when I see myself as being just as superficial as they see me.

I interrupted my studies; I have survived one ridiculous and one serious suicide attempt; I still can't claim a single secure relationship to my credit; I don't have my own apartment; and my first novel has been rejected. I mustn't hesitate to come to grips immediately with most of my problems, since I really don't have all that much under control yet. I don't want to scatter my energy with silly things. I often think about where I might be in ten or twenty years. It may be that I think too far ahead, and therefore forget those tasks nearest at hand. That reproach I hear now and then from my mother. Instead of digging right in, I consider intensely what might happen, what might not, and contemplate a thousand possibilities. I often sketch in my failure from the beginning and then do nothing more. My first priority is my own apartment. A sort of place of rest, a bastion from which I can approach things more calmly. I must find a lover, and not until then can I mature—mature properly—as Uncle Doctor so nicely said.

A relationship in which sexuality and partnership were both present has never existed in my life. I may be all the poorer for that, but this insight is as useful to me as is blaming myself. Sex I've found, but little beyond that to interest me. My ego has never been affirmed. On the contrary, should I begin to tell of my interests or how I imagine my future—I'd get a big yawn.

My longest fling lasted a week, just about. I ended it because it soon annoyed me. Thanks to alcohol we spent the first couple of days in a daze. When the third day again started off with alcohol, I was taken aback. I wasn't able to cope with another drinker in my life. My withdrawal occupied the rest of the week. What do I get out of filling my time from one fuck to the next with alcohol and sporadic conversation?

He must be able to muster up some interest in what I do. Not just: "How are you? Yesterday I was here and there." I insist on substance, and from that I won't be swayed. I won't race around and won't fall into a panic any more because I haven't met "him" yet. I would consider someone my own age or a bit older. And no pretty boys, whom everyone would run after. Interests are more important to me and aren't actually tied to study. I could imagine someone who has lots of contact with people in his daily life, who has a good knowledge of people. If he knows many, he'll be able to tell what kind of person I am and value me, above all, for my good qualities. No, no, he must definitely be more than cute. Knowing that Rewatex[2] is open till such and such a time, and where we can later get spare parts for our Volvo isn't enough for me. I also won't be a dictator, deciding everything financial and organizational in our life. Not a chance. I don't follow rules in my apartment, and I won't rule someone else's life either.

At difficult times, when I'm inclined to throw in the towel, when I become discouraged and would like to hang myself, he should stop me in any way he can. He should take me by the collar, shake me, and straighten me out by saying: you've got to go through this—this is life—enough of this foolishness. You're talking nonsense. Relax for a week and later we'll see. He should say it softly and take my hand as he says it. In a nutshell: each must be a pillar to the other. We must stand by each other, especially in difficult times, during which one doubts oneself and doesn't quite know what will happen next. That seems to me the most important. While one evolves, the other should move along with him and automatically achieve equilibrium. Then I'd like to acquaint him with my uncertainties, how things will proceed. If I had an attractive profession and lots of money, and someone should fall in love with me, I would have to be suspicious about whether he loves me or just all the trappings.

Assuming I were to come back into an active phase, starting my second novel, for example, he shouldn't immediately start whining and feel neglected. He should leave me alone, withdraw tactfully and do his own thing. When I've come to the end of my project several days later, I would then like to go and drink coffee with him in peace, and, naturally, we would discuss what each of us had been doing. All the better if we both have progressed with our plans—I mean with work. We would have to find our way to one another with that as the culmination. Yes, yes, would have to, would have to. . . .

I won't lie in bed for hours just for fun. For me that's not profitable in that it's just laziness. Yes, there must be some of that, but the meaning of a partnership should not be lost in that. I don't have to be together with him every night. Nothing comes of love-making. To me it's a riddle how one can do nothing but screw, day after day. The years are screwed away, and what then? It is just a sensual pleasure, which never progresses beyond a certain physical satisfaction. What I can have in one hour I don't need to have over three. I can spend the time more advantageously. I also won't rush it, but it seems to me that sex is for most people a substitute for meaning in life. What should I do with such a hot-blooded guy who would clear the desk and not let me finish the page I'm working on? He'd be as good for me as one who waits quietly and ashamedly in one corner of the couch.

Another dream: I've worked hard all day and sit in a chair with a stiff neck. He approaches, I feel his hand at the back of my neck. He says in a calm voice: "That's enough for today; again, you've done more than enough. You toil and toil." Afterward we lie down (for relaxation, without sex) and now and then we caress. Already I'm fit again for the evening because I sense that here is a person who knows how tiring my workday was.

In the first few years he would have to accept without much fuss that I must sacrifice a lot of extras because of my work (for example, swimming and traveling). He knows that I don't wish to involve him at all directly in my difficult work. First of all, I would never fall in love with a type who lets himself go. Someone who already as a young man hangs around idly and without purpose will certainly be very troubled by forty. These midlife crises only occur when there's nothing satisfying in life, and such people realize they've frittered away their time. Only someone with strength can offer support. I associate idleness with being fat, hanging around sense-lessly, and eating ice cream every day. I would depend on his strength when I'm in over my head. Our different capacities balance each other out well and create a kind of protective skin around us. Together each would be less vulnerable.

I value not being identified at first glance. I would demand that of my partner as well. I can't imagine that the active, stable, engaged person I desire would have another view on this issue. I have a normal appearance—that has often been confirmed to me. Only to someone who observes more closely does it become obvious. I'm not the type who can wear a bright red jacket. With my face and glasses I would appear ridiculous. Suppose I'm thinking something over and knit my brow and add a red jacket to *that*? Never.

I'm the type who wears a suit. Yet it wouldn't suit me to do certain things dressed in a suit: I've also staggered drunk out of the subway in jeans and a leather jacket. I'm real picky about glasses. With my pale face, a neutral sort of glasses doesn't go too well. I share this hard look of mine with my whole family, all the way back to my grandmother. These days my face isn't quite so pale because I snuck a little of my mother's rouge. What, you don't notice? Good, huh? Often I don't bother to do it. But when people see such a pale and colorless face, they think: "Such a young man and already half-dead." Who wants to talk with such a corpselike, pale type? I certainly don't.

A similar paleness covers the face of the main character of my novel. I've introduced my hero as "Hophi, the tiger with the little granny pussy face." He views the world with the strained look of a nearsighted person. Hid behind "Hophi" is the formulation "homosexual philosophy student." Just a moment. We can laugh later.

In the main figure I somewhat idealized myself. I draw him ironically, of course, when I have him reading fifty pages of Kant on Monday and an equal amount of Marx on Tuesday. He also resembles me when he has difficulty starting a conversation with people; he's suspicious of the masses and becomes immediately didactic when someone has dealings with him.

Now he has a relationship with a waiter named Silvio. I won't tell about how this relationship came to be—that is left up to the reader's imagination. Hophi has his own apartment in the Prenzlauer Berg section of Berlin, the second entry in the left apartment house, up three flights of stairs. Only the stereo is new. The wide bed and the stereo dominate the room and lend it its atmosphere. Naturally, all of the problematical characters of the younger generation in recent GDR literature live here in Prenzlauer Berg. Where else? Silvio is sexy and uncomplicated. He has a small apartment in a new highrise in the Marzahn suburb of Berlin with petit-bourgeois furniture and carpets with bold patterns. Naturally he must continually defend his apartment against Hophi's arrogant invectives. Hophi makes a claim to dominate on the basis of his intelligence; Silvio earns the money. There is no shortage of conflicts.

I direct the main characters in such a way that through the mastery of their conflicts a transformation takes place. Both of them change. Silvio's character becomes problematic and Hophi becomes more physically aware. Silvio decides that the next renovation is to be done more stylishly, and Hophi dusts regularly.

I haven't negotiated my way through the problems yet. It's nonsense, of course. Extensive rewriting obscures more than it clarifies. I've left enough room for the fantasy of the reader, above all in the erotic scenes.

Friends ask me sometimes: "Are you still writing? Is it still fun for you?" My answer is always the same: "Fun is rare. I experience moments of amusement or fun, but writing usually has more to do with drudgery.

When I had the completed novel, I took the pages in my hand, rustled them through my fingers—ssssst—six hundred pages, a novel, by me, something you can grab on to, it can be read.

One more word. Before I begin my second novel, I'm going to mature nicely first.

Interview completed 1984

V. Body and Joseph

Introduced and translated by Jeffrey M. Peck

Translating these interviews is more than a staid academic exercise; it is a movement between two cultures and two sets of differences. The word *translation* comes from the Latin *transfero*, whose past participle, *translatus*, means "to bear across." The word's literal meaning describes the activity that takes place when the text "goes" from German to English, but it also alerts us to a similar movement back and forth by the two men in the following interviews. For me the shift is made easier, narrowed as it is to linguistic translation. For Body and Joseph, whose worlds are constituted by different sexual preferences, "translation" is much more problematic. This metaphor of movement draws our attention to all confrontations requiring comparison and differentiation: from one culture to another, from one experience to another, from one sexual practice to another.

Given the resonances of this metaphor for accentuating the difference between cultures, it is nonetheless striking that the national distinctions between the experiences of gay men in the GDR and the United States seem to be erased, at least in these translated documents. To be sure, the original language is colored by the idiom of the GDR and checkered with expressions and coloquialisms immediately recognizable to anyone familiar with East German culture. In addition to using GDR-specific language, the two men express social and class differences in their tone, word choice, and sentence structure. Yet at the level of personal experience, the socialist political ideology of the GDR does not appear here to have had a striking impact. These two men—one a worker, ex-convict, social dropout and the other an educated, cultivated, and rather bourgeois economist—struggle with the experience of coming out, an experience that seems to transcend class, status, and, from our perspective, national or political identity. In short, one expects that socialism would have made a greater impact on expressions of personal and sexual identity.

The stories of Body and Joseph are very literally (his)stories: narratives by men about their lives. This play on the word, so common among those people working toward unveiling male power and authority in the writing of history, mandates a different turn, however, when it addresses gay lives. (His)stories require us to defamiliarize the male viewpoint in order to differentiate between male heterosexual and homosexual investments in patriarchy and to distinguish between the kinds of stories they tell. Gay men (at least those who are "out") do not share in the privilege of dominant culture. Their stories are marked by the recounting of experiences that are seen as strange, immoral, or even "sick," and they are composed by the often compulsive retelling of early inklings of their sexual orientation, new sexual experiences, and ultimately their coming out.

Their lives are different because of the prominence of sexual difference. Often producing alienation and rejection, their difference makes storytelling an almost existential necessity that establishes coherence and meaning in what may otherwise seem a fragmented life. Perhaps that is why their stories are not dominated by what may seem like major events. Seen against the repression and oppression they have experienced, mundane incidents assume an unusual immediacy and dimension in their lives.

Representing their lives in such stories is an additional act of translation. These particular experiences told through the events of everyday life can move us to see the universality of gays' experience and what it is about, even if we do not share their sexual preference. We might expect the lives of gay men in the GDR to be exotic, unusual, or unique, either because it is an authoritarian state or because homosexuality is legal. However, when Joseph reflects on the fears of Nazi denunciations in a different Germany, he is drawing on the anxiety of living as a gay man even though the situation of gay men in authoritarian states like the GDR is no better or worse than in states with more formal freedoms such as our own.

The disappointment that runs through both of these interviews comes less from the gay experiences of these men than from their loss of faith in a society that ultimately rejects them. How much that disappointment has to do with the political system in which they live is not made clear. Depending on our own political standpoint, our prejudices may be questioned or confirmed by the lack of a more positive response and support from a socialist society that guarantees not only certain human rights but also full incorporation of all its members.

But whatever position we take on homosexualities under socialism, we cannot help but get caught up in these men's individual stories. We are both excited and disappointed by what they have to say. We read on to find out if perhaps their experiences will be different from our own or those of our friends in West Germany. We want to find out what happens to them in the hope that these men will find a world more congenial to them than we have found in the United States. These interviews make us want to compare and differentiate, no matter how similar Body and Joseph are to people we know. These lives are exceptional both because of and in spite of their difference. Perhaps it is precisely in *translation*—linguistic, social-psychological, and political—that these men's lives can best be appreciated, for uniqueness and universality are constituted in the movement back and forth across two worlds, both theirs and ours.

8. "You don't get points for drinking"

Body, born 1947, worker

When I was back in jail, it became clear to me every time that my time outside was wasted, senselessly wasted. I somehow just killed time. Always the same. Four weeks before my release—I decided this time it would be different, very, very different. The first time out, you'll see! I avoid the old circles of friends, I don't step foot in the bars. All the same bums and crazies hang out there. I can do without them. This time I am a lot smarter.

Two weeks after my release, I had it up to here with *Kaffee* and *Kuchen* and I went back to the bottle. Glass in hand, I sat back in the middle of the same bums and crazies and felt really good. Aside from two or three new faces, the rest were all the same.

In jail you can't find anybody to talk to about your real problems—I couldn't anyway—and so you deal with everything yourself, in the dark, under the covers. That says everything. Under the covers you discover a world for yourself in which you'll live after your release, really different than before. You have time and you sketch out a life for yourself into the smallest corners with beautiful colors. These dreams have no relationship with the outside, with life as you had lived it until now. But you realize that soon enough, and you don't waste any time thinking about that before you get out.

During the day the others tell you their crazy tales. They talk for hours about what kind of incredible dudes they were outside, women standing in a line that long. That day will come again, they promise everyone—for damn sure, never back here. Since they're all doing that, you go along with them. So at the end of my twenties, I was the typical *Abo-Knaster* (jailbird).[1] In and out, back in again and out, sometimes longer outside, sometimes longer inside. I already had the same prison syndrome as the others.

As a young dude, I was looking for a place where nobody questioned me, and you find that easiest in bars, in the local tavern, with people who don't have any expectations of you or anyone else, with people you can bullshit with for hours, while your brain slowly but surely gets soaked with booze. I was satisfied.

You come in: "Hello, Body, heh old man, what's up? Get pissed, buddy." You have the feeling they're all just waiting for you, it's high time for you to show up. At least they act like it and soon Tortenspritze[2] will stop by and lisp, "Do you have a buck? You're getting pretty late here. It's already ten."

Anyways, if you have money on you, they can't be happy enough that you're around. You sit there, stand at the bar, have no obligations, drink and kill time. A real discussion is way too demanding. You feel cool because you're part of the scene. If someone we know from school comes in for a cigarette or a beer, everybody breaks out laughing: heh, this guy works full time. And someone heard that he'll get married soon too. Then it's all over. Everybody goes wild. Back at your own job the boss complains; one problem after another. The other workers are getting tired of you, but here in the bar you're still somebody. Suddenly it hits you—my god, it's already been three days since you've worked. Trouble's around the corner again. To go quickly to the doctor doesn't work, impossible, too drunk for that, so another round and the tight spot in your stomach goes away. Your buddies scream and hold their sides from laughter when you mention what's going on at work.

Days go by, and once in a while it bothers you that they could pick you up again, but that goes away and finally the day comes when you don't even worry about it anymore. Everything sort of moves along. At home your mother complains: you are a bum—if you don't go to work soon, do thus and such, you'll be as bad as this one and that one from the street. For a while you listen to this crap, then it's enough and you're off to the tavern. It's still morning but the place is full; some of your buddies are already there, you still have a hangover from yesterday and for that a fresh Pilsner is the best medicine.

How meaningless it all was, I only realized many years later. I became dependent, addicted to the meaningless bullshit, to the bar jokes, I felt really good in the crowd at the bar. It was often tighter than in a tent, and I needed my alcohol.

In terms of my growing up, there wasn't anything special about me. After my birth, I went to a Catholic orphanage until I was eight years old, then three years back at home, which I didn't like either. My father was a total alcoholic. When he was drunk, he was a simpering, nasty, sentimental asshole. I still feel today his snotty tears on my face. When he was sober, he was both authoritarian and brutal. Mother was a good person in her own way, but weak and she also drank.

I couldn't stand it, ran away from home, and moved back into the orphanage. There I tortured myself with the question: why me? Why couldn't I live at home? Others could do it. I always had the feeling that something very important in life was being kept from me—a family, a more or less intact family. My complaining turned me into a loner. I rejected the world around me, reacted with aggression, and withdrew into my shell. My thoughts only focused on my home.

At fourteen I was back with my mother, 1961. A crazy year, especially in Berlin. Everything was upside down; the schizophrenia spread to us children. I went to school drunk, missed an exam, and got kicked out.

My father belonged to the so-called *Grenzgänger*.[3] He worked as a laborer in West Berlin. After August 13 he stayed there for good. Suddenly he lived in another city and I could "view" him twice a week. After work on Tuesday and Friday he climbed the viewing tower that was on the other side of the Wall and we stared at each other. It was like a zoo, and if we wanted to talk to each other, the cops got in between and chased me away. Naturally I turned against the state, and that father I couldn't stand turned into a saint. Now I was longing for the same thing I couldn't tolerate before.

My mother convinced my school principal to take me back into the school. At the end of 1961 a school class from Leipzig visited my class in Berlin. We sat nervously on our benches and grinned. I was thinking, how can one talk so loudly, in such a weird Saxon dialect? Suddenly I heard one of them say: be glad that you finally have an antifascist democratic protective wall that lets you study in peace.[4]

I simply let my fists fly. I didn't know what to do. I just let 'em have it. I had plenty of energy. At seventeen I was put away for the first time. Resistance to the state. We were a gang on our street and felt that we were being treated unfairly by the cops. You can imagine how such a group functions. In the beginning we just talked back; then we fought back. The result: some wound up in prison.

At nineteen I found the gay scene. Here I didn't have any inhibitions. Even though I had to hide my orientation from my buddies in the tavern, here it was a trump card. From my time in the orphanage, I had my sexual experiences and with the way I looked I was a hit. I got offers one after the other. Maybe I got involved with the wrong ones. In any case, after a short time I was in the middle of a mess. My confidence was crushed; I let myself go. The superficial sexual contacts, without any depth, made me feel worthless. When I awoke out of my numbness, I felt sick as a dog. I felt sorry for myself, but I still ran back again. Sort of a vicious circle.

At that time there was nobody with whom I could have talked about my life. Older ones who could have helped me I rejected. Anyone over thirty was too old. We made fun of them. Whenever we had a free chair we let one of these vultures know from a waiter that we wanted him at our table. The waiter had to let him know what we were drinking, and when the new round arrived, he joined us. These guys never noticed how we took them in. After it was over, they paid the bill and that was it. We really preferred traveling salesmen with suits and ties.

The more miserable things got, the sooner I punched somebody. It's schizophrenic, but for some that made me only more interesting. I stood in a corner where I didn't belong at all. Rough and butch on the outside, I longed deep inside to be taken in someone's arms. Hard shell, soft core; maybe a woman could have handled that but not the guys I was running around with. They were irritated when I told them what I wanted. Such a big guy and then this. . . . So I didn't let myself get into it anymore, since I didn't get anything from it except frustrations, and aside from that everybody gossiped in those circles. I became more and more aggressive.

I don't want to brag, but no one can tell what I am, and I don't give it away in how I come across, that's not my style. I always hung around with manly types. I wouldn't be seen with queens. Never. "He hangs around with queens, so he must be gay." That's the way it works. So that my close friends didn't suspect anything I made up a story about a married woman. I was careful in getting away.

That's the way it is; normal people look down on the gays and feel superior. We feel good when we see a queen, because we're at least not that bad. Nowadays I'm somewhat friendlier toward them, somehow more liberal. I distinguish myself from them only in that I am not so obvious. Basically we all want a man. I guess they need to camp it up in order to feel good. I mean, maybe they experience themselves best that way, that they have a body. I like to wear washed-out tight jeans best, because I feel butch in them. Everybody plays around in his own way, that's how it is, and always a little bit with himself. We all want to show what we have, whether we're normal or not, right? I've compromised before, only a few times, of course, but I can camp it up and not bad at all. It's not my style, because I don't want it. I tell you, every one of us should try to become like the ideal picture he has of his friend, and most of us want a real man, the way he looks and the way he acts.

I accept a lot of the queens because they have a practical attitude toward life. They don't worry what people think of them. That doesn't faze them at all. What impresses me is that they let the men they like know how they feel, whether they like it or not. I would never be able to do that.

In jail a real queen really goes for it and lets everybody know. For most of them there's not much choice anyway, because of the way they look. They realize very quickly that they have nothing to lose and take their place at the bottom. They are the lowest, doing the shit work, but in the dark they have their fans. Sure, becoming someone's property is real common in jail, with sex, of course, and jealousy enough to kill. The wildest types watch each other constantly, just so sugar daddy can't pick up another one. During the day they make fun of the gays. That's just as much part of the jail schizophrenia as the fact that they get angry and defensive, denying everything if you would ask them about it. Never, not me!

In jail you have to be a man. Textbook virtues aren't called for here. One of the hottest customers, a guy with incredible biceps, today is a feared bouncer in a bar. He has probably never got it on again so passionately and with so much show as there. Christ, if only one person had mentioned a word about that pair.

My first real experience with a man started after my second release. I had two more years of not being allowed into Berlin, which I spent in a tiny place near Zwickau.[5] I went to work regularly, but I stayed away from the people there. Evenings I read or sat in front of the television. Jail had made me shy away from people.

After a few weeks I got to know M. I was glad that he wanted to get in touch with me. I wouldn't have gone after him. He courted me and persistently got rid of the garbage that had piled up in me. He didn't take off insulted when I rejected him a few times. On the outside, I seemed calm and cool, inside I was nervous and torn apart. His patience had an incredible effect. Slowly I caught on; it was like learning the alphabet all over again. I understood that something must grow if something is to come of it, even a friendship. Up until that time, everything had to happen right away, and if not, I dropped it completely. All at once I felt like getting to know another person slowly, to approach him and to do things together with him. I hadn't ever allowed these desires to surface in my superficial life in Berlin.

After two months we were a couple. The more I accepted the relationship as a given, the calmer I became. I was amazed that I was capable of this. As silly as it may sound, I was really quite proud of myself that I was capable of completing something on Friday that I had planned on Monday.

Other people didn't interest us very much. I didn't know them and they knew that he was "different." That such guys like he and I got together didn't seem to surprise them. I don't know what they said behind our backs, but in our presence not a mean word was said.

For a year and a half I was finally on the sunny side too. That changed me. Most of all I wasn't envious of those who had no problems at all. That the relationship fell apart after one and a half years was really my fault. At the first signs of wear and tear I panicked. I totally overreacted and got out. Today I know that they were signs of wear and tear as you see them in every marriage, wherever one has an everyday life. The honeymoon was over and, I thought, that was it.

As if without provocation, I started fighting again. Explain that to a court. I felt that he didn't pay enough attention to me anymore. If he talked to a young dude in a bar, I went nuts; if he came home one hour later than he had said, I sat in my chair and didn't say a word. I got more and more unbearable because I didn't want to believe that the honeymoon couldn't last for a lifetime. Because I kept beating people up, I went back in and that was the end. I couldn't find a balance because I expected everything from him that I hadn't got in my life.

What can I tell about the next few years?

In prison everything was the same as before. I wasn't a newcomer anymore and I knew how things worked in there. I read everything that the library had—most of all fantasy books because I could lose myself in those. Before my release I planned, this time for real, . . . I've already talked about that.

In the middle of the seventies I had enough of the laying around. I wanted to get married, really get married. A few of my old buddies had since managed to leave the scene by way of getting married. Of course, those were "normal" buddies. On the weekend they now took their kid to the soccer stadium to see the Union Club play,[6] and when I couldn't avoid them in the street, they told me that they were giving up smoking and drinking—except for a glass here and there with their father-in-law or at a family celebration.

The attempt with Kerstin was another fiasco for me. After a year and a half she told me to my face: "You don't need a wife, you need a psychiatrist." So, that was that.

The fear of disappointment grew in me. I had disappointed and been disappointed, and I said to myself the best protection against more disappointment is withdrawal. I have a tendency toward depression. I know that. If someone laid into me, I was deeply hurt and felt that I had been mistreated. It was already like that in the orphanage. When I let the others have it, I didn't think about it twice. It has to do with my getting shortchanged in life. Since my childhood I haven't been able to get rid of that feeling.

I am introverted and try to do everything by myself. Because I am not always successful, I seem to block my feelings and I become totally helpless. At that moment I would like to speak to the first person I come across in the street: "Hey you, do you have a little time for me? I need your help."

Try that once! Those stupid faces that stare at you. After that I went back to the bar, and after a few schnapps life seemed already more bearable. Drunk, I would march to one of these meeting places sometimes, and if someone came close, I would hit him. Back in court, once again I couldn't explain why.

Without the help of my doctor, I would never be here today. I am certain about that. He understood me; he listened to me and didn't give me a hard time. You know, as soon as I feel any pressure, I am gone. He didn't throw his hands up in the air or roll his eyes as I laid my innermost feelings on the table, and he didn't judge me to be a monster when I told him I was homosexual. He accepted me as I was: a person who out of despair tried to kill himself because he couldn't get things straightened out for himself and had to be helped because he couldn't do it by himself.

He said to my face: "Alcoholism is a sickness, homosexuality isn't. Combined in one person, they as a rule lead to catastrophe, as with you. We have to do something *against* the disease and *for* your orientation." If I had up to that point thought at all more deeply about myself, then my thoughts had gone exactly in the opposite direction.

In addition he said: "You will stabilize when you accept what you are, alcoholic and homosexual. You will change when you develop a strong will to stop drinking altogether and when you live out your orientation as you find it in yourself."

For hours we analyzed my life up to that point and we came to the conclusion that the situation was pretty bad, but only half as bad as it looked at first glance. Other people were also messed up, not only me. He didn't get impatient and helped me sort things out, whenever I didn't understand everything right away. I had to first get in my head that all this was about me. A chronic drinker in an advanced stage with the typical symptoms: daily, continuous drinking, the typical withdrawal symptoms that go with a falling blood alcohol level, headed for cirrhosis of the liver, loss of control, social problems.

After he had heard my whole story, he corrected himself. The way in which I had lived out my sexuality up to that point indicated that it also made me a medical case. The conflict was preprogrammed: a passive homosexual from whom everybody else expects the opposite and who is on a macho trip. Christ, try to deal with that!

After one month the first setback took place in the therapy group. Without talking to me about it beforehand, the therapist asked me to talk about my homosexuality in front of all the group members. He had gotten this information out of my file. I was speechless. Why should I suddenly expose myself in front of all these strangers? My sexual life was none of these people's business. I resisted until I couldn't hold out any longer. I knew what they thought about gays. Why should these people think otherwise? I didn't dream about arguing against the conventional fixed prejudices. I will choose the people with whom I discuss these things. Even today I don't know of anyone who has had positive experiences talking about it, either in the work collective or in school. Maybe some do have positive experiences. If so, so much the better. If, for example, homosexual alcoholics would get together, then I could trust them. But such a group doesn't exist—not yet.[7]

After four months I was released from the clinic. Two years later I was back in. The same circumstances, the same fiasco, a bad relapse and fewer chances for recovery, since they are reduced by relapses. Only I knew that in the meantime I had become another person.

I had started drinking again, regularly and abundantly, but with a bad conscience. When I thought about my doctor, I felt terrible. We were still in contact and I called him once in awhile. On the telephone I told him that I was okay, and I always invented a few lines about a friend who didn't really exist. After those calls I felt so bad that I ran straight to the next bar. A year after my release, I didn't call him anymore. I rarely missed work.

The second stay in the clinic began like the first: intensive care, consciousness, detoxification, withdrawal, fears, depressions—the usual. After I was more or less back together and slowly showed that I was ready to be treated, he began to talk to me again. Feeling totally guilty, I told him about the last two years, always ready to get a lecture from him. Nothing of the kind. He asked me if there had also been positive experiences in this period. I was surprised and looked at him astonished. I had nothing to say. He reminded me of our talks over the phone, and with hesitation I started to answer his question. An apartment of my own, almost finished, problems at work weren't so bad anymore, and—I couldn't help but smile—not one fight, really, not one. I had nothing else that was positive. I knew he would ask about the friend I had mentioned on the phone. Without thinking very long about it, I laid the cards on the table. I made up the friend for you. I wanted to assure you, because I was ashamed that I had failed again. There was a man but only for a very short time, then I withdrew. The person who drinks finds everything else to be a burden. I am sorry that I have disappointed you. The telephone booth is less than twenty steps away from the bar.

He reacted soberly, not at all surprised or unfriendly. I only sensed disappointment in his voice. The situation was really only bad for me. Suffering here, suffering there. Fortunately he had had a few positive experiences himself—a few make it work here and again, thank God. And I should get rid of my embarrassment: my chances would be a lot better if I could find in myself a deeper reason for my rehabilitation. But for that I would have to think more of myself, be less careless—with my health, with time, and with men. He could never be more for me than a crutch, which I, I hoped, one day no longer would need. I buried my head in a pillow and started to cry wildly. He stood up, stroked my head and left.

The next few days I lay in bed like a mummy and tried to make sense of what he had said. It couldn't have been clearer. He had made it clear to me that I, including my calls, was a bother. He could never be anything more than a crutch for me. With that everything was said. My calls he had taken as signals. Here is someone calling who has improved and he wants to get rewarded, with love. I hadn't admitted to myself that I was in love with him because it was fruitless. Again he knew more about me than I knew about myself.

You know, my so-called mentors always operated on a wavelength that I couldn't and wouldn't accept. That started in the orphanage. Their demands went in one ear and out the other, rarely otherwise. With a few the tone was enough and I switched off: "You must understand, you learn for life and not for the teacher. One doesn't get into fights, nothing can become of you, no, no, get yourself together, everybody wants only the best for you, but you . . . come on, get a hold of yourself, you are so ungrateful, if everybody was like you!" Later they addressed me with "Mister." Words, words, words. In the name of the orphanage's leadership, in the name of the school's leadership, in the name of the collective, and in the name of the people. I won't even deny their good intentions, I am only describing how it appeared to me. Before anyone in the orphanage had realized that the tough guy was also sensitive and vulnerable, my childhood had passed. By at least seventeen I was proud of it when nobody around me noticed that I was a real softie.

The long and the short of it is my doctor thought of me as a person, without any qualifications. For him I was not a thing to be disciplined or played with. I never had that feeling with him. He accepted me as a person who, quite simply, had to have help, as a matter of fact. He had made it very clear to me how far I could go with him, only to here and no further. But to there I could count on him. What he said hit me because he didn't just give me words. When I needed to, I could go to him. I'll say it again: he was dealing with me, myself. Back in the orphanage, I reached out to this or that teacher, in my own way, more indirect, not always easy to read; nobody ever told me to my face, but I felt it always: "This tough guy also wants affection, that's a little too much to expect."

The ones who got praised were those who didn't stand out and I beat them up for that. That was a vicious circle because I got punished for it.

My buddies who managed to make the jump did it through a person they could relate to, usually a woman—a woman who aroused in them a feeling that they were worth something. I am talking about the buddies I've known over the years and have observed. They got themselves going for only two reasons, love and money. It was best if they had both; sometimes money was enough. I accept that, just as I accept the people who put an idea first. The worst ones are those hypocrites who are driven by the same trite reasons but want to convince others that they operate for noble motives. If you don't accept their bullshit, they shut you off.

Believe me, a person needs a reason to change. It has to be worth it for him. The one who is held down for years, whether it's his fault or not— he doesn't think much of himself. Self-awareness, feelings of self-worth are hardly there anymore, and if so, only a tiny part.

When you get released from prison here, no one is alone. I mean, apartment and work. The state takes care of that. That certainly is worth something, but the good intentions often evaporate very quickly, in spite of a roof over your head and a secure job, because there isn't a single person who cares. It is difficult to pick yourself up without any help. A good work collective can help you, but it can't do more. You need someone who cares, and to find him is not easy. The state doesn't help you with that, especially not us homosexuals.

Since I realized that you don't get points for drinking, I have changed. The upstanding citizens say, "Good for you," and those who could care less about the rules say, "Body is trying to be classy and will soon have his place in the union."[8] This attitude is confirmed when I meet my ABV in the street. I'll greet him and ask in a friendly way: "So, Comrade Deputy Schmidt, everything rosy?" And he answers: "For the time being, yes, I hope it'll stay that way." Of course, he means me with that remark. He doesn't really seem to believe my transformation.

Nowadays I don't push as much as I did years ago. I face reality as it is. It's not always pleasant, and often I would rather put my head in the sand and give up, but I force myself. Perhaps the most important change is that I have stopped trying to blame everyone except me. That also happens, but I am responsible for myself.

What's better is that I am more at peace with myself and have accepted that I have to compromise. I can deal better with my aggression. I fought before because I hadn't learned to solve my problems with reason. On the other hand, if I had arms like twine, I would always have negotiated rather than hit first.

It's nice that I can enjoy my work and enjoy the little things in life. I don't claim to be over the hurdle; the cravings are still there, especially for alcohol, but I am trying. I have to get a hold of myself whenever my conviction gets weaker, and above all whenever I ask myself: what's actually waiting for you on the other side of that hurdle? Do you really want to get there?

I would prefer a kind of compromise: not to give up the drinking entirely but control it, a friend I could see two or three times a week. No living together. With my work I am satisfied. I already said that. As far as the drinking goes, my doctor told me clearly, I can do anything but never another drink. Anything else would be an illusion, and possibly a deadly illusion.

Through my work I have met people with whom I never had contact before. I like those people best who take me as I am: someone who does a job and would like to be paid well for it. I find those people funny who act as if we were all one big happy family in our socialism. When they get into a conversation with one another, they just about apologize that there is still simple physical labor in a socialist country. If they had it their way, all social differences would have been eliminated a long time ago. I find it amusing, because they just don't understand that they're no better than I am.

In some apartments you have the feeling that these people surround themselves with a hedge like Sleeping Beauty and then quickly move a few thorns to the side so that you can polish the windows in their castle for them. Once in a while I do meet people with whom I'd really like to spend an hour.

Interview completed 1983

9. "Society could have gotten more from me"

Joseph, born 1944, economist

My sexual life has required an incredible amount of energy. Strength, which was lacking in other areas of my life, wasted meaninglessly. The expression *sexual order* comes to mind. An awful term, but it strikes the core of the matter when I say that I needed about ten years to accommodate myself more or less to that. At twenty I learned in a rather brutal way that I was "different," scum. Suddenly the "Sunny Boy" with the glowing future stood on the outside, among the disrespected. Inside of me arose layers of sediment, a mixture of guilt feelings, inferiority complexes, self-pity—a fundamental pessimism that held on for years. I will never be able to free myself from that completely.

I still react sensitively whenever anyone asks me about my sexuality. I don't know if dreams reflect inner states, but sometimes, shaken with fear, I awaken from a dream. Inside me is fear, which cannot be put aside as easily as in the saying: so what, it was only a dream. The craziest things go through my head. For example, from floor to floor I think about each of the tenants and ask myself, how would this one or that one react to us up here on the tenth floor if we could roll back history about fifty years? You could be denounced at that time for the most insignificant reason. It was enough that someone really wanted the apartment of an "enemy of the people" because his didn't have a balcony. These are crazy thoughts, quite absurd nowadays. But what this one or that one has let on about the two gays up there on the tenth floor, I don't even want to know. It has always only taken one person for a denunciation.

Let's not kid ourselves. Even today the first reaction toward someone who is recognized as a homosexual or admits to being one is covering him with a net of prejudices. It's possible that this net has become looser in the last few years, but it is still a net for catching people. At first my generation panicked and struggled to catch its breath. The most rational have, after a moment of despair, regulated themselves true to style, in the most recent fashion, and made modest careers. Those with a more passionate nature went wild under the net, as if every day could be their last. In the end, everybody has lost out, because in their own way, everybody has had to come to terms with a homophobic environment. For those who were hard workers, the professional advancement suddenly stopped; barriers that they couldn't see formed a wall. The passionate ones ran incessantly after the perfect love and haven't seen that there are other sides to life.

Before my medical studies I was in the army. I went directly from high school to the army, into a tank unit. Around me were plumbers, tractor operators, carpenters, and masons—all practical trades. My reservations were quickly dissipated. I felt great among them. I was athletic, not very ambitious. What was important was what my buddies thought of me. I didn't give a shit about what my superiors thought. We soldiers were in this unique transition phase from boyhood to manhood. Play and seriousness changed like the weather and no one knew exactly if what had just occurred was play or for real. Why should we have cared? Most of us had stuck our girlfriend's picture on the inside of our locker door. But your roommates and your tank crew, with whom you at times were together for fourteen days and nights straight, were closer to you than anybody else.

In male communities a large part of the relationships are mediated physically and sensually. Homosexuals, who observe male communities from the outside, imagine that behind every affectionate touch is sex. Heterosexual observers find it harmless. What they see are pure friendships among men, pure affection for each other, no more than that. Both are fantasies. In my experience the climate in male communities helps integrate sexuality into the interpersonal relations in an uncomplicated way. The one who puts his arm around the shoulders of his buddy is far from wanting to sleep with him. But he can find himself in a situation in which the desire for more affection toward the other hits him like a ton of bricks. I've experienced it.

My two other roommates were on weekend leave. And right away we opened a bottle and envied the two on leave who were now with their "women." When the bottle was empty, we got into bed, into my bed. During the entire night we didn't say a word. Only after several days did we find the old intimacy again. We were both afraid that the other would be brusque and distant. Carefully we approached each other again. Weeks later we suggested to our roommates that they keep their established leave schedule.

After my time in the army, I began my medical studies in L. I rented a room from an old girlfriend of my mother. My landlady was a doctor, a very intelligent woman with whom I could discuss the most varied topics, sometimes all night long. It was great. I adored this educated and understanding women.

One evening I came from the university. There sat the council of the goddesses in the living room together. My mother's unannounced visit signaled danger. Her expression indicated that they had discussed this for a long time and seriously. I still held the door handle in my hand when the tirade began. Without warning mother fired away. Pig, homo, sow, bastard. Strange, but gay boy hit me the deepest. Mother must have agreed on the vocabulary with my landlady in their lengthy consultation. Yes, she was calling this filthiness by its real name. Every excuse would be approval. There was only one thought in my head: this woman is not your mother.

As my paralysis left me, I screamed back. I don't remember anymore what I said exactly. Up to that point I had destroyed all the letters of my army buddy right after I read them. Only the last one I kept. I had put it in my drawer among my underwear. I couldn't understand how such a cultivated woman with the best manners could have in such a slimy way stuck her nose into my private affairs, looking through my underwear. I realized that it wasn't only curiosity that drove her. Apparently it always takes just an argument of higher purpose to make a noble act out of cheap snooping. In this case she had done it in the name of national health. Already the next day they dragged me to a doctor. They had put their gay boy between them so that he couldn't get away. Everything was arranged, no waiting. Both of them would have most liked to storm into the examination room.

Without being shy I spoke to the doctor about my feelings for my friend and that my feelings for him were much, much stronger than what I up to that point had felt for girls. No comparison. He listened in an interested fashion and took notes. After ten minutes he sent me out again. After that he called my mother into the room. Five minutes later she was out again, pale as a ghost, completely speechless. She first had to sit down.

The doctor had told her earnestly and precisely that it was my decision if I didn't want to sleep with women, especially since I was almost twenty-one. His experiences with other patients indicated that there wasn't much one could do. I was not sick, and any therapy would only do damage. And if the patient himself doesn't want it, there was definitely nothing to do. And this was that kind of situation.

Shaking her head, the landlady received my mother's report: That cannot be true! I began to grin inside, since I already regarded myself as the final victor. My landlady got up, and with a glance at the office door, she said: "Let's go. Unfortunately we have run into a medical nitwit. If Professor W. were not at an important congress abroad, this would not have happened to us. There are blunderers everywhere, unfortunately among doctors too. It was only sad that such dramatic misdiagnoses have irreparable consequences. People without the right connections would have to give up at this point and go home. Thank God, we don't have to." Mother crowned it all: from the start this doctor hadn't appeared very trustworthy. She had had a bad feeling from the first sentence. In the end he might be one of these clever closet gay boys himself.

In the evening the council of the goddesses convened again, fortified with an old girlfriend of my landlady, also a doctor. After the meeting my mother came to me in my room and let me know in no uncertain terms that she wouldn't leave this house before everything was back in order again. She would count on my help. Oh yes, Dr. M., that was the third member of the council, had brought in a new aspect that was very enlightening. She diagnosed the whole thing as stemming from laziness. People would withdraw more and more from their natural obligations. Probably a result of the liberalization and certainly not limited to the sexual area.

The very next Monday I was taken to the professor. The landlady didn't come along since she knew we were in good hands with the medical professor. When she had given him a description of my disease, he had calmed her: "Send me the boy. We'll take care of that."

Mother had regained her confidence. Our taxi stopped in front of a beautiful *Jugendstil* villa, surrounded by large old trees, everything stately and the best. A female receptionist led us in and told us to take a seat. The professor would be ready any minute. Everything was very much according to my mother's taste. All doubt was laid aside without question. What could possibly go wrong here?

I was called and asked by a nice older gentleman to take a seat. He asked me simple questions. I told him how I understood it, willingly and in detail. After a half hour he shut his folder with a satisfied look and asked his assistant to give me another appointment. At the end he patted me amiably on the shoulder. Mother was slightly irritated when she heard that still another meeting was necessary. Well, if it has to be.

At the second meeting he asked me to sit on the couch. I lay down and started talking. As I started to speak about my friend, he stopped me abruptly. He was interested in my relationships to my father and my mother. He had to hear everything, everything about it and as a doctor he would not be surprised at the most unusual sexual desires, which I had possibly carried around with me, for my father or my mother, or even both. Every minute detail could be of great help. I was rudely interrupted as soon as I dismissed my sexual desires for my parents with a brief observation and came back to talk about my friend. I didn't yet know Freud and didn't know what he was getting at.

It didn't take long and he let the cat out of the bag: "You are sick and you have to get healthy again. You are suffering from a sickness that we can heal. You only have to want it. Together we can do it." Monotonously and aggressively he repeated the same sentences again and again, like a minister: "We both will conquer this malicious sickness. You are young, strong, intelligent." As if bitten by a spider, I winced, as I suddenly felt his soft hand on my head. Fortunately he pulled it back right away. He wouldn't allow himself to be deterred and continued to talk. I caught myself at that point. My eyes checked the room, bit by bit; in the farthest corner of the room my eyes stopped at that wonderful picture, a river scene in morning fog. Willows on both shores, and a fisherman in his boat. I closed my eyes, quite tightly, tighter and tighter. Above me a purple heaven took shape. I lay in the grass on the shore and felt how the fisherman left his boat and came to me. In no way was I supposed to open my eyes. Everything would be lost. I breathed more evenly. The fisherman was he—my friend. I was certain, for only he smelled like that.

From the soft murmurings behind my head, words emerged again. Nature, spring, seeds, reproduction, will power, man, woman, marriage, children, sports, intelligence, and one sentence: no one with such an orientation can become a doctor.

Slowly I came to. It was terribly hot. With a soft voice I asked him to open a window. Suddenly I felt a hot flash through my entire body. I tightened my neck muscles, lifted my head a few centimeters, opened my right eye, and saw what had happened. The most washed-out place on my jeans showed itself clearly. I closed my eyes and felt terribly embarrassed. I asked him with an even lower voice if I could sit up. But no, he would open the window and I could cover myself with a blanket so that I wouldn't catch a cold.

It became overwhelmingly clear! He connected my erection to his encouraging words. He became more and more friendly. I repeated my request. Clearly more severe in tone, he made it clear to me. Sit up? No, that wasn't possible. Did I want to carelessly jeopardize what had been accomplished? I got up and asked him to end the therapy for today. Clearly dissatisfied, he agreed.

I went to the next appointment and explained to him that I could only converse with him if I could sit across from him. I had to look people in the eyes when I talked to them. Yes, he answered, that is the case with healthy people, but in our case I should let him decide the appropriate method. Again more friendly, he added that the time would come when he would talk to me looking into my eyes. In spite of this, I was committed to sitting and our conflict came to a head.

During the next few days I felt very bad, torn in two. Mother threatened that she would cut off her financial support. One couldn't become a doctor with this orientation. I relied emotionally more and more on my friend, but he still hadn't responded to my call for help. I sat in my lectures apathetically, in front of me a piece of paper that I had divided from top to bottom with a thick blue line. Left, on the side of the heart, I gathered the arguments for him; right, on the side of reason, I put mother's. In one moment I decided for the left, in another for the right. I couldn't get out of this brooding mood.

Mother intimated that she was willing to "reward" a cure appropriately. The professor had agreed to another session. Then came the letter from my friend. I locked myself in, ripped open the letter, and couldn't read because everything got black in front of my eyes. Slowly I calmed down. I read the last sentences again and again. "I will always be your buddy. My girlfriend and I, you remember her from the picture—we'll be getting married in the fall."

I have never again in my life felt this alone and abandoned. I cried miserably.

The next morning I felt incredibly matured. I wanted to deny everything, treat everybody with disdain. I hated everyone, even him. I just wanted to be cold and distant with others. For days one picture danced through my head: her, as she moaned beneath him. Something had broken inside of me.

The next day I lay down on the couch without being asked and didn't expect anything anymore. He tried to get me to react, but I didn't. Five minutes later he demanded my participation or he would discontinue the treatment. I stood up, put on my jacket and left without saying goodbye.

Mother received a written notification that caused her to attack me again. Incorrigible, unthankful, stubborn, only creating problems for others; this hadn't been exactly cheap. He who doesn't want to be helped has to face the consequences: I could choose between one year's interruption in my studies and work as a nurse in the women's ward in my father's hospital or continue my studies in J., a smaller university town.

After that she took a deep breath in order to add: I had to leave L. in any case, at any cost. After all, everybody knew that L. was the mecca of homosexuals in this country. No wonder, given the city's international population. I shouldn't expect any more mail from this guy. She had written him a letter that he wouldn't forget his whole life.

I shuddered. Was that the reason for his rejection? I got up and screamed at her: "I don't have a mother anymore. I don't even want to see you again." I packed my things and left the house. I stayed with a fellow student from the university and on the same day I wrote a letter to my friend. I never received an answer.

The treatment had repercussions. I accepted myself—as a sick person. I wanted to live like someone who accepts his illness and learns how to deal with it. People were really upset when I laid my university withdrawal form on the table. Why this, when you are doing so well? My answer was short and to the point: "I found out that I won't make a good doctor. My decision did not come easy."

No one understood me; everyone just shook their head. In the meantime my mother had stopped financing me but didn't know about my withdrawal. I found work as a nurse and was from then on financially independent. With shift and night work overtime I earned rather well for the circumstances at that time.

And then the inevitable took place. I looked for contacts and found them where they are still available for homosexuals today—in their dark meeting places. These places intensely mark in their visitors the difference between sex and love. This is a basic experience of homosexuals and in my mind the key to the behavior of most of them.

At that time mother proceeded from the following consideration: financial worries would force the spoiled child back again into her arms. After two months had passed without any petitions, she got nervous. She couldn't take it anymore and came to L. At the university she learned that her son had withdrawn. On that same day she managed to get an appointment with the dean and get me registered again. She caught me at work. Soberly she told me that I would get support again on the day I would continue school. Yes, at the university here in L. My answer devastated her: "I could never be a doctor with this orientation. That would be irresponsible. Aside from that I feel very good doing this work as a nurse. I don't have any more to say."

Months later she wrote me a letter. She was in a bind. My brother wanted to get married and she didn't know how she should explain the absence of her youngest son. She couldn't think of a good reason. I answered that I wouldn't leave her hanging but that I would leave again on the evening of the wedding day. I kept my promise.

Four weeks later I wrote her a letter. I expressed once again my deep disappointment, explained my reasons for ending my studies. If she ever wanted to be called mother by me again, she would have to force herself to accept me as nature had made me. Neither son nor mother could choose the other, but one could try to live with the other. I had told her that I had found a man with whom I was happy. If she had the desire to see me again, I would come, but only accompanied by him. A week later I had the invitation on the table.

During the trip I was about ready to jump out of the train. We arrived at the station bathed in sweat. I was feeling sick as a dog as I pressed the bell on our front door. Mother opened the door and was shocked. She looked at my friend and couldn't believe her eyes. In front of her stood a man like out of a magazine. Big, strong, curly black hair on his head, and more of it sprang from his open shirt. She didn't know how to get herself in control. That didn't fit at all with her image of the gay boy. Now she was the one who started sweating. Later she admitted to me that she would have gone after him if he hadn't been with me. As far as men go, she had never been shy.

It was amazing how quickly she adjusted to us. From this day on there was no longer the problem of having a homosexual son. She didn't try to give any big explanations about being tolerant. She also didn't insist on lengthy discussions where she tried to clarify her position. From this point on, our relationship was based on trust in every way.

From the beginning Father had kept out of it. That he never really accepted me, I only heard about years later. When I confronted him with the unfair way he treated Mother, he dismissed me quickly: "Maybe I should discuss this with a gay person. First you clean up your own life!"

Once I read in a book a sentence that has stayed with me ever since: people are only rarely better than the circumstances in which they live. That made sense to me; however, it remained open why some were better. Were they more clever than most, did they see through the conditions better? Mother was addressed as "Frau Doctor," even though she had never seen a university from the inside. Father was the one who had studied, sheathed in an aura that came with being a doctor in such a small town. Father was smarter, but he had never tried to approach me. There still was his other son who had turned out right, who chased skirts, as it should be—a stud like his father.

As pathetic as it may sound, Mother and I, we found each other again.

I am very certain of that, because we loved each other. One doesn't become tolerant from one day to the next. The individual doesn't and certainly not society, not even by decree. That requires motivation and expectations, occasions. Father put up with me as long as I didn't question him. I know: his chances to act in some human way toward me were fewer than Mother's, since we didn't love each other. Why should he want to understand me? Why should he have experiences with his son that would make him uneasy, experiences that society for centuries has repressed into the subconscious and maintained as a taboo? Only fathers who love their sons do that.

For the majority of people there are really no compelling reasons to change their perspectives about us. Tolerance will move ahead to the extent that living together in general becomes more human. And what that depends on would have to be discussed separately.

With my mother there was peace, and now I could have started my studies again. She didn't push but let me know her opinion. What mother doesn't like to have a son in a white coat making visits? Without comment she accepted my decision to start studying economics.

I lived at my friend's. For the older ladies in the building we were the friendly, nice, and likable young men who lived together because it was cheaper. And we also looked good. I in my jeans and army coat, he in his black carpenter's corduroys. Well camouflaged, at least we assumed so. At the end of the sixties I carried, instead of the army coat, an old leather jerkin from my grandfather as a Thälmann jacket.[1]

At our home there were acquaintances of my friend. I felt good in this group. Here my problems were discussed, extensively, sometimes all night long. I couldn't get enough of it. Books were pressed into my hand and I ate up every line, which only tangentially dealt with relationships between men. I was fascinated by Hemingway's macho heroes and their strange relationships to each other. I was deeply impressed by Cocteau's aestheticized male world and the explicit representations in the novels of Gide. It was incredibly important for me to find out that this or that famous person from the past should have also been one and that certain contemporaries had been rumored to be that way. That felt good. Our get-togethers had a feeling of intrigue. We were among ourselves. Soon I could discuss as the others did. Us and them. They were the normal ones. I understood that my difficulties were really not so unusual. The problems of the others were similarly patterned. We were bound by our suffering. With one or the other I could also talk about the relationship to my friend. Aside from my mother, that was otherwise impossible. In our discussions we always returned to the one point: humanity wants to be deceived, the truth is only annoying. Typical for the homosexuals in the sixties was: outwardly hide yourself and live inside your own four walls. It became clearer and clearer to me that I was compelled to hide an important part of me from others. One time I had asserted myself with my mother with an enormous effort. Then it was only successful because we loved each other. Hiding was also a lot of trouble. Being up front would have required more strength than I had.

In this environment my damaged self-confidence recuperated, more or less. On one hand, I felt protected; on the other hand, the ghetto consciousness in this group made me increasingly nervous. If hiding was the only alternative, then why not do it right? I observed individuals more closely and realized that it was quite apparent that they were gay. I couldn't understand these so-called queens who obviously looked gay from a distance. They were a puzzle for me and I disliked them. I stayed out of their way and despised them. By their provocative behavior they literally asked for discrimination. Why couldn't they control themselves when my friend and I could do it?

I was proud how well I disguised myself. Years later it still felt great when somebody said: "You? With you one cannot tell at all that you are like that." A lump of sugar for one's adjustment: I always reached for it. Just don't be soft. I think the way I presented myself is hardly different from the macho stuff of heterosexual men who are constantly worried about their masculinity.

I caught myself starting secretly to observe my friend. Whenever he stood up, he put his right leg forward, like a dancer. I criticized him. He brought his tea cup quite acceptably to his mouth, but why did he close his eyes after he had taken a sip? For a while he accepted my tips with a smile. But when I started constantly to correct all of his acquaintances, he got very angry. He told me to my face that I should use my profound analyses in the bedroom instead. I lost control. Feeling cornered, I started firing.

I was a mess, one big pain, my body dried up, I withdrew. What had happened? I think I had reached the end of my naïveté. The hopeful young man from a good family had finally realized that society had given a little place for him at the bottom. Anxiety about the future and fear of being exposed as a laughable figure got stronger and stronger. I didn't want to belong to those who were disrespected.

When I said that my friend and his circle had built me up, that was only true for the first two years. The more I learned about myself, the more I was affected by the poison of public opinion. I stood at the bar of some tavern and began to talk about the topic with a complete stranger, just to find out how he would react to it. If his face changed in disgust and he started to examine me, I quickly changed the conversation.

From my perspective today, the reason that my friend and I separated is quite ridiculous. I walked in once as he was showing my photo album to a friend. I tore it out of his hands hysterically, ran out insulted, opened it to a certain page, and destroyed a photo that showed me as a ten-year-old dressed as the Queen of Hearts at a children's Fasching party. I was convinced that both of them had made fun of this photo. Three weeks later I moved out for good.

At this time in L. the first weightlifting clubs started. I joined and began to work out regularly. I wanted to become like the men in Hemingway's novels—physically strong, taciturn, take action when it became necessary, at times slightly melancholic too. Small versions of this type were working out right around me. I glorified "maleness" and despised everything that only remotely appeared gay. For the next two, three years I liked the role of the guy with the secret. My sexuality became increasingly concentrated on my body.

What before had been the circle of friends now became the sports group. In another way it was a retreat into private life. I realized that neither my studies nor a social organization could satisfy my needs. I felt terribly alone, abandoned in the world. A typical heterosexual commentary on this situation is again and again the following: life isn't just made up of sexuality. However, for those who as young persons have to carry around a ridiculed sexuality, it sure is. Which one of my fellow students ever had to consider whether his feelings for the girl next to him would be socially acceptable or not? His only problem was whether she wanted to or not. And that alone was enough for it to become his first priority. If society at that time made a statement at all, it was a negative one. Isn't it a logical consequence under these circumstances to withdraw into a private sphere or into a subculture? And it remains unpolitical. Its members have enough problems as it is. When I said at the beginning that I was forced to waste energy pointlessly, then society is primarily to be blamed for that. Society could have gotten more from me.

I was almost thirty, completely unhappy. I felt the fear of getting old, and besides I was convinced that I had missed out on a real life. The atmosphere in the sports club was slowly getting on my nerves. I had seen through it. Many of those people were only interested in correcting their masculine deficits because they confused soft with wimpy and weak with unable.

And at that time something happened to me that changed my life at the very core. At one of our club's dances, the sister of one of my workout partners spoke to me. After a few glasses she explained to me that she was only here because her brother had asked her. Up to that point I followed her. But when she told me that most of the club members thought I was gay, I was shocked. Her brother had asked her to talk to me about it because she was lesbian. I lost my composure. When I looked over to her brother's table, he raised his arm demonstratively, indicating that I could really trust her. I almost began to cry.

After the dance we wandered for hours through the city. She promised to introduce me to a friend from D. whom she had met at mutual sports competitions. The last few days before this meeting were awful. When the time came, she had to virtually drag me to the station. Hours later I was in love.

Love that doesn't have the world's blessings quickly falls apart or intensifies into rare passion. But that one has to learn first.

"Love moves mountains," "love gives you wings." Such proverbs aren't exactly original; however, they describe the strength that love can set free. Every love is concrete and has its own character. Ours got me on my feet and opened a world for him that he hadn't known until then. Big words, but I can support them. His sensuality made me capable of love again. I awakened in him interests that had been unavailable to him until then: theater, books. My crazy desire for masculinity no longer hindered me from living.

After three quarters of a year I moved to D. For a year we lived without problems in his parents' house. Then I got an apartment and we moved in and still live there today. Most of our friends are heterosexuals, married couples, unmarried people. Because of this, we often are confronted with the fact that difficulties in our living together rarely had anything to do with our homosexuality but rather with the fact that two different individuals are living together. Sometimes a GDR yuppie will laugh at us and reproach us for desperately trying to maintain a life-style that heterosexuals have long exhausted. To that I can only reply: I don't know anything better, at least not better for me.

Heterosexual friends also say again and again: "Actually you're just like we are." I think that's only half the truth. It's only that way for those who didn't give up, who have worked through it and found a partner. But he is difficult to find if you live in a community with a thousand people, whether in the south or the north or in the middle of the GDR. As far as maintaining our love is concerned, I agree with them completely. There we have to apply the same method—to work on it. What that is concretely, both partners have to find out for themselves. Since we don't have children, we have to perhaps be more creative.

Well, and what if . . . ?

I would be a doctor, would have a family, a different circle of friends. My homosexuality forced me into confrontations at a time when others were still living unquestioningly according to the Communist party slogan from the late sixties, "Faster, further, higher." Even back then, I had lost faith in the belief that socialism would overtake capitalism.

Interview completed 1985

VI. Theodor and Dieter

Introduced and translated by
James R. Keller

In translating the two interviews with Theodor, I encountered two different people. In the first interview, in 1981, he was only eighteen years old; in the second interview, he was twenty-four. Theo's language changed significantly in those six years, and this change itself indexes his development from an East German adolescent to an East German man. Hence these interviews serve as a kind of seismograph of the evolution of a gay identity from 1981 to 1987 and thus provide a window into the coming of age of a great number of other young gays in the GDR.

As an eighteen-year-old in the first interview, Theodor looks back on the four years since he took a field trip with his class and for the first time really became aware of his homosexual attractions. As he describes those adolescent years, the account is of a difficult and painful gradual realization, accompanied by alternately tragic and hilarious ritual travails—known also to this translator and probably to many readers. Theo candidly retells the epic: the discovery of intensely interesting graffiti and the public restroom scene (in Alexanderplatz, the main square in East Berlin, perhaps known to the reader from Alfred Döblin's novel and Rainer Fassbinder's film); the first time in a gay bar and the disco silliness; the problems with parents and the visit from the woman psychologist; lying and chasing after girls in spite of it all; perking up ears when the "topic" is mentioned; and, finally, the mixed emotions of excitement and fear in the subculture, ridicule of overtly effeminate gays, and the growing importance of friendship for him.

Theo's situation is at once typical and unusual for a young gay man in the GDR. The desire to move to Berlin, the only city in the country with more than one million residents, is common to many. Theo grew up in a small city quite near Berlin, and his sister also lives in Berlin now, not far from him. Theo's constant references to the apprenticeship years show the importance of training programs for East Germans who do not attend the university and the integral part the workplace has in the daily lives of trainees. On the other hand, an occupation in the restaurant business is rather desirable, especially in Berlin. Moreover, a position as waiter has relatively high social status because of waiters' power in allowing customers into often overcrowded restaurants and bars. And the restaurant to which Theo often refers, and where he eventually got a job and still works today, is the Opera Café located on the main central-city thoroughfare, Unter den Linden, across the street from the Eternal Flame to Victims of Fascism and scene of the weekly changing of the guard.

In the second interview of 1987, there is a more mellowed approach to life expectations. At home and work, Theo says, he has reached a certain equilibrium, but he still wonders how important that awareness of being settled actually is. He claims that being gay makes him no better and no worse than the others, just different, and that aphorism can serve as the rubric for both of his interviews in this collection. At another point, he tells of never having thought of suicide, contradicting what he had said six years before. Here the entrance of AIDS into the consciousness of gay men in the GDR may be apparent; AIDS chronologically separates the two interviews. In the second interview, Theo alludes to it with slight caution in his assessment of what it is like to be gay now and what the future holds for gay men. The beginning of a discourse on AIDS in the GDR was accompanied by other liberalizations, including a general opening to the West. Many young people applied for emigration visas, Theo's acquaintances among them (and in the fall of 1989, Theo himself would apply). One former lover Theo describes lives in the West. It is well known that in applying to leave the GDR before 1989, one of the major reasons listed by young men was that they were gay and wanted to live in the more openly gay atmosphere in the West. Concerning AIDS, however, GDR authorities handled the crisis much less hysterically than most Western countries.

These two interviews are revealing to us because they show how Theo— GDR resident, waiter, young gay—has a unique perception of his own past, a strikingly familiar view of his present and future (at least until he reaches forty), and a homosexuality probably defined by us, the West. There are differences in conceptions of sexual identity between him and us: for example, there has been very little commercialization of homosexualities in the GDR. Yet gay East Germans, especially those in Berlin, know much about the West through frequent contact in bars and restaurants, and through West German television and radio. For Theo, his personal sphere has become most important for coping with daily life, and a telephone is a necessity indeed, along with a relationship that has to "click." For me, the act of translating became a reacquaintance with someone I know (quite well, in fact), correspond with, hope to meet again, and know will "make it," in spite of it all.

My second translation, of Dieter's interview, begins in the present, as he describes his life with H. and how their relationship revolves around having free time for each other; the next third of the interview presents the long process of Dieter becoming aware of his homosexuality (which lasted most of his lifetime, until age thirty-five); the last part tells of how Dieter found H. again later in life and of their pleasant domestic existence since then. Translating Dieter was a very different experience indeed: he comes from an older generation than Theo, was married for seven years and has two children, and was convicted under sodomy laws that existed through the 1960s. His homosexuality is quite different from Theo's and that of most younger gays. Moreover, I do not know him personally, which made the process of translating more detached and more similar to a case study than an interpretation of testimony. Finally, Dieter's many career changes, his moving around, and his childhood spent in an orphanage make his life experience vastly different from Theo's and my own. However, this account is probably more representative of East Germans who grew up directly after the war and thus is valuable for decoding a homosexuality different from the one that structures Theo's identity.

Dieter stresses the concepts of masculinity and femininity more than Theo; he views himself as a masculine man who "wants to live with a man." His main goal in life is apparently to arrange a domestic existence most optimally structured according to certain expectations of monogamy and permanence. Dieter perceives the family as *the* "seminal institution in socialist societies," which is interesting in that the GDR has one of the highest divorce rates in Europe, three times higher than West Germany's. Dieter seems to view his homosexuality as a variant on fulfilling the role socialist society has set for him. The history of growing up in an orphanage and having been convicted for practicing homosexuality would substantiate his need to feel that way.

The American reader might be puzzled by Dieter's obsession with vacation time, coinciding time off, and scheduling shifts. In the GDR there are certain allotted vacation locations and times for many workers, and the East Germans pay keen attention to this aspect of their lives. In addition, the stores, as in most of Europe, close early or have short hours, which can create problems for couples in organizing time off together (apart from time shopping together).

There are similarities between Dieter and Theo that deserve comment and suggest differences between life in the GDR and the United States. Both interviewees recount a story of a woman colleague at work who tells everyone about the gay man next door. This unusual coincidence may be only chance, but I was interested in how the break room seemed to serve as a forum for feeling out the ways that the workplace set the parameters of acceptance there and, by extrapolation, for society as a whole. The break room I know from working in American factories was different, in that most fellow employees discussed what was in the newspaper or sports, for example. Unfortunately, both Dieter and Theo felt uncomfortable and realized the impossibility of discussing their own loves after these comments from workmates. Only now, at age forty, does Dieter finally feel secure enough about himself in his relationship with H. to be more open in the work atmosphere—something I imagine to be cross-cultural, East–West indeed.

In sum, it appears that Dieter and Theo are more determined in their homosexualities by their respective ages than by any other factor, be it ideological, familial, or life-situational. The age or generational difference is also very obvious in American and West European gay groupings. Of course the backgrounds of the two cannot be overlooked either: Theo grew up in a family headed by a civil servant; Dieter was an only-child orphan who views the Soviet Union (at least its hospitality and film culture) positively and is less questioning of the "system" in general, interested instead in creating a pleasant domestic life. Perhaps the reader will recognize himself or herself more in the one than in the other speaker. But at least the translator hopes to have conveyed an idea of different life conceptions and values, patterns and goals, of two gay men in the "other" Germany that might provoke new reflections about possibilities and constraints in our own society.

10. "I am not a banner waver"
Theodor, born 1963, waiter

In the summer of 1977 I went on a school field trip to the Baltic Sea. That was four years ago; I was fourteen. At the nude beach there, I caught myself looking somewhat unwittingly at nearly every man, mostly older ones.[1] The first one I saw I rather liked, the next one not as much. I became conscious that I found men more attractive than women, as far as their build goes, you know. I didn't think about it after that. At particular times I caught myself staring, and immediately thereafter my thoughts went back to what was going on at the moment, whether that was playing volleyball or teasing the girls.

I had already had sexual adventures with men in my dreams: I woke up in the night drenched with sweat—yes, that really happened. But try putting things in perspective at that age! Who can do that?

The graffiti in the toilets at the train station worried me. I studied the scribbling. Never once did I read a book so attentively as I read that. Each time I started sweating and ran out, until I simply decided to try it—I wanted to know—but by then I was already sixteen.

I let myself be picked up by a guy, went with him, and it happened. After that I felt miserable. It was as though it was written all over my face. Now everyone knows, I was afraid. You cannot imagine what kind of thoughts raced through my head. Sick, degenerate, degraded. For days I went around confused, until I figured out a reason for myself that relieved me somewhat. That was pubescence, not really so bad since your classmates also did it with each other. I thought I'd grow out of it, I'd turn out like the others.

It was a hectic time. I desperately tried to get the girls. Even though I was not very direct, I wanted to sleep with them right away. I wanted to prove myself, and it worked, at least well enough for me to feel okay for a while. But as soon as anyone said anything about the subject, I was terrified and perked up my ears to listen in more closely. This lasted for one year, and then everything fell apart. Something happened, and I was back to where I'd been the year before. Totally confused and bewildered, I went through it all again, severely reproached myself again. But one thing helped me through it more than in the year before: my certainty that my desire was much stronger than I wanted to admit to myself.

I hesitantly headed to Berlin. The worst of it all is the feeling of helplessness: you cruise along and have to realize that not even those you do it with want to talk with you about it.

The web of lies began in my second year of apprenticeship. I was at the age when everyone goes nuts, and when someone has an experience, they usually blow the story up a lot. In telling my stories to people, I presented the guys I met in my time off as women. Followed by looks of amazement. Who meets at least three women in one week? But I was only lying in one detail: I made the men into women. Whatever could have given the truth away was left out.

Now I'm in my last year of apprenticeship, and it's difficult for me to hang out with a lot of people my own age. I feel more grown up. I can talk with them, not that I feel any more intelligent, but when we fool around during break, or when I listen in on their discussions, there's an unmistakable difference: they're simply not up to my standard. I feel more mature. It makes sense. I move with a different crowd, I've done a lot of things—not all good, by the way—that they couldn't have done yet. Gradually, the boys hooked up with the girls, and I cut myself off from them more and more.

At home everything was much more problematic. Of course, my parents noticed how I had changed. Whenever my mother wanted to start a conversation with me, I'd cut it short and mumble. The greater the distance between us grew, the better I felt, the more she suffered, the more aggressive I became. At that point, my father had no idea at all what was happening. I intended to keep them both in the dark. Every now and then I brought a girl home, acted it out in front of my parents, as if whenever I wanted to go into town, I was going to see her. I even did visit her for a short while, and then I beat it.

Somehow I was able to keep everything under control, or so I thought. Until one morning the doorbell rang. I was taking sick leave and still in bed. I went to the door with bloodshot eyes because I'd been out all night, as always, and I opened the door. In front of me was a middle-aged woman dressed in the most chic, now look. She said, "Good morning, I am Mrs. Meyer, marriage and sex counselor from the state counseling service. I would like to speak with you. Your mother has told me that for the time being you are on sick leave." To which I replied, "With me? You want to talk with me?" I knew right away what was going on.

"Yes," she answered, "your mother called me. In her despair, she didn't know what to do next, so here I am." Actually it was a polite request, so I politely let her in.

I hopped back into bed and grumbled at her, "Go ahead, shoot, but please make it quick if you can, I don't feel well at the moment." She blabbed on like a broken record, "You can't do this to your mother, stay out all night, at your age, run around, and with men like that, what will become of you?"

I propped my chin under my right arm, looked at her like I was ready to bite her head off and said, "Thank you for your offer, but this would go over better with your grandma instead of me. She might even listen to you. Goodbye, there is the door!" I rolled over onto my other side and refused to look at her anymore.

That might have been rude, but it was a way of deflecting it all away from me. The slightest criticism and I immediately showed my claws. Whenever my mother started saying "Boy, you can't do this to us, we didn't raise you so that you would sleep with men," I would holler back, "Leave me alone, your bitching is getting on my nerves, beat it, you make me sick." I would get really offensive, insulting, downright mean. She would burst into tears, and in my rage I would add one more punch: "Get out, if all you're going to do is whine." At that moment I went ice cold. After she'd left, I felt terrible and sobbed into the pillow. Actually, you are right, I thought, why are there men and women, after all? But what should I do about it?

I couldn't get it together and would have just as well done myself in, really. I've considered that often.

At home, in my familiar surroundings, I constantly cut myself down; in Berlin, I shot off like a grenade. I turned more and more promiscuous. That definitely has to do with the fact that in the meantime I had become convinced that with this orientation, I would surely never reach old age. Those are real states of panic. You go for it all; you want to get something from life before it's all over. At times I was really a pig. I would pick up a guy, demand a fifty, and then dart real fast around the corner, leaving him standing there, or else do a quickie, pull my pants up, and split without a word! Today I can only laugh about those things, and that wasn't even two years ago.

But I really didn't know any better. I traded in a brand new pair of jeans for black satin women's pants, forced myself into them, and then pranced out onto the "fashionable boulevard." Crazy, but I really and truly didn't know better.

As a young man, you are open prey. They're hot for you, let's say for your fresh meat, at least most of them. They get involved with you, but really it is just a fling and they leave you again. Because they are afraid— sexual offense with minors and such. So scared they're ready to shit in their pants, they won't invite you into their apartments, and when they write down their telephone numbers for you, they're usually wrong. Or they whisper to you, "Wait until you are eighteen, and then . . . " But actually that means wait until you are human. Less than eighteen and you're a dangerous monster for them.

Yes, I was used and thus formed—for all I know, deformed. At home I told them I had a girlfriend in Frankfurt/Oder and, because it was so far from here, her father picked me up in his VW Golf. Surely no one believed me, but I kept insisting, stubborn as a mule. My mother looked at my new jeans and my stylish leather jacket and only shook her head. I screamed that the girl's father bought them for me. If you don't believe me, ask him yourself, he's sitting down in the car. I served that one up ice cold. For me these things were the world. Eating in the best hotels, racy cars, on the weekend off to Budapest, high life.

Our environment is homophobic, certainly. Clearly, we are discriminated against. Hatred of gays is par for the course. The average person reacts aggressively toward us. I noticed it among my colleagues at work. If we pass by one of those conspicuous gays on the street who is real queeny, then it starts up immediately. "You should castrate that sow" is the way they talk. It's not meant quite as seriously as it sounds, of course, but it is still said, and pretty often. Whenever the topic comes up, I listen in very closely. They must get these ideas from somewhere. They're not innate.

I imagine myself calling my colleagues from work together during a break: "Listen, I'm not interested in women. Those were all lies I told." Oh boy, that would be pure terror. As much as I can, I suppress dealing with this animosity toward gays because it depresses me. I would rather not hear it at all. I think what I think and I go on. As a single individual, I would fuck myself over if I would admit it while I'm still an apprentice. It could be that I'm not the only one at work, according to statistics definitely not, but that's only on paper. The fact is that no one at work is out. And I'll continue on like this, all that revelation stuff is not for me. I am not a banner waver.

The prejudices come from there not being enough explanation about it, but also because there's a lot of history connected to it, the Nazi era, the church. I am not surprised that the masses see things through blinders; they can't help it.

I'll give you an example. An older colleague moved, and as chance would have it, a gay lived across from her at the new apartment. She came to work the next day all upset and burst out, "Imagine, my God, that is amazing, in the new apartment, on my floor, there's a gay man!" She looked around the table, as though Dracula personally had met her. The others chatted among themselves: "A gay, really, what does he look like, how does he dress, does he have a high voice?" It was a zoo. One of them asked, "How were you able to detect it so quickly?" "Yes," she answered, "I was warned when I signed the lease. The person responsible for people signing the leases lives on my floor, and he told me."

No one thought that it was indiscreet. Everyone agreed that it's a good idea to be warned about someone like that, the earlier the better, you just never know.

I didn't say anything, I have to be careful. If I had said something, I could have gone ahead and said, "Me too." Sometimes I act cool and mimic the laid-back type, sort of like this: "What people do in their own beds doesn't interest me." And some agree, as long as they think it's a man and woman.

Weeks later this colleague told the same people, "You remember my neighbor, you know, the homosexual who lives on my floor? By the way, he's really helpful. If I'm not there, he helps my mother with the shopping and carries coal for her from the basement to the apartment. Actually he's not really so bad." The other women sat up, put their sandwiches down, and looked at her. Their looks betrayed their thoughts: there must be something wrong here, what was she saying?

She insisted, "Really, he's quite nice." The other women were speechless. They looked at each other crestfallen, picked up their sandwiches, and continued chewing. The conversation ended. I think that's very typical for our situation. Only someone who is gay, or who knows people that are, really knows what's going on.

Gays among themselves are a completely different story. When I picture the scene in this way, then my hair stands on end. Really. That the straights say things about us doesn't surprise me at all in those moments. When I'm at Alexanderplatz I observe the situation, of course. There are guys standing around there, at the johns, for hours, the tips of their shoes soaked through. Looking and cruising with great devotion and perseverance, as if under a spell. The older ones kneel on the slimy tile floor and give blow jobs, others masturbate like crazy; no one is there to go to the bathroom, and if someone comes in who really has to go, no one pays any attention to him. That's normal.

In the bars they aren't so nice among themselves either. They hardly stick together; they put each other down. When I stood in front of such a bar for the first time, my heart was pounding, and I didn't dare go in. By the tenth time I went in. The first thing I noticed: as if on command, all heads turned toward the door. All through the room there was a nervous twitching, I was sized up, appraised, like at a meat market, at least I felt that way. My ears were ringing, and I walked through the place as if in a trance. I thought at any moment I'd fall to the right or left until I saw the door to the toilet; I knew that was my rescue. I went in and breathed a sigh of relief, luckily I was alone. I looked in the mirror and thought: everyone is waiting for you to come out. Another deep breath and then I'll be back in the ring. I felt like a zombie. I focused on the exit and had to leave. I ran the last two meters.

Sure, the excitement passed. I understood what the scene is there. Yes, first of all, gossip: he's going with him, they are together again, that surely won't last long, he's gotten fat, rather like that. A meaningful conversation never comes up.

The bargoers are wound up. So many gays at one spot makes everyone nervous. They chatter superficially, always face in the direction of the doorway, and expect something. At Opern Café the people are always seeking approval. They always have to show up. It is like an obligation. You are "in" when the daughter of Dr. Whatshisname greets you and the nephew of the ambassador, one really ought to know them: only people who are truly "in" go there.

Opern Café is rather like a fashion show, and woe if you fall behind in that beauty race! Jeans with braids, jeans without braids, stonewashed jeans, dyed hair, undyed hair, tennis shoes. Everyone agrees: you can really only go to Opern Café to be seen—where else?

Presently the disco show reaches its climax with "Rain, rain, rain," you know, the disco hit. I get goose bumps just thinking about it. Three guys stand in front of the disc jockey in a pose, raise their right arm in the direction of the rain clouds, steer into the cigarette smoke and plea for rain, singing and dancing.

One of the three calls himself Amanda Lear. I visited him once at his home. Amanda is all over posters, record covers, stickers, wherever you look: Amanda. He was really silly: observe her index finger, the way she forms her lips, isn't that wild, look. And then he demonstrated it to me.

When I came out of the bath, he was lying naked on his imitation bear rug, pointing his finger at me, wiggling his little bottom and moaning: follow me, follow me! It might be that most of them go there to be seen, not to find a friend. I go there now and then. I am not a regular and don't want to become one either. I imagine I have figured out the subculture. I know my way around, know what to make of the people. A permanent friend is out of the question for me, and I haven't found one yet either. The kind you meet there are ones I just can't approach. It is not a matter of their appearance but rather their behavior that gets on my nerves. This bad way of drawing attention to oneself, so la-de-da, you know, then I am all clammed up.

I don't know whether I could make a partnership for life work out. I cannot stand being regulated and controlled. I'd like to be able to come and go as I please. Right now there are two people I see from time to time. I like to see them, I know what to expect and don't have to put on airs. I can't expect, with that one there it's got to work out, with him I want the great big event, indeed right now. I suppose one grows into a relationship without doing too much or too little. Forcing things never works. When I think of the couple I know, those so-called stable friendships, I would rather just forget the whole thing, because if it means setting an example or living an ideal, I'd rather remain alone. On the other hand, I tell myself I'll never get to know those with whom it could work, they never go where I do.

B. recently told me: love means that it has to hurt. Just wait, there is no hurry. In the next few years, I won't start a family, I won't build a house, I'll see. I am curious enough.

As for relationships with people, I would really like to learn more. I include a lot by that: my parents, the other apprentices at work, the adult colleagues at work, and the men I'll meet. I know where the problem lies. I want to give you an example. When I'm interested in someone, I feel ridiculous, I have the feeling I'm becoming pushy and my deepest desires keep me from courting a man. Making out in public, so common among straights, seems strange to me among men. When I see two men making out with each other I feel embarrassed, and I say something. Without saying something negative I can't watch. That's not normal. I would like to be together with B. for a whole week; maybe I would see things more clearly after that. Perhaps I would have the courage to tell him that if I were drunk; at any rate, I couldn't tell him sober. But it shouldn't be that I first have to drink in order to do what I want to.

Interview completed 1981

That was six years ago? Oh boy, that is a long time, I was eighteen, six years is a long time. What do I think when I read through it now? That is the way it was. I've told the truth. I remember well, that's how I started, my first steps. Sometimes I have to smile, the next five lines hurt. Oh well, now I am twenty-four and feel it. This and that spot is still there, less hair in front. I have become more careful. I don't go right to bed with just anyone. Not only because of AIDS—I expect more. All that excitement— those days are past.

I think I have found a good mode, I mean, how I have organized myself. I have a job I like, earn good money, am financially independent, and rely on nobody. Today I value other things much more: friends, traveling, now and then culture. Senseless running around is not for me anymore. I no longer have the endurance. If I stay out for the whole night it takes me three days to recover. After the third large beer I begin to see double.

If someone had predicted six years ago that I would work at Opern Café, that high-class place, I would have said they were crazy. Now I work there. A lot has happened, in private and in my career. At that time I was still in training and working on the conveyor belt, then a few years as a sales-man, six months taking care of senior citizens, and now here. I am working where I can earn the most. I'm not extremely materialistic, but money is nonetheless important. My needs and wants have increased. Being a waiter is hard work, but not monotonous.

You work with people. Some are nice, others unpleasant, but at least it isn't working at a knob, dial, or switch all day. Studies are no measure for personality, I mean, the way I define it. A simple person often knows more about what is going on, is more open and more real in his own way than a person with a degree. That has to do, of course, with my expectations. I tip my hat to people who spend their lives behind a desk and perform hard intellectual labor. As people I am indifferent to them; they seem dry to me. I wouldn't have the zeal, I have always been easily distracted, and I also have problems concentrating. Such bookish types don't interest me in the least. I rely on my experiences, and I don't mean by that that they might not have some qualities that I value—it's not that—but maybe it is just that a streetcar driver can more easily deal with being gay than a professor. At least here in Berlin and in those cities with streetcars. I don't know about other places.

I also think that I could have taken a different course the last six years.

Without B. I wouldn't have gotten to know these people, he wouldn't have influenced me, I would have had different experiences. Maybe I would've hung out, not done anything; in an extreme case, I might have become antisocial—that was possible. I consider it pure chance that I fell in love with B. and he with me. Still today I consider B. the most important person in my life. Actually he was my mentor. He influenced me, and I still miss him, although the separation was well over two years ago. The experiences I had with him, that we had together, they live on in me. It was a happy time, very pleasant. This or that misfortune was also there; on the average, though, it was great. I still have snapshots from that time, and I often think of him, but I must look forward and can't run back, nor do I want to. I live in the here and now.

As long as I can remember I haven't had such a good conversation partner and lover. Someone like him I haven't found again, at least not yet. Most of the time they are one-sided affairs: if we didn't talk, we made love, or vice-versa. I have to have an impulse, in some way be inspired, then I talk too; I rarely offer my own words. In our conversations I sorted out what I thought was important, what would be of value, what I wanted; then I got really enthusiastic and worked on getting it—for example, in my relationships with friends. From B. I know that friends are important; a group of friends replaces the family for us. But one has to work on getting close friends. A normal guy of my age automatically has a family on display with the marriage license. Of course that can backfire. People are not forced on us, but I think that finding a good group of friends is the hardest thing for a young gay man. You can quickly end up in a bad group.

I have friends and know people I like but I don't value highly as friends. I associate with them, go out for a beer with them or to the movies, but that's about it. With friends you don't need an occasion; you just regularly meet with them.

Sure I make compromises; without them nothing goes smoothly. That is something very important I've learned. One thing is for sure: we have to learn to deal with society, not the other way around. Gays who don't realize that are dreamers, and if you don't make your own "power," you cannot be helped. It's not easy for me to be the motor. Energy alone is not enough; you have to learn that too, I think. I notice it in relationships between men my age and younger men. I could image a relationship like that—why not?—but I could never play the part of a daddy. Actually I am really lazy, and if someone came along who is twenty years older (like B.), I would run into his arms and get the warm fuzzies. Assuming, that is, that it "clicks." I felt quite comfortable in this role without being childish. Maybe I need a few more years until I am ready to be the motor in a partnership again. At the moment there is only enough for me and not for a second.

Having a partner is not the most important thing right now. My motto now is: wait a bit and look around. In my relationship with B. I was quite the troublemaker. Among other things, there were a lot of fights. I don't mean to make excuses, but I was inexperienced, stupid, and curious. I approached people like a young pup and . . . yes, I felt trapped, I mustn't allow myself to be chained down. After work I wanted to go somewhere for a beer or two, or into a café, visit with people, without having to report home. I hate it when everything is always planned or has to be agreed on first. Of course it is always harder for the one who sits at home and waits, but I am that one too sometimes. Last year when I tried to make things work out with K. it finally became apparent: I flip out when the other one waits in the front hallway with a stopwatch. I don't have any breathing room. If I came home an hour late, I was given inquisitive looks. "How could you?" I listened to the nonsense and thought silently: tonight I'll be spared from one hour of television.

The rest of the problem came from having too many material needs met. If I had said I wanted green pants tomorrow, he would have moved heaven and earth to get them. With B. we never had money at the end of the month, yet in spite of that we still did more. We went across Bulgaria, without a car, with a backpack, unsure of a room for the night. I was usually the one who got upset. B. would just straighten up and march on, head held high, like Mother Theresa. Five minutes later my complaining even got on me, and I shaped up. I could really talk to him, from deep conversations to vulgar chatter.

When I moved out from K., it was clear to me whom I had lost, and yet I wanted to leave because I wanted to liberate myself from limitations and pressures, even if they were pleasant ones. It was important for me to break off the relationship with K. after several months; I still believe that today. He was a great guy, but I don't want to hole up in a luxury apartment and collect objects. I get turned off by economic games, I laugh at wealth, I am not dependent on a car and a house, I want to live. At least once a month I have to get out of Berlin. When the sun shines, I go to the lake. If I feel like going to Weimar, I go to Weimar. People are more important to me than a bank account, and at twenty-four you can't have both.

Whoever wants to get along with me has to have similar views: that is a prerequisite. In graphic terms, if I have twenty marks left in my pocket and I know that a visitor is coming, I go shopping and don't worry about saving.

My parents learned a lot from my sister. They were invited to her parties along with my friends and me. They know who my friends are, and for years Mother has asked about those she likes; she doesn't ask about the others.

We are on good terms again, but open? No, I would say not. I don't talk about the topic, I would feel silly telling her: "Hey, yesterday I met such and such a person . . . he is like this or that." If she wants to know something, she should ask me. I won't start it up.

It makes her a bit sad. I avoid it too; I don't want to talk about it because deep down it still bothers her. Sure, she accepts it, in her way, but she is generous about it only because I am her son. Perhaps she is only waiting for me to let her know more about my life; that is possible. We talk a lot about my job; she is happy that I am moving ahead in my profession. We have a common language on this topic. For her it is important for me to advance at my job and to have good friends.

What should she advise me? Try to remain human, make the best out of it!? She cannot say much more: what would she base it on? My problems are not the same as my sisters'. Father knows that I am the way I am. Up to now he has not said a word about it. He is very discreet and avoids the topic. Our relationships have improved since I have moved out of the house.

Everyone knows at work. I am accepted because I do my work, and I think I do it well. Sometimes I am motivated and at other times I am less so, just like the others. As an untrained employee I bring in profits, and that is all that counts. I am not the kind of person who relentlessly works myself to death in order to prove that in spite of "it" I am really okay. On the first day the head waitress asked me right off the bat whether I was gay. I replied with neither a yes nor a no, but, rather, simply shot back, "Why, honey, just so you don't get your hopes up?" After that she fell silent. At work I don't have any problems. I am at ease, a little joke here, a little joke there. If I were ever to notice that something was going on behind my back or against me because of my attitude, I would snap back immediately. The restaurant business is different from a large company.

When five waiters work at one cash register, the tab is totaled for all five together. Each of us throws every last coin we have in tips onto the table, and then it is divided between us. When your colleagues work with you at this level, you are accepted, whether you are gay, lesbian, or anything else. You have to be buddies. If someone is having a bad day, I take over two tables from them; and the next time they would in turn help me out. It is up to you to create your ideal conditions at work. Anyone who doesn't fall into the rhythm, and instead complains and acts stupid, is not accepted. All the waiters have to keep their own stations under control. If I do something wrong, then I hear about it from experienced colleagues, note the criticism, and don't feel attacked. I think about it and correct the mistake. In the end it is not a matter of the waiter himself, but of the collective enterprise of the whole place.

I am not too good to do the dishes when the dishwashers are gone and an extra hand is needed; I just roll up my sleeves and get it over with. If the people who clean don't show up, we do the cleaning ourselves and don't complain. But if I have to sweep the terrace, that's it. "What?" I say, "have I heard that right? I'm supposed to sweep the terrace? File a complaint, honey, otherwise I'll do it myself." There has to be a limit somewhere.

Next year I am in the training program. I am earning the waiter certificate through the adult training program once a week. Whether I'll work as a waiter my whole life I don't know yet, although at a good restaurant being a waiter can be a good job, not just a way to earn money. When I was a salesperson, I enjoyed my work too, but now I earn a bit more. The work isn't a piece of cake: twelve long hours on your feet is hard work, especially in the summer when the terrace is open. By the end of the day you are completely exhausted.

I have already worked several different jobs where I got along fine because I didn't become disappointed and asked of the others just what was demanded of me. I can judge situations well and I have a healthy bit of self-confidence, not exaggerated and not out of perspective, just quite normal. Just because I am gay does not make me better or worse than the others, I just live differently.

You ask strange questions! At forty, what I would like to have accomplished? A nicer apartment, not just the furnishings but more room, my own bathroom, here in Prenzlauer Berg, if possible. At forty I might need more money to sleep well at night. Now I do my best without. At forty I would like to have a bank account. I would like to be able to have a partnership for several years or at least be in the middle of one, and a job where I think that I'll work until I grow old. Until I am thirty I'll leave myself time to try out different things here and there; after that I would like to find a position where I can stay. It could be that I will be a night watchman or sit in a wheelchair—dead.

I haven't thought that far ahead and I don't want to either. Oh, yes, one more thing: I can't allow myself to get fat—no gay dares let *that* happen.

As far as other things go, I do not expect any spectacular changes. That will all just fall into place; everyone lives as freely as they are able to. I won't live to see the day when you can approach the one you find attractive out on the street in broad daylight, definitely not. We'll be dependent on our meeting places for a long time to come, and all gays will go there for their tasteless rendezvous, sometimes often and sometimes less often. In towns and villages they'll remain hidden forever; to be able to experience something they will have to go to the larger cities, even fifty years from now. I hope that it doesn't get worse: that is not such a far-fetched idea. After all, though, AIDS has not yet mowed us down. Hopefully it never will.

I refuse to be harassed by authorities anymore if I choose to live with a man, and if I am stopped by a cop at night in the park and asked what I am doing there so late, I answer, "I am gay."

My neighbors leave me alone. Those two people who give me funny looks, well, I think to myself that they always look like that, that it is their nature. I live really well in this city. I have never thought seriously of taking my life. After the rain comes the sun; if something isn't working out, I go and stand in front of the mirror and paint and smear, leave the house, and feel rejuvenated. Each day is a challenge, especially when you are gay. You can nose-dive a lot faster as a gay man because there are none of the safety valves that married life offers. There a lot is prescribed and determined by the rhythm of married life; I have to force things again and again on my own. A double life would drive me crazy. At work, nobody would be allowed to know; to each office party you would have to bring a front; you couldn't meet friends in the open—no way. I would rather not lie; it is too much of a strain for me.

I would advise each person to accept him- or herself and not to try three lives at once. Many fail at that and become resigned or worse. I can only laugh about those who fool their peers day in, day out, and are even proud of it. The poor loonies can't get it into their heads that everyone has known for a long time and has merely refrained from mentioning anything, out of tact. I don't play the hetero, nor do I wear a sign on my forehead proclaiming my sexual orientation.

There is a lot that could be done among gays. Instead of hanging out in bars, bored and waiting to be asked for the next dance, they should approach each other and talk to each other. Gays are masters at cutting their own kind into shreds, beyond recognition.

I refuse to yield to those pressures anymore and prefer instead to go out with a group of friends. It is not that I am afraid to go alone; it is just that I don't feel like standing in a corner, pretending that I could care less about anything or anyone. When I go I feel I have to be really in good form, incredibly at ease, and yet that is a kind of pressure too. At work I am much more comfortable because everyone knows about everyone else and game-playing has no place there.

Since I have gotten my telephone I can find out the latest news without even going to the bars. I call up friends or they call me and we talk about the latest gossip. A telephone is important, at least in a city as large as Berlin where it takes so long to get from one section of the city to the other.

It would be nice if things would "click" again. Love is the supreme, but it can't be forced; a nice romance is something I wouldn't turn down. I have two or three possibilities, but my pulse surely doesn't speed up when they arrive at the door. I say, "Hello, please come in. Are you hungry? Are you thirsty? May I offer you something? Do you have a problem you would like to discuss?" They simply stop by; they are merely there; sometimes we go to bed, but there really isn't much more to it. Yes, I still feel that it has to "click."

Interview completed 1987

11. "I'm a man and I want to live with one"

Dieter, born 1946, worker

There was nothing worse for me than sitting alone at home. When I was alone, I was lonely. Since being together with H., I've changed.

I no longer suffer when I'm on my own now and then for a few days. I know that he's thinking of me even when he's at his parents', or when our work schedules make it difficult for us to see each other. He travels home quite frequently during the summer months. His parents have a farm, and there's especially a lot of work to be done there in the summer. In the winter we live here in this apartment.

We both work in four shifts. Our weekend is decided by the shift schedule, not by the regular calendar like most people's. But a work rhythm such as ours also has its advantages. People who work a regular shift have to run to do their shopping either before or after work. I'm able to get my shopping done at a leisurely pace on my days off.

Nine months ago I was transferred to another shift because a shift foreman was absent. Until then, we, I mean H. and I, had worked in different positions, but we had the same shifts. Now he comes home, and I go. When I return, we have twelve hours together. Naturally I have less time for sleep. When the four shifts are over, we have a free day to spend together. That is his last and my first day off.

Whenever I come home from the night shift, I bring fresh rolls or cake home with me and we have breakfast together. If we can, we sleep until noon and then we spend the hours together until he has to go to work. Whoever has the early shift makes coffee and wakes the other one to eat breakfast together. The one who has the day off can then go back to bed afterward.

Every three months we have a few consecutive days off. I prefer to plan those days well ahead of time—he rejects the idea of long-term planning. The exception to this is the annual vacation. We are forced to plan for that because of how they allot vacation spots at work.

I know that we cannot live with different shifts permanently. The danger of missing out on each other's lives is great. Recently I reminded my division foreman that I want to return to my old shift.

After you've worked for a while in this huge factory, you realize that in order for the production to keep rolling you have to roll right along with it. That's precisely where the term "rolling week" originated.

No, I haven't yet reached that point: to go to them and say that my relationship with my friend could be jeopardized if I'm unable to return to my old shift. I'm not yet able to do that. But today I've come far enough to be able to answer anyone in my daily life who would politely ask me about my private life. Three years ago that would have been impossible for me.

I also want to return to my old shift because I felt better there. The whole atmosphere there was more pleasant. The conditions within a socialist brigade are damn important. Now when I meet a colleague from the old brigade, they ask me: "When are you returning? How's your friend?" I think they like me and need me. I was the dynamo of the collective. On the one hand, that bothered them sometimes. But then again, I was the spark.

They know that H. lives with me. They also know that he doesn't have his own apartment and has to drive a long way from work to home. We suspect that they all know about us. But we are not sure. That's nearly the same situation with the others in our apartment building.

I think I could count on a positive reaction if I were to tell people in my old brigade.[1]

Whenever his brigade had a party or outing, I was naturally invited along. My colleagues also invited him without even asking me. To them we belonged together. We never worried about what they might have been saying behind our backs. The important thing was that we were together and could have a good time. Unfortunately there are no more good parties with my colleagues on my present shift.

Sure, there were hints. They live together, go shopping together, there must be something up. One of my colleagues once confided as much to me. At that time I was unable to speak about my sexual preference. I just listened and that was all.

You can't take so seriously what colleagues say about gays at work. In a twelve-hour workday, there's bound to be a lot of talk. Gay jokes are always popular, and whether a pop singer is "like that" or not is of interest to everybody.

I feel that this topic is too much for them, that they really have no idea where to start. And how should they? No one has enabled them to deal with it. And not everyone makes derogatory jokes about us gays. When a colleague starts in on one of those types, you can also hear other workers say: leave him alone, each to his own, some are one way, some are just different.

For our colleagues it is not an issue anymore that we go on vacation together every year. That might be because we constantly alternate driving. Last year I drove him, and this year he is driving me. It dawns on people that during the winter he cannot drive back and forth so many kilometers by motorcycle every day. So he stays with me. And whoever lives together in the winter should be able to spend vacation together in the summer. Now that's pretty obvious, isn't it? It could be that many people need a crutch to guide them past bothersome realities.

On another shift there is a lesbian couple. One of them is very pretty, the other has more of a tough, masculine air about her. People joke about them, but not because they live together. Most men can't get it into their thick skulls that such a pretty thing could fall for a butch woman, something to the effect that she would be so much better off with one of them.

Then there is the gay man who lives in the building of a woman colleague of mine. "Our gay," she begins each time before letting him have it. "Our gay" takes care of the house duties and works on all sorts of stuff. He really needn't bother. "Our gay," then she looks each and every one of us in the eye at the breakfast break, "most recently he repaired the hall light again." "Our gay" seems to be quite mechanically inclined. Surely none of us in the break room would have thought that. Knit and dance well, indeed, even cook well, but a handyman? That was surprising. Therefore they had best not comment on this latest bit of enlightening news.

I can't really say much about the people living in our new apartment complex. Most of them work at the plant. That makes us all close somehow. You end up saying hello to each other after you have boarded the same shift-bus to work for some time. Early in the morning at 4:30 one might say something about the weather. It seldom leads to anything more. The only ones who really have something to chatter about are the young girls. Surely, though, only until they get married.

On our last vacation we made the acquaintance of a young married couple. They live only ten minutes from us. We were a great group. During the day we were together at the beach; in the evening we socialized in the motorhome. When H. and I played the flute, they crawled out of their camper and came over to ours. After two days we came out to the young couple. It turned out that they had already suspected as much. When a forty-year-old vacations with a young man, then it is either his son or his friend. And when they both go jogging in the same kind of T-shirt, there's no mistaking.

It's possible that problems might arise from the age difference. Until now we have been able to solve all of them. I've also lessened my demands. I've come to accept not receiving an answer when I touch on the question of the next day off. He just doesn't want to plan ahead. He feels that the workday offers enough regularity. I don't force the issue because I know that I upset him with my Prussian thoroughness. After all, I *do* want to keep him.

You know, I am a person who has difficulty holding things in. When something is bothering me it has to come out, otherwise I suffocate. It doesn't matter whether that is at home or in the work collective. As soon as it is out, I already feel better. If I could only be more patient I would accomplish more. At home and at work.

Initially I was perplexed whenever he tried to convince me that nothing bothered him, nothing at all. I sensed his troubled mood and couldn't accept it. Ten times I asked him and ten times I received the same answer: it is nothing, really nothing. Instead of waiting I became angry and hurt him. I got all worked up, became louder and louder, and he increasingly closed himself off from me. We were both better able to deal with things when we learned to compromise. He must simply learn to deal with certain situations on his own, and I have to learn to control my moods and not demand that he answer me right away.

And something else. I can give praise, but for him it is very difficult. When he came home today, I was in the middle of dusting. He comes in, looks around, and comments, "You missed some over there." I know he doesn't mean to sound angry, he just is that way. And it hurts me. I had, after all, only slept four hours after the night shift. I am repeating myself, but it's very important. Being considerate of the other is the key.

H. permits me to let my feelings out. Before, I would have had a guilty conscience whenever my feelings even began to rise inside me. I owe it to him that suddenly I am experiencing emotions outside of the usual range of feeling—emotions I had up to that point only felt at the movies. They range from anguish when he arrives ten minutes late on his motorcycle to physical satisfaction to that good feeling of being busy in the kitchen while your loved one sits in the living room and knits. Yes, he enjoys knitting, but he enjoys equally as much working in the garage on his motorcycle. From our relationship I have quickly forgotten that the masculine has to be hard and the feminine soft. There are activities that are pleasurable and ones that effect the opposite, namely, boredom. Just what is typically masculine, typically feminine? I would say that too many clichés hinder us: that is typically masculine.

Our household chores can be easily assigned. The one with the most convenient shift does the shopping for those few days. Balancing bills and mailing things off is my job; he does more in the kitchen. Our finances are never botched. I write down every expense and keep exact records. I have to calculate very carefully because I am also paying for my two children. I do the laundry, since I don't mind it as much as he does. By that I do not mean, however, that he never touches the laundry basket. Our work schedule demands that we be flexible at every chore.

What does masculine mean for me today? Ten years ago I would have given an easy reply. Masculinity affects me erotically—when I see an athlete on the racetrack, for example. I find lanky, sinewy men very attractive—also outside the sports stadium and in a three-piece suit. You know, what my friend looks like. Of course, in addition to these physical attributes there must be personality and views that are acceptable to me.

Brutal, hard, aggressive, dominant: these only fit for a few men. It will not be long before these characteristics are not attributed to men alone but instead to all characterless people, whether men or women. I am a man and I want to live with one. His appeal is not lessened by cooking, knitting, or crocheting.

H. is the center of my life, and I hope that he will be for a long time to come. It's difficult for me, but I also have to allow him his personal freedom. I had to adjust to being his first real relationship. He should remain autonomous; this also holds for experiences with other men. We do not reproach one another if one of us sees someone else. We belong together, and as long as we love each other, we know how far we can go.

Neither of us is desperately looking for another man. Since we usually socialize with other couples, there does occasionally arise the possibility of casual encounters. I think that is relatively harmless. My jealousy sets in as soon as I notice that someone wants to separate us. Then I naturally step in. I could not change his mind if he would want to leave me. Who has security when it comes to love? I am convinced that this freedom keeps us together better than pressured attempts to stay together. We really do not have a violent marriage. A secure bond, with distance. Those are his words.

I will also not be able to talk him out of going home in the summer. His family needs him there; besides, my new "standardized" apartment at that time of year can hardly compete with a large country yard. I go with him whenever it can be arranged.

Yes, H. is really the center of my life. What then was going right in my life before I met him? When I was released from the orphanage at fourteen I was a weak, sickly boy, whom the strong ones had trained to bow to their whims. The boys my age were always a head taller than I. All of them had girlfriends; no girl wanted me. I was constantly teased. Before going to sleep I would secretly undress, and when the group went to the communal showers, I hid myself. Everything about me was so small that I inwardly agreed with them when they predicted that I would never become a real man.

In order to be accepted I played the class clown, and during group games I always volunteered for the thankless spots. Secretly I hunted birds, prepared them and stuffed them, and proudly displayed them to our class leaders at the dinner table. They accepted them and then proceeded to smash them against the wall in the corner.

My mother was an aunt to me who visited me now and then and brought things along for me. The more the better. I did not know my father. He was with the Soviet occupation troops. Today I say that the Soviet Union is my fatherland and the GDR my motherland. I'm serious. I feel very attached to the USSR, and trips there are always a great event for me. The people's hospitality there appeals to me, and I like their simple and direct ways.

As a child I was proud of the fact that my father was one of those who had liberated Germany from fascism. When our orphanage took a field trip to the Soviet Memorial in Berlin–Treptow, I explained to everyone with bright eyes, "The one standing on the top is the brother of my father."

As a child I was deeply moved by Soviet films. I'll never forget the film *The Secret of Two Oceans*. In the movie there is a father figure who brought me to tears. The films about Makarenko also stirred me.[2] I saw myself in them. The whole Timur movement I held dear to my heart: a community of people, living for each other, with one another.[3] My ideal was stated best by Ostrowski: "The highest thing that a person has is life. . . . "[4] Later I wanted to become a male nurse or a teacher. To be there for others, be accepted and loved by them, I imagined that to be wonderful.

I was not unhappy in the orphanage; I did not long for a family either. I was only unhappy because I was not accepted by most of them since I was too insignificant to them. I suffered a lot because I wasn't given enough affection. Sometime, I thought, that would surely change—later, when I wouldn't be overlooked anymore. My great longing for people and love was not diminished by this experience, not at all. If a man had come along, like the fathers in my favorite films, and made me his son, I would have gone along with it. On the spot. Both of the men my mother married were not to my liking.

After eighth grade I left the orphanage and moved in with my mother. Her second husband had indeed adopted me, but he never really accepted me, probably for the same reasons that made it so difficult for me at the orphanage. After tenth grade I went to study agriculture. During the week I lived in the boarding school; on the weekends I was at my parents'. This was also the time of my first experience with a girl. It ended in catastrophe. She could only laugh hysterically about my shy and awkward approaches. Shortly after that I was caught masturbating and had a bucket of cold water poured over my head. In panic I hid in a barn. I felt terrible and was convinced that I would be forced to quit the apprenticeship. I didn't find out until days later that the boys had played a practical joke on me.

I could have finished my apprenticeship, but I was physically too weak for further work in agriculture. So I started to work in a warehouse in a large plant. There I met F. He was a lathe hand and showed up three or four times a week at my distribution center. A friendly relationship developed between us. He was the first adult who respected me and accepted me as a whole human being. I was happy. It led to sexual contacts, but he was not ready to devote himself entirely. Sometimes I was permitted to rub his body from top to bottom with suntan lotion and more; on other days he wasn't around for me. When everything was going well between us, I was happy and felt secure; when he withdrew I felt terrible. In the end I became such a bother for him that he broke the relationship off completely.

I didn't know what to do, cried for days and felt deserted. I was alone, all alone. At home I had problems as well. Mother had decided to side with my stepfather and was always supporting him. Thus, on a whim, I packed my things in a bag, boarded the train, and went to Görlitz. I decided on Görlitz because an aunt of mine lived there. I got off the train and knew I would never return home.

On the way into town I stopped in front of a poster. It advertised employment for the large new energy plant. Instead of going to my aunt's I went to the work crew department of the plant. I immediately got an assignment to the employees' apartment building and started the next day as an assistant boiler attendant. I wrote to my former employer and quickly received my release. By the way, F. has been living together with a man for many years. We see each other every now and then.

Before long I had become qualified as a boiler attendant. I was a hard worker and had a positive attitude. They were impressed by my work, and I was elected as a functionary in the Free German Youth club. Now I really hit my stride. I had earned enough trust to get a socially responsible position. Me, of all people, that little wimp. I dove into my work, and after just a few months I was delegated to the city of Neu Brandenburg for further training.

I enjoyed my time at the school. All around me were young people with whom I could talk about things, sometimes all night long. Life with young people really appealed to me. I forgot all about the bungling with F. and my parents at home.

Shortly before the end of my training, tragedy struck. A classmate attempted suicide. During the investigation things came to light that had been going on. I had befriended him, but he was in love with someone else. He wanted to kill himself out of lovesickness. In his desperation he told everything. That included that there had been intimate contact between us. We were told to break off our studies and made to promise never again to have homosexual experiences. Out of fear we agreed to everything. In my files it says, "Termination of studies due to health reasons."

I went back to Görlitz and was employed for several months part time as the director of a youth hostel. Meanwhile I had also become a member of the Communist party, the Socialist Unity party. As director of the youth hostel I took care of everything and constantly strove to make things as pleasant as possible for the guests. Mostly I had young guests, but older people also ended up in youth hostels in those days.

I tried to make things happen there. Just one example: each group had to sing for the others at least once. Upon their arrival I told them: "Here it is customary to prepare two or three folk songs." In the evening before retiring, the windows were opened wide and we had singing competition between the groups. The highlight was a song sung in unison. In addition to the official guest book I had my private guest book. If you like you may page through it.

I lamented to a married couple from the city of Neurupin that my days as director of the youth hostel would soon be over and that my one desire was to study education. They spontaneously asked me to move in with them in Neurupin. I could work whenever I wanted to in the husband's business, and if I stood the test the plant could possibly delegate me for a position to study to become a teacher.

I didn't need to reflect long on the offer. In Neurupin I worked for the civil engineering department and as a truck driver. I was certified for various driver's licenses, and I had acquired yet another during my apprenticeship at the agriculture collective. After just a few months, however, I was stricken again with ill health. I had overworked myself. Although I'd recovered physically, I didn't have enough energy. I was offered a position at the archives and accepted. I had already accepted my fate when one day my host stood before me, beaming and smiling with the letter of acceptance for me to study education. I was accepted. Me, the failure.

My promise, never again to have homosexual contacts, was something I had broken in the meantime. In the youth hostel I had already had several occasions for that. My time as a student was one of the best times of my life, and yet as early as then the patterns were set that led to my gravest mistakes. My grades were good. The classes were interesting to me, and I learned quite easily.

When one studies education, one of the oldest and most important claims of pedagogy is drilled again and again: setting a good example is crucial to being an effective teacher, a tested and well-proven theorem. I was also aware that the family is the seminal institution in socialist societies. All of these were good reasons for me to begin the search for a wife. I did not feel I was a homosexual; thus I was able to fulfill my intentions without a second thought or a guilty conscience. Moreover, I was already twenty-six, and if I intended to be successful in my occupation, then it was time to marry. Said and done.

I got along quite well with one of the girls in my seminar. We could make it together, as they say. Without much ado I asked her to be my wife. She said yes and I was relieved.

The marriage was official, but not actually consummated. I had been assigned to work on the preparations for the 1973 World Games, ended my studies prematurely, and left for Berlin for several months. I wrote her flattering letters in which I told in detail about the city and my activities. There was surely no real desire for my wife in those letters. When I returned home to her after the games, she explained to me that she had met a man in the meantime who was in love with her. I was at a loss to respond and immediately agreed to the divorce. We had simply made a mistake with each other. It happened like that to many young people. But I still had no idea about myself.

I had little time to dwell on the situation, for I was drafted into the army. I was divorced and felt right at home in the all-male environment. I did not have to forget my wife; there was nothing to forget. I was a good soldier.

In those eighteen months I received more awards than in my entire life up to that point.

After my time in the service I met my second wife. I literally married her away from the speaker's podium. I was impressed by the way she argued and in discussions rigorously attacked petit-bourgeois stances. I was a Communist, and the fact that she was also a Communist was obvious. After the roundtable there was a dance, we got to talking, and I immediately noticed that she was a good conversationalist one-on-one as well.

I was not really in love. She became pregnant, and I wanted to marry her. Today I know that it could not have worked out between us. The mother-in-law had hoped for someone with higher social standing for her daughter, so she went on the attack against such an insignificant teacher as myself. My wife constantly picked on me. I attributed that to her pregnancy. When she lost the child, I felt guilty. I finally came to the realization that I was not a fit husband. Yet compared to a drinker or a man who always lies to his wife, I wasn't bad. Now I know that a woman gets bitchy if she is never embraced or when she discovers that her charms and overtures don't knock her husband on his ass.

She became pregnant again, and when the child was born, I felt relieved, downright rehabilitated. Now I was a real man, with wife and child. It did not matter how the marriage would work out, the main thing was that I was now a father. And for those around me I was finally a man like all others.

Unsatisfied as we both were, we threw ourselves into raising the child and struggled bitterly for his favor. What would be more natural for this situation than a second child? On vacation on the Baltic Sea I ran up and down the beach with my son. It was a kind of showing off. My wife lay in the beach chair, and everyone could see that she was pregnant again. What was really going on behind the scenes was something even I would rather not have known.

The sexual aspect was forced into the background more and more by both of us; I delved into my work so much that in the evening I was completely exhausted. On weekends I invited colleagues over from work and acquaintances, if only to have men around me, regardless of whether anything happened or not. Two years ago a proverb from a calendar fell into my hands: "The years petrify into lost time." With a jolt I knew that this was the motto of my seven years of married life. A life like that is hellish.

She testified to the divorce judge that she had caught me with another man in our apartment. And that was correct. After the divorce she had it arranged that I was not allowed to visit the children. That made everything clear to me. The reason: a father like me damaged the children in their development. I shall never understand why there is still such an arbitrary law on our books. I am still permitted to pay child support, of course.

The payments were a burden in the first few years after the divorce.

Now I just become upset when I think about it. How can I know what she is doing with the money? Who can tell me that it is being used for the children's welfare? Naturally I am quite curious about what the children are doing and about what will become of them.

I was convinced that I was at fault for a long time after the divorce. Today I don't view myself as guilty. It was my environment that had taught me to abuse my sexuality because it devalued anything homosexual and denied it as unnatural and illegal. And women who for years play along with us also become victims of the official morality. The fact that I learned so late must be because I am not very perceptive.

I got to know H. in the dormitory where I worked as a teacher. We liked each other at once. I tried to be around him and told him about my children. Later he admitted to me that he only listened to my stories so patiently because he wanted something more from me. He was seventeen years old and I was his teacher—two reasons for keeping the hands above the bedcovers. Soon our conversations turned to his approaching eighteenth birthday and his completion of the apprenticeship. We both waited for that without ever mentioning what that meant. But even then I did not believe I was homosexual. I associated filthy images to the word. Homos: to me, they only chased after the male organ, hung out in public restrooms, and acted effeminate. That wasn't me, not like that!

My relationships with men were platonic, friendly, and clean and proper. I enjoyed being around them. In a circle of men I felt physically good and sheltered. I went to the movies with them, played cards, or partied. I liked men, and when THAT even occurred now and then, I felt best. But friendship was in the foreground, and tenderness was like the dot on the i. No reason to consider myself homosexual. I was never drawn to the meeting places of homosexuals. I always avoided those whose proclivities were obvious at first sight.

When I was eighteen I had observed them at one of their meetings, together with a friend of mine as we looked at them through the window of my mother's apartment. We were convinced that those people were criminals; there were organized things going on there; they had to do with money and prostitution. We chased one of them on our motorcycles, the one we thought was the ringleader. He was faster in his car, but we took down his number and reported it to the police. We thought we had caught a dangerous pimp.

All those feelings mentioned above ended at once: my marriage and my friendship with H. I was tried on paragraph 151 and sentenced to several months. I would rather not repeat the whole story. The bottom line was that, based on the psychiatric test, I was informed in writing that I was most certainly homosexual. I was duly recommended to admit it to myself. I had to wait thirty-five years and receive a written confirmation to finally comprehend my own feelings.

After serving time I had two wishes: get away from my wife, in other words, get my own apartment, and find H. again. I was completely unhappy. He had entered the service in the meantime, and I was probably going to get my own apartment. There was hope after all. When after several months we met in front of the plant gates, H. was so horrified that he avoided me. He did not want me anymore, looking like I did. I was outwardly and inwardly in a pitiful condition. He left me standing, hopped onto his motorcycle and called after me, "I'll give you a call." Weeks later the call came. We set a meeting time, but he didn't come. In my desperation I drove to his home. I was obsessed with the certainty that everything would be through for me if I could not win him back.

His family knew me and had always treated me in a friendly way. I talked with his mother the entire evening while he looked at me. During the night I found the opportunity to finally get everything off my chest. The next morning he told me he would try again with me. Things were looking rosy for me. He took me to a clothing store and bought me an entirely new wardrobe. He ruthlessly threw away my old, unerotic clothes from my married years. He paid attention to my diet as well, and soon after that I got my new apartment. So we spent our first winter together.

His love for me developed with my emotional recovery. He wrote poems of joy, which he later gave me to read.

In my love letters I invented names for him that I'd never before heard or read. Whenever he went home in the summer to his parents' farm for a few days, we exchanged cassettes in front of the plant gates so we could listen to each other. One side of my tape would be for his family, the other side for him.

For each member of the family I taped a musical greeting and then read or said something personal. For him, I compiled a program made of music and stories that occurred to me whenever I was alone in the apartment and thinking of him. Before going to sleep we would listen to the suggestively erotic tapes, each one alone in his own bed. . . .

I am a person who loves to dance. Whether at parties for our brigade or at home, my legs pulsate and want to dance whenever I hear good dance music. I can't control myself while dancing. I let myself be carried away by the melody and move the way the music stirs me. In public that sometimes created a scene. A dancer, a gigolo—he must be gay. When I am dancing, such names never hurt me.

I'm not a woman-hater, but when dancing, a woman is for me only a dance partner. But when I dance with him, there is a resonance there that makes dancing a real experience. I can dance in both directions equally well, but I like to lead, because I feel the music so strongly, not because I like being the man. We dance often in our apartment. Wham-bang, we put a record on and off we go. Whoever is in the mood takes the lead and whirls the other through the room. Three, four dances, then we're quiet again.

I'm telling you these insignificant details so that you understand that H.

is the center of my life. From this center, I then view the other important tasks of life: my work, my function in the brigade, and whatever else there is to do. At forty I have finally arranged my life in such a way that I can say, "I am happy." I could also work again as a teacher, but I don't want to anymore. In the next few months I must definitely try to get back into my old shift again. We really miss time for each other. If I had more time I would also like to work again as an interpreter of sign language. That job was really enjoyable. I also would enjoy singing in a choir or dancing in a folk dance group.

Interview completed 1985

VII. Nicholas and J. A. W.

Introduced and translated by
J. D. Steakley

These interviews with Nicholas and J. A. W. are, I would submit, among
the most provocative and significant texts in this entire volume—an as-
sertion that may well strike some readers as a trifle exaggerated or perhaps
downright unfair. After all, they might argue, are not all men, and thus
all interview partners, created equal? Furthermore, is it not the very aim
of this book to document the remarkable diversity of male homosexualit*ies*
under socialism by assembling testimony from the widest possible range
of gay men? And if all that is so, how could one have the temerity to rank
any one interview above any other?

These objections are plausible enough, but consider for a moment the
history of the project. The typescript that Jürgen Lemke originally submitted to his East Berlin publisher contained not fourteen but twenty-four
interviews. In the best of all possible worlds, all twenty-four might have
been published, creating a tome considerably thicker than the present volume. In the really existing world, however, Lemke and his editor performed
triage on ten interviews that they jointly deemed expendable. The texts
that make up this book were arrived at by a process of elimination, a
powerful counterargument to the proposition that all interviews are equally
important.

The process of sifting and winnowing could be and indeed was extended
even further, as evidenced by a second circumstance. Just a short time after
its release, this book was adapted for the stage by Uwe Hübner and, under
the direction of Vera Oelschlägel, *Men's Biographies in the GDR: I Am Gay*
was premiered on January 14, 1990, at the Theater im Palast in East Berlin.
Lemke collaborated closely with both Hübner and Oelschlägel, and ultimately they found it expedient to reduce the fourteen interview subjects
who people this volume to just four dramatis personae. Of the two following interview subjects, Nicholas survived the cut.

As the sole interview partner who bluntly declares that he would prefer
to be straight, Nicholas gives voice to gay self-hatred in its most succinct
form. The internalized homophobia at the core of this self-hatred goes hand-
in-hand with Nicholas's blatant misogyny; and indeed, how could it be
otherwise? Alas, this unpleasant brew is anything but unique to socialist

society and is familiar enough to us in the capitalist West. One senses that Nicholas's gloomy outlook on gay life will be changed very little by German unification.

Nicholas's tone of outright despair is supplanted in J. A. W.'s account by utter resignation. A muted, more mature tone may prevail, but it merely serves to shroud a profound melancholy. J. A. W. has the distinction of figuring in the original East German edition of this book in two roles: as interview subject and cover artist. He created a stylized, rather somber portrait of a pensive young man split down the middle into halves and capped with what appears to be a child's make-believe soldier cap crafted out of a folded sheet of newspaper. On his right half, he is clad in a stiff, vaguely Prussian military uniform, while on his left he is decked out in a clown's costume, whiteface, and a heavy application of mascara.

This image tellingly captures the split in the collective biography of East German gay men, the uneasy balance between double lives that they— along with their Western counterparts—have typically been obliged to lead. Apropos of the military uniform, it might be noted in passing that gayness per se has never constituted grounds for dismissal from the East German army, the NVA; with single-minded devotion to conscripting as many able-bodied young men as possible, NVA authorities have generally been willing and even eager to overlook an individual homosexual soldier's orientation as long as his serving did not diminish troop discipline and morale. In a broader sense, however, the cover figure's uniform symbolizes all forms of accommodation to the pressure to conform, to pass as a "real man."

The role of clown or fool, on the other hand, is one for which gays have long felt a special affinity. The name of a pioneering American gay rights organization, the Mattachine Society, revived a medieval epithet for a type of court jester whose serious jokes held up a mirror to the foibles of contemporary society. In nonaristocratic circles, the clown has traditionally functioned as the butt of rude humor, a brightly colored freak who is secretly crying behind a painted-on smile.

Yet after having devoted so much effort to decoding the cover illustration by J. A. W., it should be emphasized that equal interest attaches to his interview. The narrative of his life and times is notable for, among other things, the central paradigm that he uses to construct his sense of personal identity. J. A. W.'s interview opens with a protracted account of the "first-class Oedipus complex" that developed from his relationship with his parents, one that fundamentally shaped his "destiny" as a gay man. It is in this context that J. A. W., almost in passing, expresses regret that he and his father "lacked a common language."

Had both father and son entered therapy, psychoanalytic discourse might have provided that common thread; but Freud's theories no doubt remained entirely foreign to J. A. W.'s stuffily proper paterfamilias. After all, Freudianism has been taboo during most of J. A. W.'s lifetime: disdained as scandalously salacious during the Wilhelminian era, attacked as Jewish gibberish under the Nazis, and repudiated as bourgeois individualism throughout the GDR's forty-year history.

The reception of Freud has followed quite a different course in Germany than in the USA, where neo-Freudian ego psychology has virtually attained mainstream status. In part because it has been so marginalized and suppressed throughout modern German history, psychoanalysis has come to exert a powerful fascination for Germany's gay intellectuals, whereas American gay liberationists have devoted considerable energy precisely to discrediting Freudianism or at least relativizing its etiology of gayness. Thus J. A. W. is willing to embrace a Freudian self-image and identity of the sort that American gays would be more likely to abjure.

In a sense, J. A. W. has turned out to be a dutiful son, after all. He has donned his father's "cynical and ironic mask," although it has taken on the peculiarly gay features of campy and bitchy humor. Behind the mask, he has lived a life of "frustration" and "inner exile." In his own way, he has upheld the respectability so valued by his parents, strictly omitting sexuality from relationships with anyone he respects or even knows very well, and confining his sex life to fleeting encounters in parks and public conveniences.

When I set about translating these texts into English, I found myself so dismayed by the outlooks and life-styles of Nicholas and J. A. W. that it (or they) began to worry me. Since the other interviews in the book were not yet available to me, I began to muse rather gloomily about the book as a whole, extrapolating from my negative reaction to the two interviews at hand. I'll admit to having felt some doubt about the editorial wisdom of publishing these two interviews and perhaps even about the project as a whole.

In retrospect, it's obvious that I should have known better. Two years earlier, I had heard Jürgen Lemke read and discuss other excerpts from this book at a gathering of gay activists in an East Berlin church. That encounter alone ought to have made me realize that Lemke was casting a wider net. But mulling over the interviews with Nicholas and J. A. W. in isolation, and contrasting their standpoints with my own more positive experience of gay life in East Germany, my reverie was suddenly suspended when I realized that I was grappling with the urge to censor and silence. All the while, I knew full well that the stifling of any and all discourses about homosexuality, be they by heterosexuals or gays, has always been the preferred ploy of homophobes. After all, homosexuality has traditionally been known as the "sin not to be named among Christian folk."

The perpetuation of that religious precept in a secularized but otherwise fundamentally unaltered form was one of the clearcut flaws in the failed East German experiment in socialism. In an amusing coincidence of history, the first East German feature film to deal centrally with homosexuality, Heiner Carow's *Coming Out*, was premiered on November 9, 1989. Exiting the theater, the moviegoers encountered streams of excited passers-by who informed them that during the preceding two hours, the unimaginable had occurred: the Wall had fallen. The joke that immediately arose was that the frank cinematic portrayal of homosexuality had caused the collapse of the state.

A final anecdote: immediately following the final dress rehearsal in East Berlin of the theater piece based on this book, Lemke was interviewed by an apparently all-gay TV crew working for the West German entertainment network SAT 1. The West German interviewer declared in no uncertain terms that he was appalled by the depth of self-loathing and internalized oppression he had just witnessed on the stage and indignantly challenged Lemke to explain the inclusion in his work of so many woebegone, even tragic lives of quiet desperation. Wouldn't all this negativity lead to an unduly poor image of gay life? And didn't the dearth of upbeat role models serve merely to bolster homophobia?

The TV interviewer from the West plainly wanted homosexuality with a happy face, gay gayness, a flattening and trivialization of the complex lives actually led by such men as Nicholas and J. A. W. But had my own reaction been so very different? Thus the following caveat is addressed to that TV interviewer, to the reader, and to myself: it takes courage to regard these tormented lives with the respect they deserve. But that is the only way to grasp the lessons they have to offer—lessons not just about the Other, about foreigners behind the Wall, but about ourselves.

12. "Every one of us is forced to reinvent himself"

Nicholas, born 1944, self-employed

Oh sure, I'm smart. It's just that I'd gladly trade in a little of that for some good looks. I'm like a woman whose problem is having too much brains and not enough boobs. Just a few inches more, and everything would be different. Quite different. Much less complicated, all at once.

You know, we gays are all neurotic, without exception. Granted, to varying degrees—one guy more, the next guy less. But we're all a little screwy. Even in this day and age, our biographies are one lifelong variation on the theme "We're only tolerated, and that's as far as it goes." And that's in the best possible case. We're shady characters, and we hang out on the wrong side of the tracks. The finishing touch is the way that what we do lacks any social consequences. I mean, the glue that bonds man and woman together. We have no set responsibility for a partner, no kids, no shared property, and—this is no joke—we also lack an awful mother-in-law. For us, there is no official acceptance into another clan. People can gripe about it as much as they like, but there's still no better adhesive.

The only thing left for us is work. There we're entitled. It should come as no surprise that the first impression we make on people is that we've never settled down, never arrived. I never have. We're constantly on the lookout, always on the edge of a neurosis that will flood over everything—at least in thought.

Everybody's struggling and dealing with it in different ways. The variations on survival extend from the harmless to the high-risk approach.

Throughout our entire lifetimes, our sexuality doesn't fit in, forcing us to waste the major part of our off-work hours organizing it. That shows up in lots of ways. We have to stay slim for day X, when we will finally meet that long-awaited knight in shining armor who'll whisk us away from this dreary everyday life to true happiness. That burns up a lot of energy, psychic energy. You'd better believe it.

Each and every one of us is forced to pull himself up by his own bootstraps and reinvent himself. I don't deny that some of us feel fine doing just that. Gay life in the fast lane, good times, no responsibilities—that may be a lot of fun for some people, but the day does come when the bloom of youth is finally gone, and then even they start to brood. Their laughter always sounds a bit hollow.

Social pressure is only one reason that we are the way we are, neurotic. Things inside us get all twisted. It's this peculiar linkage of primal male drives with elements of the female psyche inside us. That's the real tragedy in my opinion. Part of me is female, and I seek security in a relationship and need someone to take care of; yet on the other hand, I just can't keep it down. If it weren't for this gay horniness, things would be a lot easier. Women are drawn more to the entire man, his intellect, the whole picture. What does it matter to a woman whether he has a big one, or his nose is a little crooked? If at all, then only in a minor way. Man and woman will never have this problem: this exasperating comparison of bodies that men who desire each other fall prey to.

I think gay men heighten the ordinary difficulty of any two people living together by a factor of one more man. Just look at lesbian relationships: they survive much, much longer. But only because two women really reach out to each other. The external circumstances, the level of social tolerance, may change, but there will always be set biological differences.

"Scram, you boring twit!" got hissed at me years ago when I dared to pursue one of these picture-perfect gays. It was a blow, a damn hard one, but it hit the mark. For years I didn't want to admit it. He said what others were showing by the way they behaved: over there's where you belong!

And I did get it. I also realized that nature would have been kind if it had equipped me with a more pleasing visage and easily visible male attributes—instead of brains.

These days I hardly ever go to parties anymore. Anytime I do go, I'm always struck by the same thing. I notice how the people are carrying on, and I feel how much I stand outside of this noisy crowd. I don't feel superior; it's not that the people are beneath me, or that I see them as flaming queens I wouldn't associate with; not at all. I feel more and more like someone who doesn't belong to any group. Like an outsider.

I'll say it one more time. Nature didn't give me what it takes to ride the gay merry-go-round. I'd be happy to be doing it; as far as I'm concerned, it'd be fun to go bar-hopping or to go from one fabulous party to another.

Years ago, I used to criticize things—flamboyant behavior, for example. I'd think: how awful, how can they run around like that, you'll never in a lifetime catch me doing that. Sometimes I was so outraged I'd get rigid as a board. Today I'll go along with anything. I don't act that way myself because it doesn't do anything for me. That's the only reason I don't get involved. In mid-life it's easier to express in one sentence what preoccupies you for sometimes days at a time, driving you into a depression: I'm not getting the guy I want. To be more precise, I've never gotten him.

Ten years ago I held up this standard that my partner had to be so and so; this trait but not that one. My God, today I can only laugh about that kind of thing. Ultimately, all I'm interested in is getting some guy into bed who'll say: I think you're neat, and let's get it on for a while. Eight weeks or three weeks, it doesn't matter; maybe even just once. People to talk to I've got plenty of.

Nowadays I can distinguish between a physical and an intellectual friendship. Finding everything in one person is something I gave up on a long time ago. In all likelihood that's some kind of a childhood fiction, a dream. Possibly it really does exist somewhere in the gay world, but for me it was grasping beyond my reach.

Just take the latest party at C.'s. For me, it confirmed for the thousandth time that I do not belong. And gosh, the parties at his place are not the worst—actually they're the only ones I even go to anymore. At least there's a select group there, not these loud queens, no show-offs to speak of. Naturally I was interested in one or two guys; I'd have to be completely nuts not to admit that. It's always the same old thing. I go up to people, after five minutes they're getting restless, start looking right through me, and they're relieved when I leave them alone again. I'm sure other people experience the same thing, but I'm not the kind of guy who constantly says oh, nothing at all interesting here. That's pure self-defense. It's the way some people rush from one opera premiere to another, assuring each other how simply marvelous it's all been. Maybe I'd be better off if I had that pattern down too? Could be.

My hard-edged realism says to me: nothing works anymore! So at the party there was this young guy from L. A terrific guy, so sweet, a little on the boring side, the kind you have to liven up, a guy who wouldn't go after anyone unless he thought he was hot. At four AM there were still two or three guys circling around him. It was no use; he was immovable. Since the two of us were from out of town, we were allowed to spend the night there at C.'s place. So then I started making my move. I did get him, but actually he would have preferred just to sleep. That's a high price to pay. It's only as long as it works to some extent that you have the strength to bear an occasional rejection, like C., who goes after a guy with the outlook: hey, if you don't want it, you must already have it. I could never afford that attitude. It's a bit like in the animal kingdom. They can sense who's weaker. Like, here comes one who really needs it.

If I were the same as most people, I wouldn't get so worked up about things. Trick out and be done with it. But the way things go, I'm totally obsessed the next day with a thousand thoughts that all point in one direction: he wasn't really interested in you.

I assume you understand exactly what my position is, even more today than years ago: I'd like to be *straight*! Heterosexual!

As trite as it may sound, I'd give anything for it. I know I'd be able to develop much more fulfilling relationships in the straight world. After all, I am somebody. I'm not ugly; I'm not deformed either. I have a respectable profession and some brains. What I lack is a kind of body presence and the extras that gays just must have. Period. By the way, as far as my work is concerned, I'm not going to discuss it. I don't need even more people figuring out who I am.

I'll say it one more time: I've never gotten a person I wanted to have, and I've never been loved back. You have no right to dispute this; it's the lesson I've learned from my experience. Believe me, I'd much rather be telling you the opposite. I'm at an age where you start counting, and I ask myself, what real relationships have I had? None. Sure, in every relationship there are quarrels and hassles; it can break up in an ugly way, or end up in who-knows-what craziness. That's true both of straight marriages in front of the TV set and for gay couples out cruising. That's a different story altogether. There used to be many relationships based on mutual attraction. This appeal, this instinctual quality, this inability to pull away from each other: that's what an erotic relationship is based on first and foremost. You have to find the other guy and yourself exciting; you both have to want to touch each other. What it will eventually turn into will be decided later on. This later on has never happened in my life.

Take R.; we both know him. It's a fact that he can look back on two or three genuine relationships. His life has not been a series of humiliations. He's a Berliner, good-looking, has an inflated opinion of himself, and isn't all that deep. Put it together and it results in a charm that he's used to good advantage. At nineteen, he already had his first big love affair behind him, while I was living in a small town, tormented about my feelings for a straight work buddy. I was totally confused and acted so too. My kind fellow humans gave me to understand that I had a defect. The friendly ones expressed it somewhat carefully: something's wrong with the boy. Others weren't quite so tactful. As grotesque as it may seem, I silently agreed with them. Compared with others, I really did have a defect; but what was it? If I'd been able to get more information, I might have figured it out. As it was, I ran witless from one trap to the next. Yes, I would have been happier if I had managed to get some understanding of my type of feelings back then. At least I could have avoided a lot of mistakes in the following years.

R. has never once in his life thought about getting married. Why should he, anyway? At age fifteen, during one of those little pubertal games, his brother—two years older—said to him straight out: hey, man, someone could sure get the idea you're queer, y'know? A year and a half later, R. came out to his brother and got the response: hey, fella, I told you that a year ago, didn't I?

Don't get me wrong: R. has his problems too. How could it be otherwise? Ultimately he too is only tolerated, and he's gotten a few hard knocks. But plainly he had the better starting point. For one thing, he had the space that big-city life assigns to gays, and for another, he had a family that didn't throw him to the wolves. His mother cried over him the same way she cried over her teenage daughter's pregnancy, and she moaned about one more stroke of bad luck, but then she got back to business again. After raising eight children, this working-class mother brought up yet a ninth, and she stood up for her gay son.

R.'s father didn't say anything at first, brooded for days, and tried to blame himself. He felt a little bit better after his best friend at work listened to his story and then confessed that his youngest boy was also under a spell. And his buddy said: don't get all worked up; after all, you've got two boxers, and they're no runts. A week later he finally spoke up at the dinner table: don't you ever bring one of those fairies home with you! One of the boxer brothers gulped a mouthful of food and corrected his father: hey, it's even more important that he doesn't turn into one himself!

By now, R. is ending up where most of us do: in loneliness. He complains about the young people and, like me, runs around in clothes that are much too loud for our age. But he'll always have a plus in comparison with me because of those years when he lived almost like a normal person. I say almost, because at most, society grants gays passions—not love. Love is always bound up with letting it all hang out. Passion on the other hand doesn't need the entire person and tends to get hung up on superficialities: age, looks, muscles. After the first go-round, the passion's spent too. If R. talks about his past, it's always about the "good times." Compared with the fate of homosexuals stuck their entire life in some kind of marriage, he's had a heavenly life.

Far be it from me to idealize heterosexual relationships, but it is a fact that there even less attractive people have a chance to be loved. At least that's how I see things, although I often quarrel about it with M., a woman at work. We're good friends. At first glance we have a lot in common: born in the same year, both self-employed and somewhat successful; both divorced, one child, and looking for a male partner. There were times when we'd spend a good three days a week griping about our fate. Whoever happened to feel better at the moment would make dinner for the one who felt worse. We would feel incredibly close, drink to our spiritual kinship, and assure each other that the latest disaster had been predestined to turn out that way. And then at some point the sentence was spoken that brought us back to reality.

It went like this.

I say to her: No matter how hard I try, I'll never understand why you don't make more of your opportunities as a woman. After all, you can choose from half the human race, not counting children and old men, whereas I . . .

Here she interrupts me: Hold on a minute. You seem to be forgetting that the other half is made up of heterosexual men, self-centered, insensitive guys.

So I break into hysterical laughter and exclaim: The queers are all so nice!
She says: Good grief, let me finish! I don't want to live with the other

half of the human race, and you don't want to live with the four or five percent who are supposed to be gay. We're looking for that one guy, the needle in a haystack, the exception. And that's a dilemma we share.

Now I'm totally indignant: Wait just a minute. You can meet your exception any time of day and chat him up if you feel like it. Assuming you get moving.

She interrupts me: Stop giving me these statistics. You know perfectly well that I make my presence felt.

I say: Nowadays a woman can approach any man.

She says: Theoretically, yes, but in practice, no.

I say: At worst you're risking a rejection, while I have to reckon with a lot heavier artillery. And besides, you all can use the personals in the newspapers. We're just not in the same boat.

Wisely enough, we broke it off at this point and went to bed. The next morning, neither one of us really wants to remember what we'd said. So we eat breakfast silently in the garden and are a little bit ashamed. After all, we're beyond the storm-and-stress age. Since the weather's passable, each of us grabs an easel, goes down to the waterside, and paints in silence. Basically we aren't really into it; we'd much rather keep on talking about our favorite subject. But in a more sensible way, more objectively, without those statements you're ashamed of in daylight. So after a short while I call over: Well, how's it going?

Not too well, she calls back, and right away we're back together again.

We reassure each other that, fortunately, we're no quitters, that we can both put up with a lot of guff, and that overall we're doing just fine, thank you.

I feel our friendship is a give and take that's good for me. She can't quite figure me out, but that's due less to her intelligence than to the range of her own experience. I get touchy whenever she lumps my boyfriend worries together with hers and turns them into ours.

You know what really bugs me? When one of my concerned straight friends says to me: you're selling yourself short. Falling for some kid! What kind of guy are you anyway, messing around with these youngsters?

Sure, from his position he's right, and I realize that his concern is genuine. But he sees things precisely with straight eyes, and that means he's assuming a man in my position always has a choice. If I try to explain myself, all I hear is: there are plenty of choices, why do you have to go for precisely that type, you know what I mean.

There simply aren't enough gays. The human race does live heterosexually. Whether deep down it really is the way it lives is another question entirely. Any time I say that, my conversation partner jerks reflexively, and I sense that he's incredibly happy to be heterosexual. He doesn't say so, of course.

I know straight couples whose relationship also isn't working out, but even so they still aren't as unhappy as I am. Straight men are much more capable of handling career, relationship, and interests in their everyday life. Smart, well-meaning people advise me to focus on other things—life has so many wonderful sides to it. All this advice doesn't help me one bit as long as I don't have a boyfriend at home who's thinking of me and who comes home to me every day after work. Or for all I care only every other day.

I know, I'm a pathetic mess.

I envy people who can sit down and peacefully read a book. I'm immediately asking myself, why bother reading? I no longer think that learning is especially useful for me. Name a book that I could read with any benefit for my life, that could help me with my partnership problems. Max Frisch, Christa Wolf, or the modern Americans? All of them just point even more directly to the fix I'm in. What does it help me to be able to say, oh, right, that's exactly how it is.

This inability to get seriously interested in anything certainly results from that. Think of Stefan Zweig's famous novella, *Confusion of Feelings*. Everything you can say has already been said there. All of a sudden the professor can do something he's been incapable of his entire life—he dictates his book from start to finish to the boy. It's because the fundamental thing in his life has finally happened, the most important thing. Naturally there have always been a few great individuals who have created art from their neurosis throughout their lives. But at what price?

You're probably thinking I'm the queer with the typical victim complex, someone who would hysterically lament his fate even in the face of the most splendid sunrise, who's much too screwed up, and a person no one can stand to be with. Sure, sure, I notice that in your questions and in your face. You may not be giving me these trite hang-in-there slogans like my mother—"there's a cover for every pot!"—but in the back of your mind you consider me incapable of a real relationship.

Here I'm going to have to digress.

As a child I never wanted to stand out; I always wanted to be industrious and nicely modest, the way grown-ups told me to be. My mother, the teachers, and the minister. Be this way, do that, then everyone will like you. If I ever veered off the proper path, my mother called me naughty, the teachers called me disobedient, and the minister called me sinful. Before I went to school, my mother checked whether I had all my textbooks with me. And on two afternoons each week, she'd ask whether I had my songbook. On Tuesday she meant the songbook for the Young Pioneers and on Thursday the hymnal for religion class. Tuesdays I sang the latest Young Pioneer marches, and on Thursday old chorales. Caption: the education of a country boy in the postwar years.

My grades were just as good in confirmation class as in school. I got a little stuck-up when the schoolteacher suggested I aim at a career as a teacher and the minister tried to interest me in his vocation too. I got attention then especially because I was so good at drawing. Or copying, to be more accurate. Especially picture postcards. I was happy when my mother would hold my work closer to her glasses, tilt her head back and forth thoughtfully, and say approvingly: how do you do it? Just try to tell those apart.

I provided my entire class with gift cards for all occasions and got a lot of recognition for that.

My face was always pale and cheesy and, according to the school nurse, anemic. Anyone who came to our apartment would usually cast a concerned glance in my direction and remark: Hedel, you ought to give that boy some cod-liver oil.

And my mother, even a bit more concerned, would sigh: he won't eat any fat, and he reads too much, if you ask me. He'll ruin his eyes yet.

The message I got was: actually, he's to blame for everything.

The other boys were constantly running around outdoors; no wonder they had peaches-and-cream skin. Wouldn't you know that they'd be so different. I could draw and was bringing home good grades, but as for being a real boy—well, forget it.

The Nazis and their war had drilled people to obey any command and had filled them to the brim with fear. I think my generation absorbed a good dose of that with our mother's milk. Fear comes in many shades. My heart still pounds whenever I enter a government office, regardless of what I'm there for. In retrospect, it's become clear to me that up until about my thirtieth year I always reacted to events according to a pattern—confusion, fear, guilt. That applies to my experiments with girls during puberty, to my marriage, and to my first encounters with men.

My schoolmates also reacted to girls in a clumsy and confused way at first, but differently: they desired them, and the girls could feel that. I remained highly theoretical and prim. That was just fine for the first and second date, but after that, fear started creeping up the back of my neck, and I retreated. I considered myself a failure and felt guilty toward the girls.

Everyone became less and less able to deal with me. If I was confused, I acted like a hooligan; if I was afraid, I clammed up; and if I felt guilty, I got hyper because I wanted to make it up. Mother expressed it in her own way: this boy's getting stranger and stranger.

Her maternal instinct was sensing danger. She knew as little as I did what direction it was coming from. She didn't have a clue; and how could she have? It was the classic conflict between parents and children, ravaged by mutual ignorance: they stop talking to each other, because they can't. The consequence is that people stop helping and start hurting each other. The mother turns into a natural enemy and the son into a huge ingrate. The son wounds his mother, and if she defends herself, he's outraged.

Like many who can't work things out with the people around them, I fled into books and escaped into the movies. On Tuesdays and Fridays they changed the show, and regardless of what the movie was, I was there.

There was plenty of the things I was missing in everyday life—romantic love, suspense, everything that happened would make sense after ninety minutes. I especially liked the underdog who keeps getting the short end of the stick but who gets rewarded at the end. Or the ugly duckling turning into a swan, defying everyone's expectations. I developed a need for harmony that could switch into the maudlin and sentimental at a moment's notice. I escaped into dreams because I suspected that I'd never be able to satisfy this need with the people around me. I still haven't entirely given up this striving for harmony, but it has died down over the years.

On the silver screen, World War II was still in full swing. I would catch myself searching the faces of the soldiers for my father. For me, Father was the man in uniform in the wedding picture with my mother. Anytime I visited my friend from school, I was green with envy because he had a father. And he would just interact with his father so calmly and easily.

For my eighteenth birthday, my mother gave me the gold pocket watch with a spring-open lid that had been sent to her from the Eastern Front in 1944. Among the items there was also a diary that she now gave me to read. I was electrified. I read every sentence three times. Under June 18, 1944, he had written:

> I can't grasp it—I have a son.
> I have made a LIFE.

His handwriting. My father had written that, in blue ink. In my imagination I would picture how he was sitting exhausted in the foxhole, slowly opening Mother's letters, when he suddenly jumped up to tell his comrades the big news, beaming with joy. Shortly before going to sleep, he had made this entry. About me.

I was confused and upset. I asked her about Father, about guilt. She turned away and dried her tears with her apron. Guilty, not guilty—should he have let himself be put up against the wall? He was a good person, and that was how she intended to preserve his memory. Among the Russians too there were all kinds. Anyone who claims otherwise is lying.

My answer bowled my mother over: so what, he died anyway!

Youngsters who don't want to be driven crazy by older people react in a sweeping way. At school, I constantly heard about people who had resisted the Nazis and who had gone to their deaths without complaining. I was completely confused in my feelings.

In the meantime I had finished my vocational training in advertising. At work I was fairly successful, but on a person-to-person level nothing was happening. I tried to become friends with one guy at work. I forced books on him, movie tickets, and wanted to talk with him for hours. Right in the middle of a conversation he'd remember that he had to go to an appointment, and off he went. I'd go home, lie down, and read the next book.

After going to the movies once he told me he was going to send me a letter. That was unusual; I was so disoriented that I worried about the reason all night long. It had to be something exceptionally important, since people who are together at work eight hours a day and live not three minutes apart from each other don't write each other letters. And sure enough, that's how it was. In a blunt way, he informed me that people were talking about us and that we would have to end our friendship. What they were saying, you can imagine. And then something happened that is still mysterious to me today. I knew right away that someone must have told him I was a "fairy." I'm certain that I'd never read nor consciously heard this expression up to that time, and yet it existed in my subconscious and was immediately at hand. Okay, I was different from the others, but not a "fairy." In my powerlessness I had only one thought: I had to go to him and clear up the mistake; I'd never made untoward advances toward anyone, not even him.

Halfway to his place I turned around.

Naturally I had wooed him like a suitor, evident to everyone; the only one who hadn't seen what was going on was me.

At my office they were recruiting for volunteer service in the army. I said I was willing to go, and after taking the fitness exam I worried that they might reject me. Everything went okay, and in early September 1961, I left home.

Where I'm from—on one hand, that means the country I'm from, and then it also means the town where I spent my childhood. You don't consciously experience a feeling of home until you return there after being away a long time. I was back in my hometown for the first time after fifteen years, and my first impression was: everything's so cute and tiny. The houses, the street with shops, my bookstore, and the movie theater. I went into the bookstore, browsed in a few books, looked calmly at all the customers, and then my gaze was glued on a boy. I was certain he was the son of a coworker I'd fallen in love with twenty years earlier. I must have been just standing there in front of the shelves, uneasy and a bit depressed. I stepped alongside him, grazed him with my arm, and looked him right in the face. He looked at me, and at that moment I wished that there were less distance between what happens in books and actually goes on in people's minds.

As I went back to my car and sat down on the cushion seat, I wanted to get out of there fast. I realized that my hometown would have wrecked me mercilessly if I hadn't managed to get out of there on time. Back on the highway, I stepped on the gas like a maniac. Sixty miles an hour was too slow for me that day.

At age thirty, I'd reached a point where I was wondering to myself: is that all there is? Eight years of marriage, one child, a decent profession. Outwardly I was a presentable person, but on the inside I was at my wits' end. I would have been a treat for any psychiatrist. My wife was too, by the way. I'm not going to tell you any details from those years. That it lasted all of eight years makes no sense at all unless you take into consideration our provincial backwardness and the most self-destructive of my petit-bourgeois virtues: trying to please everybody.

Basically, we shouldn't have spent even eight months together. From the first day on, we were missing the most important thing—intimacy. How can there be any human warmth if one side is on hold and tolerates at most a hand on the shoulder?

During my university years I went on to have my first fleeting experiences with men. The meeting places attracted me magically; what I experienced repelled me. They were the only kind of encounters possible in those places. I was pulled in two directions at once and each time had the feeling: something awful is about to happen. I despised the types who didn't want anything from me anymore, and I myself had nothing more to offer from sheer terror. Back at home I was seized by a terrible hangover; I hated myself and felt guilty. Like a seizure, I was overcome with a need for harmony and order, and for a few weeks I was the model husband and father—until my next visit. This is that same triangle of confusion, fear, and guilt that I spoke of once before. What's crazy is that I didn't want to hurt the people I lived with, but in reality I was doing so. Including myself.

To put it crassly: I used my wife all those years in order not to have to live as a gay.

The collapse had to come. In the summer of 1973 we spent our annual vacation at the Baltic Sea. One sand castle farther lay a young man who was obviously interested in me. We got acquainted and walked along the beach for hours. I fell in love and was defenseless. After four days, my wife made the inevitable scene. I let it all out, and the next morning we left.

Three days later we filed for divorce. I spoke with Mother, informed my father- and mother-in-law, and in the written affidavit that accompanied the request for a divorce I named the real reason.

All it took was one sentence, loud and clear, and I was out the door. Everyone was thoroughly confused. From that time on, I belonged officially to a minority and was treated correspondingly. As an inferior. In contrast to C., I was delivered over by my kin to be shot down. Mother was fussing about damage control: for God's sake, do you have to trumpet it out to the world; it's already enough of a disgrace.

My mother-in-law was convinced that I had dreamed up the cruelest possible thing to torment her daughter. My father-in-law detected a lack of regret: you seem to be proud of your perversion.

I had done something horrible to everybody. Obviously everyone's first priority was to protect the mother and child from this monster. Of course, no one—including me, at that time—realized that the real monsters were located somewhere else entirely.

And there was no regret from me, no promise to try to change, just the stubborn sentence: that's the way I am!

Back then, I was basically just like the boy whistling in the dark forest out of fear.

My disclosure was an act of sheer desperation, not a conscious decision. It was a first step, and I expected that things would get better in the future. That was sure a big mistake. As for the guy from the beach, I didn't even have his address. And, in my new existence as a single, I still had to carry on a double life. I was searching for love and was coming upon people who were afraid of the light of day for fear of being found out. Thin-skinned as I was, I couldn't deal with that. I would go out every evening, as faithful as if I were looking after an aged grandmother. Rain or shine, come hell or high water, I'd meet J. I can still remember how we froze one time when it was zero outside. Afterward we warmed up at my place over a hot bowl of bean soup and bemoaned our common gay fate into the wee hours. Those we wanted didn't want us, and the few who were after us, we snubbed. They were either too old for us or too queeny. Between us there arose a kind of emergency support system. We agreed that our rational insights didn't help us one little bit and that our failure at the meat market was caused purely and simply by superficialities.

When I think of the huge effort I used to put out years ago . . . at my giant New Year's parties, for instance. . . . Only the cream was invited, good-looking and educated. Flaming fags were strictly forbidden to attend. The invitation list would get drawn up at the beginning of November, scratched out, put together again; for days the New Year's program would get worked up and rehearsed with lots and lots of energy. The queens would hiss: he's not inviting us.

Of course they did crash the party after midnight. God and all creation were there, picking each other up. The next morning J. and I, totally hung over, got to pick up a hundred empty bottles and clean for two days. Really, that's how stupid I was once.

Right now I can't stand having happy people around me. I get mean, cynical, and sometimes really nasty whenever I see a couple carrying on. Recently I canceled a barbecue in my backyard on short notice. Sorry, I can't stand your contented faces, at least not right now. At the end you'll sweetly leave with each other, and the next morning I can hear you saying on the phone: great time at your place again. Besides, I know myself: two, three drinks, and I'll start playing the clown for you. I just can't do it now, maybe next month. It's a shame that friendships suffer because of that.

I think I've reached a low point. I seriously wonder what the point of all this is. All that's left for me is putting the make on straight guys like some kind of predator. I'll draw a guy into my orbit, treat him in a way so that he gets to like me. All that works out fine to this point. They call me up and arrive from God-knows-where on their motorcycles: man, you're a cool guy, your records and everything.

But what's the point if the most important thing is missing? At some point they look at their watch and notice: hey, man, it sure is late, I've gotta get home to Katie. They don't understand why I suddenly turn nasty and cool and keep it short the next time they call up.

In the back of your mind lurks the thought that maybe someday some guy may really go for you. If I stay out here in my uniquely decorated little house, nothing at all will happen. I can't go wandering the streets every day, or hang out in those bars. I used to have hope, this instinctive hope that it might just happen today. I've also lost any sense of satisfaction that material things used to give me. A great car, a fabulously furnished house, super sound system, VCR. Then what . . . ? Nothing, that's what. Everything in place, nice and comfy, and that's that.

Everything is happening like in a movie I've already seen thirty times. You know that guy, and that guy; their faces confirm what you already know.

I see complete loneliness coming my way, and I hope that by then my soul will be calloused enough to survive.

Now and then a quiet voice speaks up shyly inside me. Toss off all these superficialities; live a quiet, modest life. Be happy that you've won back your child; be happy that you've painted three, four pictures that really turned out. I can hardly believe it—could that be my voice?

Interview completed 1984

13. "The harlequin and the faun"

J. A. W., born 1917, painter and art educator

Back in the early twenties, in the train yards of old small-town railroad stations, there were these upright rollers with hemispheric tops. They were made of solid porcelain, around ten inches high, five inches in diameter, and had red and white stripes. They must have been part of the signal system back in the early days of the railroad: guide posts for the engineers when switching tracks. I wanted one so badly. I admired it the way I now like my East Asian figurines.

One hot summer day, my father and I were out walking. Mommy had dressed me up especially nicely, in white overalls with embroidery. At the train yard I spoke my wish: I'd really like to have one of those!

Father nodded, much to my surprise. What I'd expected was a stern no, stuffily proper and reproving. All right, just take it, he said.

Was I ever happy! Giving no thought to my white overalls, I got down on the gravel and went to work with my little hands. It was no use: the thing wouldn't budge. Solid, top-grade industrial porcelain. I refused to give up. At the very moment I was given permission, I was unable to do anything with it. I was getting worn out and disappointed, so I looked to my father for support and . . . found myself looking at a bemused face. He'd been just letting me root around like a dog in a molehill.

I've never forgotten that.

From the vividness of my account, you may detect how much that incident still preoccupies me, even now, a good sixty years later. I'm not criticizing him; he was also intelligent and a good man. But what immaturity this behavior shows. He was relishing an easy victory over a small, helpless boy. But the victory had its aftereffects. Often I felt he was treating me like some little dog, something you like for being funny and cute, but you don't take seriously. Even when I was a university student, something as crazy as this could still go on: I was on my usual weekend visit home and was having a conversation with my mother. We read a lot of the same things and would talk about them. Father walked in, broke into our conversation, and dismissed me with one sentence: and what, boy, makes you think you have anything to say?

That hit like a pail of cold water. After all, I was a student of probably twenty-two. I stormed out, slammed the door, and was livid. . . .

Fortunately, he left my day-to-day upbringing to my mother. He probably realized that she was better at educational matters, more empathetic.

My mother and I were a unit from early on. She was a real partner and treated her children as having equal rights. From my childhood right up to her death, I was joined with her by a deep and close friendship. As a child I was quite naturally jealous of my father, and it wasn't long until the effect became evident: a first-class Oedipus complex.

Back then, I didn't realize that my father was also involved in my intellectual development and was closely supervising it from a certain distance, as was often characteristic of fathers in that era. Both of my parents provided whatever I needed and could somehow manage to integrate in terms of my development. I didn't even notice how supplies for painting and sculpting simply materialized within my reach. When I first showed an interest in art as a twelve-year-old, I found a book about Dürer under the Christmas tree.

My father secretly participated in my artistic experiments, but sadly from such a distance that no father–son dialogue ever came about. Not later, either. I mustn't hold back one thing, however: as a sixteen- or seventeen-year-old, I violently rejected his initial attempt to reach out to me because it made me uneasy. That connection was never made.

He died at an early age, and I didn't fully realize until decades later just how much richer our lives might have been if we'd ever managed to find a common language. He himself had grown up without a father and had never learned to show love to his children. He was jealous of them because they put a claim on his wife, whom he evidently needed very much. He hid his intellectual cultivation from me behind cynical remarks and an ironic mask.

My father was born in 1885 to a teacher's family in the old town of Thorn on the Vistula River. He was entirely a product of late nineteenth-century Prussia. As a state-employed civil servant in the customs division, he quickly reached a financial level to sustain a family. With a government-backed pension, of course. The total security and reliability of the civil-service hierarchy was the credo to which I was born.

On a material level, we could scarcely bear comparison with the average craftsman. The modest level we lived at is unimaginable today. But the Prussian civil servant knew how to compensate for a small income with a cultivated bearing and social dignity. The bookcase of such a family was a good measure. By the way, even today I still regard a person's bookcase as the best indicator of his character. Not his bank account, or even his car's horsepower. I learned at an early age that culture is not primarily a matter of material outlay, but rather of intellectual and personal pride. It's interesting that the German language still separates the concepts of culture and civilization.

Self-control, a dignified bearing, sublimation—these were required of me at an early age, but they were also modeled in a way that gave them credibility. The sex drive was curbed by education and channeled as much as possible into other interests. Young people were supposed to get plenty of outdoor exercise, to postpone sexual gratification until later in life. I believe that this is one of the reasons I survived during the dangerous years from 1933 to 1945.

I was born in 1917. By one full year, I'm still a part of the lost German Empire. It's curious: I was one of the last to be enrolled in "One-Year Insurance." You have no idea what that means? Prussia had created the so-called One Year for the sons of its indispensable civil servants: a single year of military service instead of the usual three—an institution that, in its own way, helped divide society into upper and lower orders. In 1918, when Germany became a bourgeois republic, the One Year was done away with. Up to then it had existed as a privilege. One Years were to the manor born: they slept in separate quarters and were largely spared the indignities of military service. After cleaning weapons, regular recruits had to show they'd washed their hands before they entered the mess hall, whereas the One Years could walk through unchecked.

You could only become a One Year if you had reached a certain level in school: promotion to the senior level, which ended with the university admission exam. That cost money—tuition money—which the "lower" orders were able to raise only in exceptional cases. As a rule, the "simple boys" would enter an apprenticeship at age fourteen in order to start earning money as quickly as possible.

Yet the One Years had to cover all kinds of living expenses themselves, and they also had to pay for their expensive uniforms. Since this was beyond the means of many civil-service families, a fine and practical institution came into being: an insurance policy. If a newborn son of a civil servant promised to be sufficiently fit, his parents could enroll him in the One-Year Insurance.

Later, anytime I'd complain about the rough times in the Labor Corps or in the service, my father would remark dryly and tersely: well, One Years didn't have to worry about that.

In 1937, I took my university admission exam. It was grotesque when my final German literature teacher, a Nazi by temperament, replaced the classics with texts from Wagner operas. I couldn't take him seriously, and I was unwilling to parrot that vacuous Teutonic babble with its overwrought wording. It took a long time for me to develop anything like an unbiased relationship to Wagner. Concerning the Hitler Youth, I once stated publicly that I was not going to join "that group." That worked out rather poorly. A gang lay in wait for me, surrounded me, and beat me up.

Like my parents, I despised brutality and thus also hated those brown-shirted big shots who puffed themselves up so much. They were the antithesis of culture. We regarded them as preposterous, yet they soon turned out to be horribly real. We viewed what was happening without comprehending, flabbergasted: this can't go on for long—that's what we were thinking and hoping.

You know, the preconditions for being homosexual were evident in me from early on. Those around me figured out earlier than I did that I was different from them. I didn't see it; I didn't realize it for a long time. As a youngster, I was often faced with people who laughed at me. I lacked a military bearing, didn't march as smartly as the others, couldn't handle a soccer ball properly. If anybody joked about the oddness of my way of walking, the others around me would smirk knowingly. I lived in constant fear that they would take me for a fairy, and that before I even knew what a fairy was. This was one of the most wrenching and crucial experiences of my life. I had to learn early on to put up with heartless ridicule. I could tell you a thing or two about what it's like to be the butt of jokes. I was forced to put up with it. I've never belonged to any crowd, never was a pillar of society. I've never felt I had the support of being in a majority. Early on I discovered for myself what was later called internal exile without ever having heard anyone use the term.

Allowing thugs to bash minorities with impunity is a feature of all fascistic systems. During my youth it was the "East European subhumans," the Jews, and the homosexuals who were in trouble. They were "degenerates" to be beaten up at will. Doing so, even the lowest, most rotten, pathetic thug could feel great.

At school I was given to understand in quite unmistakable terms that I could give up any hope of passing my university admission exam if I didn't wear the brown shirt in some form or other. So shortly before the exam, I had myself transferred from the civil defense league into the SA. I skipped duty as often as possible. During my university studies in G. and in M., I simply ignored my membership. I officially resigned two days before my army induction.

The Nazis had established compulsory military service, and like all my school classmates, I had "volunteered" for military service months before my exam. All the others were called up for active duty immediately after the exam; I was the only one who wasn't. I was waiting for that letter in fear and trembling. It never came. Somehow, my petition must have gotten snagged in some office. Military service repelled me in the extreme, but I wanted to get it over with to avoid having to interrupt my university studies at some future point. My fellow students were rejoicing: they assumed they'd be able to study undisturbed and in peace once they finished their hitch in the service.

Not one of them was even able to start university study. What was waiting for them was the battlefield. They were mowed down in droves, for the war began two years after that exam.

Thanks to a private connection of my parents, I did, however, show up right on schedule for Labor Service in the filthiest and dampest area of

East Prussia. The noncommissioned officer corps there was the dregs of the entire Prussian military and ranked even lower than the usual service. Anyone who got turned down by the regular military was sent to the Labor Service to try to make it there. And now there I was, smack in the middle of it.

Every Saturday afternoon, the command for base cleanup boomed out: college brains, fall out left; route step, march! Woe to the pivot man who didn't immediately turn in the direction of the latrine. That was our field of action. Quite a hilarious joke—the college-bound servicemen double-timing it right into the crap. They couldn't get enough of this regular Saturday gag, those Nazi Labor Service pigs.

For many years I was in a sort of sexual and erotic hibernation. For more than half a century I was successfully sublimating. Those were strangely amorphous, dead years—a time when I was blocking everything. Our bourgeois upbringing had put us through the wringer, cranking out a product that was expected to know what was respectable, what was seemly and proper, and what was to be rejected. After all, parents seldom realize how much their kids do realize or at least suspect, despite all attempts to shelter them—and why should they?

I can't have been more than six or seven when a gentleman whom I didn't pay too much attention to was visiting us in our apartment. I was playing quietly in my corner when suddenly I heard him say: my man (*mein Mann*) is waiting for me.

It was an electric moment. Up to the present day, I still don't know what he meant. A business partner, a workout buddy in an athletic club—I just don't know. Since my parents reacted to this remark completely normally, it must have been insignificant. In a peculiar way, I became intensely preoccupied with this "my man" spoken by a man.

After finishing my stint in the Labor Service, I was allowed to attend the university for a while at the end of 1937. I'd received a provisional discharge. I began studying language and literature in K., where my older brother was starting a career after finishing an engineering degree. As is so often the case with brothers, we didn't really communicate with each other until we got older. We discovered each other as brothers during wonderful weekend outings in the countryside around K.

Once this happened: it was a spring day warm as summer, but for safety's sake we'd brought along our heavy jackets. He was carrying his, folded over his arm. My jacket was cheaper, more modest than his. In order to hide that, I threw it over my shoulder casually, and I kept it from sliding down by sticking my hand in a back pocket. So my cheap nothing became a little toga, a wrap that was "chic." My brother looked at me and said: God, the way you do that. . . . He, the big, good-looking guy, gladly yielded to me: without any apparent effort on my part, something worked for me that he was incapable of—me, the "little shrimp." He conceded this.

You know, one institution played an important part in my childhood: ballroom dance lessons. Without these dance classes I never would have overcome my deep, panicky shyness. During these months I received instruction on how to move in "society." I learned to walk across a polished hardwood floor and how to carry a chair across a dance floor. Just look at today's youngsters, the way they drag a chair across a disco. You have to learn how to make an entry. From the Renaissance up to the nineteenth century, the dancing teacher played an important role in the education of aristocratic children. Without learning how to walk, the women of earlier centuries couldn't even have worn their big crinolines. Those enormous masses of skirts would start swaying terribly if you walked in the normal way. A small intermediate step catches it, making it possible to sweep across the floor. Wearing the outfits of baroque lords also required such small touches. It must have been a splendid time for our kind of people, since they can generally do that sort of thing without lengthy training.

In short, I had this knack for staging a scene from early on, and the dance lessons were not without their use. I learned to cover up my shyness, lost my fear of socializing, and to top it off received the confirmation that I was quite an attractive, good-looking little fellow after all.

For many people, it takes an exhausting effort to change from insecurity to a self-assured manner. It's like learning to speak extemporaneously. It may well be that you have to learn to pull yourself up by your own bootstraps from the swamp of fear; incidentally, the same is true in bed.

My dance-lesson partner was a sweet, good girl, sadly not very attractive, tall and skinny, daughter of a silly, arrogant mother who worshiped her son and who must have been pretty herself once. This girl took after her father—which is why she was so homely. Well, this father, who had no power within his own four walls, loved his daughter very much. Naturally, the poor kid was overshadowed by the other girls, whom the young cavaliers swarmed around.

Then I began to look after this poor thing. I had found a meaningful task. I surrounded her with attentions, which finally caused the others to take notice. She gained self-assurance, was happy not to be a wallflower any more, and suddenly others were coming over, too, and asking her to dance. To a very small, modest extent she even became stylish. This girl, actually quite homely because of her skinny angularity, learned to smile and in her own way even became pretty. She came through the dance lessons well, and I came through the dance lessons well.

Every society has its rituals, and the entrance is of great importance. Anyone who is out of step from early on tends to keep on stumbling along.

What you in today's jargon call "coming out" or entering the gay scene happened to me very late. I was a university student and was on vacation at the seashore. At that very time, location shots were being filmed in our dunes landscape for a big Ufa movie, *U-Boats Westward*.[1] Movies were terrifically important at that time, especially in the small towns. Movies were the bridge to the wide world outside. People had their idols, for example, the young Wolfgang Liebeneiner, Hannes Stelzer, and others.

So there in the romantic isolation of the dunes came a man in a sailor's uniform who later turned out to be an actor from the theater world of Berlin. This sailor knew very well what effect his movie costume was having and wisely enough didn't pack it away after the day's shooting. I was the clear proof that the sailor gambit worked, even in remote East Prussia. This was my first lapse into sin.

From that time on, I would occasionally go to Berlin. After a short time, my sailor—a well-known habitué of the Kudamm—had directed me further. Not even discreetly so. My country innocence was savored as a delicacy; I was consumed for breakfast—but not for long. You know how things go in life: having once been deceived, I learned to deceive. . . .

Certainly, the Nazis did drive our people even deeper into illegality. Many were murdered in their barbaric camps. Yet despite all that, there existed in that era what today is called a "scene." The sex drive can't be suppressed for long. Certainly not if you're young and good-looking and for a time seem to consist of nothing but sex drive. Besides, young people always think that the worst can only happen to the next guy.

In this web of experiences, one person suddenly turned up who was not like most others—my first great love. We've kept in touch up to today. He was the prototype of the cultivated homosexual—smart, subtle, playful too. He had a beautiful baritone and could camp it up marvelously—and do it with charm. And—he was a decent guy. I loved him. He made me aware of the link between intellect and eros, and through that I learned to cope with my differentness.

A close relationship of trust arose between us, and that has continued even when we can't see each other for a long time. I could count our sexual contacts on the fingers of one hand. When we met again after the war was over, we did try it one more time. We cut it out right away; it was no more than a kind of politeness on both sides.

My real friendships usually entailed sex only in the beginning phase, and sometimes not at all. Long-lasting, erotic, and intellectual friendships would arise when the animalistic was excluded. Generally, a real bond didn't become possible until we were past sex.

I found out early on that sex and eros can never be harmonized for me. I have to get beyond sex, whereas I cultivate and honor the divinity of eros.

Now as in the past, I take care of my sexual business at places that, by the way, are not completely devoid of a certain romanticism. All you have to know is how to find them. One thing I do know: beyond a certain stage of consciousness, any false sense of shame is ridiculous, a sham. What you do with full consciousness with another person cannot be "indecent." The desired body has no "pure" and "impure" zones.

I told you that I served as a medical corpsman throughout the war. I was stationed the longest period of time in G. There I met a fellow who opened up a whole new world for me. He was coming directly from the Eastern front to spend a few days home on leave. We found each other with the total absoluteness that is possible for our kind.

I'll never forget that summer night. He was just swept off his feet by our acquaintance, and up till then I'd never been able to give and receive such joy. We immediately made a date to meet the next day. I couldn't go—unexpectedly had duty; I was desperate. In the next days I tore through the town like a madman. He was nowhere to be found.

It's as if something in me snapped at that point. I believe the social pressures gradually produced in me a psychic response that left me unsuited for building up any firm, long-lasting love relationship. I don't know whether this human capacity can be destroyed, but if so, it happened to me back then.

There were encounters with other people. The word expresses it fully: we encountered each other and separated again. You'd schedule a get-together and then not show up. If you did show up, the other guy wouldn't. There was so much fear in us. It was a terrible, appalling time. As a corpsman I met a young physician in my unit, an oddly tormented individual. One day he disappeared—something not all that unusual in the middle of a war; I assumed he was probably transferred. So I didn't give him any more thought.

Months later I was on duty taking care of a simple medical treatment in a penalty stockade. And suddenly the two of us were standing facing each other; he was only a shadow of his former self, a skeleton. I was deeply shocked, in despair about not being able to help. I never saw him again. The linkage was fear—self-control—sublimation.

After all, what did I know at that time? To what extent did I think through what I occasionally heard and make connections? It's astonishing how little we knew in distant East Prussia about the development of things and what was going on. There weren't many Jews in our area; I had heard the term *concentration camp*, but I didn't begin to imagine what it actually concealed. The inhumanity of the regime became apparent to me only gradually, like a puzzle; for a long time my experiences lay there next to each other like unsorted pieces, out of order; the real pattern remained hidden from me for a long time.

I got an idea of what had really gone on only in the very last weeks of the war. I learned the final story early in the summer of 1945, during an inspection of the concentration camp in Buchenwald.

You younger folks so enjoy handing out grades retrospectively for our behavior back then—usually in a reckless way, since you're overhasty to project later knowledge back into the past. Things you're not supposed to know—things you don't want to know: the origin of a lot of human tragedies and anxieties is located somewhere between the two, it seems to me. A lot of guilt came about because people knew, and yet so many ignored what was happening.

At the end of 1944, I was transferred to the Rhön Mountains. At the battleline you could no longer tell the front and the rear apart; everything was gradually crumbling. And then came May 8, 1945, and I saw more than a few men crying when they had to cut the braid off their uniforms. Even though everyone had figured that the end was coming, we were surprised when it really did arrive. The army was passé. . . .

The American prisoner-receiving camps were overfilled and wouldn't take us in. We made up what was called a precapture camp. Even in defeat we maintained order, that's how long we'd been drilled. For two weeks we vegetated, dozing away and just starving, until we were distributed to the surrounding villages. After two weeks of nettles, finally potatoes again.

My release came quickly, and I met my mother at the home of relatives in W. We were standing facing each other, what remained of our family. Father and brother dead, our possessions lost, no prospect of employment. But work squads . . . and hunger. That time has been described often enough.

Our situation turned catastrophic when the savings account passbooks from the former Eastern territories were devalued. Right at the beginning I had bought myself watercolors, remnants of which could be bought cheap in paper goods stores. In the summer I would sit with my painting stuff at the edge of a grain field, in autumn at the outermost furrow of a potato field. And, depending on the time of day, I'd paint sunrises or sunsets. In the evening, when the colors could no longer be distinguished, I would creep onto the field and collect whatever was growing on the soil and my pockets could hold. At home I would record the date and what I had harvested on the back side of my watercolors. In pictographs: cabbage, ears of grain, potatoes.

From an earlier visit in W., I remembered an antique store run by two charming older ladies. I went there, and they immediately recognized me. As usual, tales of tribulation were exchanged. When I told them that I was producing watercolors in my abundant free time, they told me firmly that I just had to bring some by—yes, people would buy them, precisely because the town was full of refugees who had money and nothing to spend it on.

The next day I put a portfolio together, "Goethe's Garden House" on top. I took the portfolio to the ladies, and from that hour on I made a big detour to avoid the shop. It simply didn't make sense to me that right now there should be an interest in my little pictures. Weeks later the two ladies called to me on the street: "Young man, why haven't you been by, we're waiting for you!" I was flabbergasted when they told me that one hundred marks were waiting for me for the first sheets sold.

One hundred marks! We were saved, and I could hope for even more. My commissions didn't stop. Among the refugees from Silesia the best selling were little pictures of saints and madonnas. I varnished them with clear nail polish and framed them.

The end of 1945. Of course nothing was uncomplicated at that time.

While filling out the endless questionnaires, I recorded, as called for, my membership in the SA. On doing so I was treated as if I had personally instigated the *Reichskristallnacht*, and it seemed as if I had been the only SA member far and wide. I owe it to two honorable and influential citizens that I was able to close the chapter entitled "Denazification" in the autumn of 1945 and to begin studying at the conservatory of fine arts.

A very productive time was beginning for me. In my first pictures it became apparent that my mental–artistic and my erotic impulses made up a close unity, that they conditioned one another. My teachers, tactful and wise, didn't reproach me, but guided me and otherwise let me be.

To my own dismay, I would repeatedly arouse female interest; my polite helplessness vis-à-vis women encouraged them more than it frightened them. It has always pained me to stir feelings and desires I cannot reciprocate, to create expectations that a word might have dispelled. Might have! I couldn't say the word—what else could I do? I got accustomed to lying.

When the law was repealed, it never occurred to me to live in a substitute family with a man. It became ever clearer to me that coupling would be bought at the price of my intellectual existence. It has been wonderful in each of my digs: in a tiny student place or now in this roomy apartment. I need only spread out my beautiful objects—manifestations of my spiritual being—in order to be myself in complete composure, that is, be able to work. The knowledge of having friends and being able to count on their occasional closeness suffices for me and makes me calm and cheerful. I've never yet felt lonely. I do fear this scourge a bit in old age. But even now I've got to watch my appointments and commitments carefully; without an engagement calendar I'd be lost. My mother, whom I lived with until her death, warned me back then: "Boy, those friends of yours are eating you up. You're like a candle burning at both ends." I just laughed at her, which I could get away with.

During my conservatory years in W., I had a thoughtful circle of friends who exchanged views in a frank way. It was a time of change, of growth. Social and intellectual bonds have always taken priority for me—a life-style I've been able to maintain up until today. Sitting right here at my coffee table, many people have drawn strength from me; they've turned me and this table into their wailing wall and thus shown how much they respect us. I've learned that he who gives also receives. It almost sounds like a Bible verse, but why not? The people who visit here really open up and reveal themselves, just as I do. I haven't been at all religious in outlook from my boyhood on. Selfless I'm not, not by any means.

By and by, life became orderly again: university degree; my term as an academic assistant; my fourth decade was already beginning. Slowly I came to realize that living as a homosexual can lead to and produce that elusive quality of refinement and sophistication in intellectual matters. From that point on, I finally really accepted my destiny. Stigma, yes, but you can do something with it. The feeling of being an outcast, of being cheated, disappeared completely. On the contrary, now I sometimes had a twinge of conscience because it seemed I had an easier and more comfortable life than do others whose eros seems to be a huge burden for them to bear. Raising children—what an unimaginably huge responsibility. If you look at it that way, then we are parasites, just going after the beautiful everywhere and complaining even so. I "father" my sons wherever I may find them, and I give the best I have to offer to my friends. This willingness to give is actually a need on my part and thus no special achievement. It isn't really selfless. People who are stingy with themselves just don't know in what wonderfully surprising ways you'll get repaid if you are allowed to give.

Oh yes, it was a real liberation, the repeal of the statute [against homosexuality in 1968], and before the other German state at that. For many long years that need to hide was an overriding pressure in my life. I suffered from having to lie and deceive—at work, everywhere. If I liked a man, I always waited for an opening. If it didn't come, I would withdraw. I think I can fairly say that I've never pushed myself on anyone. Without wanting to, people lived in illegality, beyond the law, in conditions of constant injustice, of constantly being vulnerable to prosecution and, worst of all, to ruthless blackmail. That state of affairs resulted in many crimes, a mass of horrible lies and their consequences.

How many mistaken and unjustifiable marriages took place because of the law—marriages in which women stood facing their partners at a complete loss, wondering what was wrong with themselves. And usually an unwanted child would be born right before the final crisis. Those poor kids who had to grow up between quarreling and mutually destructive parents. I've often had to observe dramas of this kind in my life. I have desperately advised young friends: don't do it—it will be terrible for everyone involved. Anytime I would meet a man and learn he was married, I would withdraw. By the way, one of the awful things I can't forgive our people is breaking up marriages. Earlier, in my time of torment, of suffering over my orientation, I envied the guys who could swing both ways. How well I could have concealed and camouflaged myself if I'd been able to do it. Only later did I realize what a gift of the gods it is to be absolutely and clearly aimed in one direction. I've learned to interpret the gaze of these self-proclaimed bi-men who respond to my imploring words by leaning back skeptically in their chairs, mulling over my words, and finally coming to the conclusion: they certainly aren't quite that queer—I use this word very consciously—quite as queer as I am. They'd work things out at home. What their marriages were like and where they finally ended up I don't need to tell you.

Each of us experiences the phase where people say vicious things about you behind your back, where the more or less subtle stabs of society cripple your soul. Weaklings tend toward short-sighted actions then, to panicked goofs, like that sort of marriage—or they kill themselves. They're still doing it. If we can manage to wait it out, the malicious interest of the conventional people will die down; they'll accept us, perhaps with certain reservations, but . . . The next attention-grabbing event is sure to come along. Nowadays many people behave weirdly, so that we with our fine feathers scarcely attract any notice. We "homos" are, after all, not the center of society.

Along with my professional activity, which I do very much love, my easel has been a dominant part in my intellectual life. Just as a musical person sits down at his piano or picks out a pretty passage while standing, that's how I treated my easel. Looking at pictures from twenty or more years ago places me back into experiences and circumstances from the time of their origin. Should I ever write my memoirs, I'd need only stroll through my pictures. Quite a bit would come back to me.

If I long sought to conceal my male-orientedness from the world, this character trait is expressed rather frankly in my pictures. The split between eros and sex that I established at such an early age has never been hidden either. The pictures say it. I've never played at being a married couple in a canopied bed, not even with the one I called my great love. In my forties I once again tried a long-lasting relationship; it didn't work out. Evidently I just didn't want to accept that I was born to be a "single"—or did I turn into one? No, love relationships in the usual sense haven't happened for me; instead, I have a love for the male in general.

By the way, this chasm between eros and sex is a phenomenon that has shaped cultural history over entire epochs: in a real sense, the bordello was probably always the institutionalization of this split. The extreme sacralization of marriage obviously made this escape valve necessary.

Over and over again, you encounter in my pictures the harlequin and the faun. The harlequin is the thinking, conscious, and therefore suffering individual; for me, the faun means the vital-animal world. And then there are Ovid's metamorphoses: Artemis transforming the hunter Actaeon into a stag, who is then torn to death by his own dogs; Apollo losing Daphne, who has turned into a laurel . . . I can't compete with Master Freud and wouldn't want to, but compared with this Artemis, the toughest feminists are gentle maidens. But enough of that—all these figurations are, naturally, a direct reflection of my world of experience and thus of my eros. My abstract works and my landscapes should also be included here. Over and over again you find grotesque, surreal elements in my work. For a time I was painting such scurrilous imagery that my mother began to fear I might be disturbed. So I said to her: if these things stayed shut up inside me, if I couldn't get them out, then you'd have reason to be worried about me. This is the way I conjure up the uncertain, formulate it, and by capturing it in my pictures I can be rid of it.

Art is active meditation, a different form of attaining knowledge, and you cannot grasp the essence of art with rationality alone. There are two possible ways of acquiring knowledge: the meditative, which the early cultures largely relied on, and the empirical, which our world has taken to the atom bomb.

It was fate that granted me the ability to incorporate elements of figurative talent in my professional work. Professional and artistic ability were linked with each other, rather like the water level at two ends of a siphon hose—the one matched the other. I'm happy that I'm still of some use even now, that my advice occasionally still has some value.

The basis of this pretty assemblage of objets d'art around us was laid in my early years. Assemblage—you heard me right. My assemblage is no collection. In the time after 1945, you found the prettiest things literally on the streets, in trash cans. Goethe in his wisdom once said that what you've inherited from your fathers, you must make your own in order to possess it. You only own things if you grasp them, understand and love them. If you can afford valuable art works, fine, but just by buying them, you haven't made them yours by a long shot. Incidentally, I'm of the opinion that things beyond a certain level of quality no longer belong in private hands.

I associate lovely memories with many of these objects, and I live with them.

At an appropriate time a man must adjust to his age. Lucky the man who succeeds at turning into a happy oldster. The misfortune of declining vital energies can be halted to a certain extent with consciousness, or so at least I hope.

The gods have been lavish with their gifts to me, and I needn't torment myself with regrets about sins I failed to commit. A smart friend once called me an attractive ugly person. Growing old is often a curse for beautiful people, while an attractive ugly person may be in a better position to grow old gracefully.

As a young man I wished to be beautiful in order to be able to turn heads. Woe to those who dazzle everyone in their youth, for what's to come later?

In order to deceive those around me, I wished I could love men and women. But I couldn't do it, and that kept calamity away from me and others. I also lacked that boundless, unlimited vitality that leads many people to neglect their own well-being. Anyone who has to work at staying healthy quickly learns to monitor his energies and to use them sensibly.

As I've grown older, I've gained the interest and even the friendship of some remarkable women. That always pleases me; the memory of my mother sets the standard here.

When I was stuck deep in my mid-life crisis, a friendly older colleague at work drew me into a conversation and said: you know, just wait till you turn fifty, and then everything will be fine again. How right he was.

Do I have a sense of humor? You'll have to ask my friends.

Interview completed 1985

Notes

Introduction

1. *Guten Morgen, du Schöne* (Darmstadt: Luchterhand, 1978), p. 4.
2. *Truth and Method* (New York: Crossroad, 1982 [1975]), p. 264.

I. Erich and Karl

1. "You won't hear heroic tales about our kind"

1. The Prenzlauer Berg was a well-known working-class district near the center of Berlin. Today this part of East Berlin has a reputation as a center of "alternative" culture.

2. Asta Nielsen and Henny Porten were the best-known silent film stars of the 1920s.

3. The back-to-nature style of the Wandervögel, who spent much of their time hiking, camping, and singing in the countryside and woods, was largely a reaction against urbanization and industrialization in the latter half of the nineteenth century. They later developed an overtly homoerotic philosophy.

4. On May 10, 1933, Nazi students in many university towns built bonfires of confiscated books by mainly Jewish or liberal authors whose works were now to be banned under the new regime. The main event was in Berlin where Propaganda Minister Goebbels himself made a speech at the bonfire in front of the Opera House (opposite the university). The homosexual Magnus Hirschfeld's Institute for Sexual Science had been a prime target of the Nazi students' raids, and more than 12,000 books from its library were consigned to the flames.

5. The homosexual chief of staff of Hitler's Storm Troopers, Ernst Röhm, was murdered along with other SA officers, some of whom had been found *in flagrante delicto*, following a raid led personally by Hitler on June 30, 1934. The reason was *not*, however, Röhm's homosexuality, but Hitler's need to remove the threat that the army believed the SA posed to its own monopoly of arms. Hitler realized that he simply had to have the support of the army to carry out his aggressive plans for foreign conquest.

6. The Horch motor company subsequently latinized its name to Audi.

7. No. 8 Prinz-Albrecht-Strasse was one of the most feared addresses in the country, for this was the headquarters of the Gestapo. It did not remain secret for very long that brutal torture was applied to those being interrogated there in order to extract the required information and "confessions" from them. It is known that a number of prisoners chose suicide rather than suffer further brutality.

8. This was Berlin's own concentration camp. Whereas most of the camps were situated far from towns, this one lay in the center of the city, next to the airfield. Prisoners were often taken to Prinz-Albrecht-Strasse 8 during the day for interrogation, but the camp itself achieved notoriety even among Nazis as a place of arbitrary violence.

9. Homosexual relations were regulated by paragraph 175 of the German Criminal Code. Under the Weimar Republic's version of this law, only paracoital (*Beischlafsähnlich*) sex was punishable (effectively, just anal or intercrural intercourse). In 1935 the Nazis rewrote the law to make mutual masturbation and even imagined advances (touching or glances) punishable by prison sentences. After 1941 those 175ers who had completed their allotted prison sentences were no longer released

but automatically sent to a concentration camp—provided this had not been a first offense. Repeat offenders were classed as "habitual seducers."

10. The Kapos were the block orderlies in the concentration camps, and this position of seniority was always given to a criminal offender rather than to a Jewish, a political, or a homosexual prisoner.

11. Flossenbürg was a concentration camp that catered especially to so-called asocials, a broad and flexible category that included the "work-shy," homosexuals, and alcoholics.

12. In the system of colored triangular identification patches that concentration camp inmates were forced to wear, red denoted a political offender, green a habitual criminal, violet a Jehovah's Witness. The homosexual prisoners wore a pink triangle.

13. This had been one of the main squares, almost the hub of old Berlin.

14. The Free German Youth invites practically all former victims of fascism, especially former resistance fighters and communists, to give talks. Gay victims, as Erich ironically notes, are not invited to speak of their experiences.

2. "This is my young friend; we're in love"

1. This was presumably a KdF cruise. *Kraft durch Freude* (Strength through Joy) was a branch of the Nazi labor union that beautified factory premises and provided subsidized vacations such as this for workers who had mostly never been abroad or on an ocean liner in their lives.

II. Reinhold and Bert

4. "The way you look, you don't have a chance of getting in"

1. Thüringen, a district in the southwestern GDR, has the highest industrial concentration in the entire country. Originally occupied by the invading American army in 1945, it was later given to the Soviet Union in exchange for West Berlin.

2. The GDR has an extensive system of marital credits and family supports, dating back to the founding of the state in 1949. Since 1972, these credits have been strengthened and include apartment preference rules, housing and household founding credit, and child care supports that favor the young married couple.

3. *Stunde Null*, zero hour, is the term used by the Germans, especially by West Germans, to describe the hour immediately after the defeat of the Third Reich and unconditional surrender to the Allies.

4. *Konsum* is one type of state-owned store; the other type is HO, *Handelsorganization*.

5. The Berliner Initiative is the housing renovation and development project started by the central government in the late seventies to improve the quality of housing in Berlin before moving on to other cities in the GDR. This project brought thousands of male workers, without their female companions or family members, from the provinces to Berlin. Many used the project to escape their small towns.

6. Teachers in the GDR are state employees, must work under strong ideological control, and are relatively poorly paid as well. Hence many private citizens look down on teachers as poor, subservient, unthinking, dependent creatures.

7. Youth clubs in the GDR, called Free German Youth (*Freie Deutsche Jugend* [FDJ]), are organized and sponsored by the state. Authorities always address youth groups rather formally as "young friends."

III. Lothar, Peter, and Volker

1. See James D. Steakley, *The Homosexual Emancipation Movement in Germany* (New York: Arno Press, 1975); John Lauritsen and David Thorstad, *The Early Homosexual Rights Movement (1864–1935)* (New York: Times Change Press, 1974); *Docu-*

ments of the Homosexual Rights Movement in Germany, series ed. Jonathan Katz, volume ed. James D. Steakley (New York: Arno Press, 1975); Joachim S. Hohmann, ed., *Der unterdrückte Sexus: Historische Texte und Kommentare zur Homosexualität* (Lollar, FRG: Andreas Achenbach, 1977); Ilse Kokula, ed., *Weibliche Homosexualität um 1900 in zeitgenössischen Dokumenten* (Munich: Frauenoffensive, 1981); Alexandra Patzold, ed., *Frauenliebe Männerliebe: Bilder und Dokumente zur "Homosexualität" in Deutschland* (Marburg: Wenzel, 1984); Gudrun Schwarz, " 'Mannweiber' in Männertheorien," in *Frauen suchen ihre Geschichte: Historische Studien zum 19. und 20. Jahrhundert*, ed. Karin Hauser (Munich: C. H. Beck, 1983), 62–80; and Hans-Georg Stümke and Rudi Finkler, eds., *Rosa Winkel, Rosa Listen: Homosexuelle und "Gesundes Volksempfinden" von Auschwitz bis heute* (Reinbek bei Hamburg: Rowohlt Taschenbuch Verlag, 1981).

2. The more traditional form of coming out in the popular press can be found in Ursula Hafranke's three-part series "Ungestraft anders?" ("Unpunished for being different?") in the journal *Das Magazin* (Heft 1, 2, 5, 1989). Here gay men speak in single sentences in order to illustrate the points the author wishes to make about the sad and unjust life that gays are forced to lead. Hafranke interviewed a large number of gay men, asking each a list of twenty-five questions relating to their childhood, their love relationships, and the ways in which they were able to live out their gayness. In this kind of coming-out literature, heterosexual "authorities" (because of their education, their scientific research) present gays to a heterosexual audience as the objects for their empathy and tolerance. The present book may also aim at precisely those goals, but it pursues them in a very different way by allowing gay men to speak for themselves.

3. Thomas Böhme has written a poem about Lothar and his museum called "Mahlsdorf Museum." In it, Lothar is referred to as "Charlotte." See Thomas Böhme, *Mit der Sanduhr am Gürtel* (With the hourglass on my belt) (Berlin and Weimar: Aufbau Verlag, 1986), 104–105.

5. *"I am my own woman"*

1. This was a period in German arts and architecture of the 1870s and 1880s characterized by neohistorical styles (neo-Gothic, neo-Renaissance, etc.). The term *Gründerzeit* refers to the period during which Germany first existed as a unified country, under the leadership of Chancellor Otto von Bismarck. This "Second Reich" was established in 1871.

2. This type of furniture was developed in Germany between 1815 and 1848 and was very popular with the middle class (a class to which the term *Biedermeier* later referred pejoratively). The style is characterized by simple lines and a relative lack of ornamentation.

3. The word for squad is *Fähnlein*, which literally means "little flag."

4. *Hart wie Krupstahl* ("tough as Krupp steel") was one of the Nazi slogans describing the male ideal of the Hitler Youth.

6. *"Married without children"*

1. This refers to the moment in Weber's opera *Der Freischütz* when Adele's girlfriends gather around her and present her with this traditional wreath as part of the prewedding festivities.

2. An area in southwestern GDR known for its forest.

3. "Neustadt" means "new town," an area of prefabricated housing projects located at the edge of the city.

4. The term Peter uses, *Lebensgemeinschaft*, is used today to signify a committed love relationship between two people. It is the social equivalent of *Ehe* ("marriage") but of course does not have the legal status of the latter. That the official agreed to enter it on Peter's application form is highly unusual.

5. This pattern is the original one used on Meissen china, so it is quite a treasure.
6. A well-known cruising area in East Berlin.

IV. Winne

7. *"What should I do with such a hot-blooded guy?"*

1. A Stresemann is a classical striped suit.
2. Rewatex is the state-owned laundromat. Although the running of laundromats is subsidized by the state, the usual waiting time for most laundry is ten days to three weeks.

V. Body and Joseph

8. *"You don't get points for drinking"*

1. Here Body uses the term *Abo-Knaster* and humorously plays with the word *Abonnement*, meaning that he has, so to speak, a regular or season ticket to prison.
2. This nickname of a friend refers to the fact that there is a space between his front teeth.
3. *Grenzgänger* refers to the people who traveled daily to work from the East to the West across the border before the Wall was put up on August 13, 1961.
4. "Anti-faschistische demokratische Schutzwall" is the official GDR term used to describe the Wall. This passage also points to the traditional competition between Berlin and Leipzig. The reference to the Saxon dialect acknowledges that this dialect incarnates the GDR, since many politicians come from Saxony.
5. In the GDR many people who are considered asocial are not only put in jail but also get a "Berlin-Verbot," that is, this person must stay in a small village and work. If he wants to go to Berlin, he must get permission from his parole officer (ABV).
6. The Union Club is a soccer club in Berlin that the working class likes very much. It is one of two Berlin clubs. The other is made up of police.
7. After the publication of the German version of this book, a state-run group for homosexual alcoholics was established.
8. The Freie Deutsche Gewerkschaftbund is the only union in the GDR. This union has places for good workers to take a vacation at a low price. This is meant ironically here, since gays do not normally visit such singularly heterosexual vacation spots.

9. *"Society could have gotten more from me"*

1. This reference is to a jacket worn by Ernst Thälmann, leader of the German Communist party who was murdered in Buchenwald concentration camp and is still revered as a national hero in the GDR. The state children's organization is called the Ernst Thälmann Pioneers.

VI. Theodor and Dieter

10. *"I am not a banner waver"*

1. Nude beaches have become the norm in the GDR, for both sexes and all age groups.

11. *"I'm a man and I want to live with one"*

1. Dieter later read this version of his life story to the members of his current work brigade. They discussed it, and afterward Dieter reported that the discussion increased trust and openness among members. Because workers in the GDR are not in competition with each other for jobs (there is an official labor shortage) and

can only rarely be fired, relations between workers tend to be much more cordial and relaxed than in capitalist countries.

2. Until approximately the past five years, the psychological theories of the postrevolution Russian scholar Makarenko formed the basis of all teachings on psychology in the GDR. Makarenko based his theories on studies of collective child care of homeless children after World War I. The socialist children's collectives were supposed to be democratically organized according to basic communist principles, encouraging individual responsibility along with an ethos of collective solidarity. Their idealist, romantic character appealed strongly to children.

3. The Timur movement, based on the literary figure in the novel *Timor and His Group* by the Soviet author Arkadi Gaidar, was part of the Ernst Thälmann Pioneer organization for children. To children raised in the USSR and GDR, Timur represented the best qualities of a young communist, consistently offering his service to others, especially the elderly.

4. Dieter is citing Pawel Kortschagin, hero in *How the Steel Is Made Hard* (1952, Neues Leben Verlag, Berlin), the popular youth novel by the Soviet author Nikolai Ostrowski. Portrayed in this book is a young generation made into steel by withstanding the storm of historical tests. Ostrowski portrays the victory of progressive forces and freedom through the grueling reconstruction work of the youth. Despite hunger and being ill-clothed, plagued with epidemics and sabotaged by foreign agents, the youths succeed in building a socialist society. The novel was required reading for GDR youths from the fifties through the seventies. Any member of this postwar generation can cite the full verse from memory: "The most valuable thing that a person possesses is life. He is given but a single one. And he should use it so that his years are not wasted without purpose, so that he will not burn from shame for a base and mean past, so that when he dies he may say: my whole life, all of my strenth, I have dedicated to the most splendid thing in the world, to the fight for the emancipation of mankind."

VII. Nicholas and J. A. W.

13. *"The harlequin and the faun"*

1. The Ufa film studio in Babelsberg near Berlin was the leading German film studio up to 1945.

JÜRGEN LEMKE is a free-lance writer and dramatist and has taught economics at the Bruno Leuschner Technical University in East Berlin.

Contributors to the English Translation

JOHN BORNEMAN is a visiting lecturer in the Anthropology and Political Science departments at the University of California, San Diego.

GEOFFREY J. GILES is associate professor of history at the University of Florida, Gainesville.

JAMES PATRICK HILL is a germanist, singer, and social worker in Cambridge, Massachusetts.

JAMES W. JONES teaches in the Department of Foreign Languages, Literature, and Culture at Central Michigan University.

JAMES R. KELLER is working as an editor in New York City while working on a doctorate in German literature from the University of Texas, Austin.

JEFFREY M. PECK is associate professor of germanics and comparative literature at the University of Washington.

J. D. STEAKLEY is associate professor of German literature at the University of Wisconsin, Madison.

STEVEN STOLTENBERG is working on a doctorate in sociology at the University of California, Berkeley.